Think of Your Future

Workbook

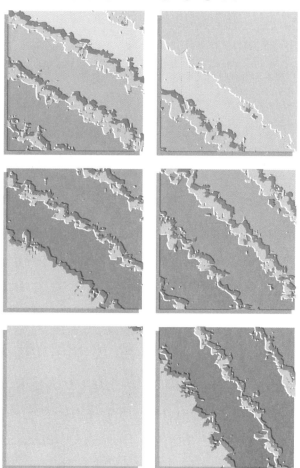

HarperCollins*Publishers*

About AARP

AARP is the nation's leading organization for people age 50 and over. It serves their needs and interests through legislative advocacy, research, informative programs, and community services provided by a network of local chapters and experienced volunteers throughout the country. The organization also offers members a wide range of special membership benefits, including *Modern Maturity* and the monthly *Bulletin*.

ISBN 0-06-263554-9

FIRST EDITION

96 97 98 99 HAD 10 9 8 7 6 5 4 3 2

Contents

Introduction

Introduction

The years between young adulthood and older adulthood can be a period of self-reflection, when the goals and ideals of the younger adult are re-examined through the eyes of the more experienced adult. We recognize that not every goal is attainable and also that, as life moves forward, goals change. Our experience and increased self-knowledge promote a more realistic evaluation of our personal strengths and capabilities. Armed with this increased self-awareness, adults can decide either to pursue the dreams of young adulthood with renewed energy and commitment or to set new goals that better reflect their current concerns.

How you handle this passage from young adulthood to later adulthood will determine whether you experience a midlife crisis or a midlife crescendo. Change provides an opportunity to pause and think about the direction in which you would like to move your future. *Think of Your Future* is intended to help you make your decisions wisely by encouraging you to seek out opportunities and plan carefully.

Successful planning at any age requires objectivity and flexibility. At age 25, it may be terrifying to try to decide what to do with "the rest of your life." At 35, it may be liberating to realize that no decisions are ever made for "the rest of your life." Successful plans are implemented in steps, reviewed regularly, and revised as needed.

Think of Your Future can help you formulate a well-conceived general plan for the years ahead. Through its activities, you will identify both your larger goals as well as more immediate goals that you will have to face along the way. Successful planners learn from failed plans and use each planning opportunity to improve their ability to foresee obstacles and formulate alternatives.

Join the Crowd

In the 21st century, the concept of retirement as we now know it will be changing in ways that we cannot even imagine. The 76 million members of the baby boom generation in the United States will be well on their way through middle age. As it has done for five decades, this population will continue to dominate popular culture and capture the attention of American business and industry.

By sheer force of numbers, and the spirit of activism that has always characterized them, the one-third of the U.S. population born between 1946 and 1964 will transform aging in America in their own image. The generations that precede and follow this massive group will absorb its influence and continue to be drawn to its values and lifestyles. Aging will be in vogue, and a revitalized mature America will be upon us.

This new nation will mirror the cultural, racial, ethnic, and lifestyle diversity among us. Programs such as Think of Your Future address the wide range of differences that is nowhere more dramatic than in the middle and later years.

You have the power to make your participation in the upcoming senior boom more rewarding. Your future will mean shifting focus, changing careers, reawakening goals, and embracing life more than it will signify halting employment, forcing leisure, abandoning dreams, and withdrawing from life. The choice is yours.

The AARP Approach to Future Planning

The Think of Your Future program is designed to guide you through the process of evaluating, judging, and determining the course of your future life from various critical perspectives.

Planning your future allows you to survey every aspect of your life in terms of the years ahead. It includes the issues directly related to moving or retiring from a primary job or choosing to undertake an alternative occupation, but it also considers the effects of family, friends, finances, health, and social and intellectual interests on a meaningful existence.

The Think of Your Future workbook addresses six life components as mainstays of productive future planning. You will see your life reflected under the following topics:

- Personal Elements: Work, Study, Community, and Leisure
- Health Factors
- Social Resources: Family and Friends
- Housing and Location Considerations
- Financial Management
- Legal and Estate Planning

AARP, which developed this program, uses its own acronym as a signpost through the four-step route to a blueprint for the future. The AARP Approach — Assessment, Alternatives, Responsibility, and Planning — follows this progression through each of the six subject areas presented in Think of Your Future.

- **Assessment** helps you compare the current status of your life components with what you perceive to be your future needs and wants in these areas.

- **Alternatives** encourage consideration of the full spectrum of options, choices, and opportunities available within each life component for your selection.

- **Responsibility** stresses the importance of assuming personal control over the decisions that will shape the future in each of your life components.

- **Planning** addresses the steps necessary to implement your decisions in each life component — stating goals, defining resources, identifying persons responsible for meeting goals, and setting time frames.

The Whole You

Thinking of your future must extend to all aspects of your life. Who is the "you" that YOU want to be for the rest of your life? What must happen for that "you" to evolve or surface?

Midlife may offer the only opportunity you get for a bona fide second chance at regrouping and redirecting yourself based on your life experience. The promise, the power, and the privilege that can come with midlife can energize you beyond anything you have envisioned.

This User-Friendly Workbook

The Think of Your Future workbook is suitable for use by individuals and by groups enrolled in future-planning seminars presented by employers or organizations. Independent study has the advantage of allowing you to focus on areas most pertinent to your concerns and to move ahead at your own pace. Group workshops encourage participants to share their insights and experiences with the other participating members. The materials are adaptable to either setting, and you may wish to supplement them as you go along, with your own research and creative ideas. Please do! You are encouraged to remain alert to changes in your environment, particularly regarding financial and legal matters and health and fitness concerns. This is *your* future you are planning!

You can reap the combined benefits of individual and group study by involving your family and friends in your deliberations. Discussion issues, planning exercises, and informational articles all profit from added contributions and feedback, especially when they come from persons you trust and know well.

Tools for the Task Ahead

Each life component unit comprises your future planning activities and includes a sequence of readings, exercises, and discussion generators. Their purpose is to work you through the process of confronting the unavoidable yet life-defining decisions that lie ahead.

- **Unit Objectives:** Your learning goals for the section.

- **What Do You Think?:** Thought-provoking questions to prompt individual, family/other network, or organized group reflection and discussion.

- **For Your Information:** Reading materials that provide basic information and a frame of reference for approaching the life component in a decision-making mode.

- **What Would You Do?:** Case studies for reflection and discussion that combine many elements of the life component review and represent typical issues faced in future planning.

The **Master Action Plans**, found at the back of this book and the final product of each life component unit, are self-contained, permanent planning tools for periodic review and revision of plans for the future in each area.

Information on organizations, services, and publications that may have continuing value in future planning appears in the Think of Your Future appendix.

Let Your Future Begin

You are at the start of what can be the most fulfilling period of your life and one of the most exhilarating times in American social and cultural history. Think of Your Future can help you analyze your options and make informed choices that will allow you to live this time to the fullest.

Personal Planning

Personal Planning

Today is the first day of the rest of your life. This statement was a popular theme when you and others were coming of age. Youth meant new starts, new directions, new ambitions. No idea was too adventurous, too bold to consider. With each new day came a new beginning.

Those new beginnings should still be coming to you as you plan now for the years ahead. Fresh starts at this point have the advantage of maturity and experience to guide them. You should approach planning for your own personal future with the same passion and dedication you give to providing for your family and satisfying your employer. What do you really want to do with the rest of your life? What have you always wanted to do that you may now be able to plan for? If ever there is a time to stop, take stock, and take action, that time is now.

The personal choices that you will review in this life component unit have to do with work, leisure, education, and community activities. They involve the interests and skills that you have developed over a lifetime and how you can apply them in the future.

If you are planning for the future together with a spouse or partner, that person should conduct an independent review of his or her hopes and expectations for the years ahead. Your separate plans can then be blended into a joint plan that ideally requires few compromises from either of you but nevertheless respects the individuality of each of you.

Unit Objectives

- **Assessment:** To assess your interests and skills; review how you have applied them to date in the pursuits and activities of daily life; and speculate on how you might use them in the future to enhance your life

- **Alternatives:** To consider alternatives in the areas of work, study, leisure, and community involvement that will take advantage of your abilities and improve the quality of your life

- **Responsibility:** To make decisions about work, study, leisure, and community involvement that meet your needs for fulfillment and balance in the future

- **Planning:** To make specific plans for following through on your decisions about applying your interests and skills to personal choices in work, study, leisure, and community involvement

What Do You Think?

The questions that follow are intended to focus your attention on some of the issues involved in planning for employment, leisure, educational activities, and community service. You are encouraged to discuss them with family, friends, or other members of your support network. Group seminars based on Think of Your Future will use the questions as workshop discussion topics.

1. When you are not working, what types of activities provide meaning to your life? What are the benefits of those activities?

2. Can you identify things you would like to do in the future — skills to perfect, experiences you would like to have, places you would like to see, contributions you would like to make, or knowledge you would like to gain? How can planning for your future help make these things happen for you?

3. You may need additional schooling to realize your future plans. What kinds of educational and training opportunities are available to adults in your community?

4. How can you find out about volunteer opportunities in your community? How can you determine which of them meet your needs and provide activities meaningful to you?

5. What leisure activities are available in your community that are affordable and convenient?

6. If you are currently employed, how long do you want to stay in your current job? Are you considering a second career after this one? What new skills or experience will you need in that career?

7. What are some of your personal strengths? Do your job and the other roles you fulfill take full advantage of your abilities and interests?

8. What decisions must you make and what skills and resources should you have before starting your own business?

For Your Information

Persons of all ages and all walks of life have become increasingly aware of the need for balance between work and other important aspects of their lives. Some individuals still view childhood as the time for learning, adulthood as the time for working, and late adulthood as the time for relaxing. A more fulfilling and more healthful pattern is to share in all three experiences throughout your entire life span. This is the balanced approach that Think of Your Future encourages you to follow as you consider your commitments of time and energy in the years ahead.

Most of your time and energy to date has probably been spent on making a living. You may not always have had the time or resources to focus on making a life by

continuing to educate yourself, by contributing to your community as you would have liked, or simply by enjoying yourself. Aspects of your life that may have fallen victim to a rigorous work schedule can be salvaged at any time, and you will want to think about doing so as you review the materials in this unit.

When you become eligible for pension benefits or other investments start paying off, you may wish to decrease the amount of time you spend in working for pay and shift to part-time, temporary, or volunteer responsibilities. You may wish to continue the education that got sidelined because you had a family to support. You may wish to share your specialized knowledge by teaching, coaching, or mentoring others now exploring the route you have mastered. You may wish to finally see Paris, take golf lessons, or participate in a political campaign. Virtually nothing is impossible with sound preparation and targeted planning.

Your financial resources will largely dictate the pattern your newly balanced life will assume, but any income level can and should support a life that brings satisfaction and structure to the individuals involved. Enthusiasm for the day ahead is critical to anyone's enjoyment of life. This is true whether he or she is still practicing law at the age of 80 or took pension benefits at age 55 and volunteers at a hospital for sick children.

You need to sort out the equation that will give you the balance you want in your life. You need to identify your interests and skills and determine how they are being used now and how they could be better employed in the future.

If your present job or occupation represents everything you have ever wanted to do, you may want to keep right on doing it. You might want to modify your schedule or change the environment in which you practice your skill, but you are fortunate if you are already doing what you love and are suited for. If, on the other hand, your job has been simply a source of income and another vision of yourself burns in your brain, midlife may provide the opportunity to shift gears and finally do what you have always wanted to do.

Midlife ideally offers you the chance to transform your life by taking control of the parts of it that you can control. Your action to reshape, expand, and diversify your horizons can counteract any of the aspects of midlife that may distress you but are beyond your control. Children do reach adulthood and move away, careers do plateau and take downturns, and bodies do rebel against unreasonable demands. You can only do so much to influence these outcomes, so you should focus instead on the many exciting and enriching areas of life that remain open to your participation.

Midlife can be seen as one big reality check. You know where you have been and where you are now. With thoughtful and thorough planning for the future, you can attempt to know where you are going. Even if your life to date has been a long string of events and experiences over which you exercised no conscious control, you can now stop this procession and take charge of your life.

Acting in support of your own decisions is always a better strategy than reacting to the choices of others. This unit of Think of Your Future will help you to look objectively at your own interests and skills and then to apply them to your own personal plans for the future.

In determining the part that work, study, leisure, and community service will each play in the years ahead, you should remember that these plans can be adjusted at any time. Change is the only constant in life, and you will want to review the plans you are making now every few years to see if they still apply to your life, your financial situation, and your wishes.

ASSESSMENT

Olga Ramirez

What Would You Do?

The case studies that follow depict situations that persons might confront as they approach future planning. Making decisions about work, education, and leisure that support one's chosen or accepted lifestyle is the focus of these examples.

None of the cases may reflect your life situation, but brainstorming options and solutions to the challenges that face other persons can bring unexpected clarity to your own plans for the years ahead. What would you do if you were in their positions? If you are reviewing Think of Your Future on your own, you may want to discuss these cases with close friends or family members. Group settings for future planning will use the studies for workshop sessions.

When Olga's husband suffered a disabling stroke, she had been out of the paid work force for 25 years. Before their children were born, she had worked as a bookkeeper for several years. While the children were growing up, Olga used her accounting skills as a volunteer with the family's church. She enjoyed the work, but she had never used a computerized accounting system before and found it intimidating.

Olga's husband has now stabilized and is living at home, but he will not be able to go back to work. He is all right on his own for several hours at a time but cannot be left alone all day. Olga and he have realized that she should get a part-time job, both to bring in needed money and to relieve her from the tedium of being at home all the time.

Based on what you know about Olga's situation, what would you advise her to do?

_____

_____

_____

_____

What are Olga's options? (Remember that balance is an important consideration in planning roles in any lifestyle.)

_____

_____

What are the advantages of each option?

_____

_____

What are the disadvantages of each option?

_____

_____

What would be your recommendation to Olga? Why?

_____

_____

Roger Brown

Roger has recently taken pension benefits from a large consumer products company after 38 years of service. His wife died shortly before he left his full-time position, and Roger is feeling very much adrift. His own health and financial position are excellent, but the midlife plans he had made with his wife now appear useless.

Roger had thought he would appreciate having all the time in the world to play golf, but he finds that just as boring as anything else that he might do all the time. His main work role was in publicity and public relations, and he enjoys meeting the public and promoting a product. He does not particularly want to go back to work, but he is having a hard time deciding on what he does want to do.

The academic environment has always intrigued Roger. He thinks that this might be because he never got his fill of it, having quit college to go to work.

Based on what you know about Roger's situation, what would you recommend he do?

_____

_____

_____

What are Roger's options?

_____

What are the advantages of each option?

_____

What are the disadvantages of each option?

_____

What would you suggest to Roger? Why?

_____

_____

Abby Nathan

Abby married right after college and spent the next 25 years being a full-time wife, mother, and homemaker. She used her degree in biology to help her four children become superb science students and kept a secret fantasy that one day she would be a medical doctor. Abby worked as a volunteer for many years at the local university hospital.

Now Abby and her husband are divorced, and their youngest child has struck out on his own. Abby's former husband has honored their long partnership with a fair and generous financial settlement, but Abby must now make a life for herself. After long service to others, Abby is eager to focus on herself. She is not quite sure how to do it, however.

Based on what you know about Abby, what would you suggest she do?

_____

_____

_____

_____

What are Abby's options?

_____

What are the advantages of each option?

_____

What are the disadvantages of each option?

_____

What would you advise Abby to do? Why?

_____

_____

Personal Planning

Bill Hansen

Bill has taken pension benefits from his job as a crane operator for a large Midwestern construction company. He is married with three grown children and four grandchildren, who all live nearby. Being a husband, father, and grandfather have been Bill's most treasured roles, and he considers himself and his wife very fortunate.

Bill has an aptitude for machinery, small engines, and appliances and is considered the neighborhood handyman. Recently his success at restoring a vintage jukebox was featured in a newspaper article. Since then, he has received offers to buy his jukebox and requests to restore other jukeboxes around the country.

He enjoys letting his grandchildren and other youngsters from the community watch him work. He is now starting to teach the ones who are interested how simple machines are put together.

Even though Bill loves all aspects of his life, he senses that he might like to do something more or different.

Based on what you know about Bill, what would you recommend?

_____

_____

_____

_____

What are Bill's options?

_____

_____

What are the advantages of each option?

_____

_____

What are the disadvantages of each option?

_____

_____

What would you advise Bill to do? Why?

_____

_____

The assessment process in planning how you will spend your time in the years ahead requires that you spend concentrated time now thinking about yourself. This may be an unfamiliar activity for you, especially if you have spent your life responding to the needs and demands of others. You should give yourself a chance to get used to the idea and then relish the self-indulgence.

Assessment is essential to any stage in life's journey. At this point in your life, you know that doing what you enjoy and what you do well brings you greater satisfaction and leads to greater productivity than anything else. Determining just what you do enjoy doing and do well and how that information translates into your interests and skills is the substance of the assessment step in this unit. You will also evaluate the balance in your life, as it has been to date and as you wish it to be in the future, between education, work, and leisure.

Evaluating Your Skills

You have developed interests and skills over your lifetime in response to your educational experience, your family and other exposure, and opportunities that have come to you or that you have created. The roles in which you have found greatest fulfillment and personal satisfaction have no doubt made the greatest use of your interests and skills. Identifying the lifelong patterns of what motivates you, what you enjoy doing, and what you do well can be the key to building your plans for the future on your current strengths.

The first step in this process is to evaluate your skills in three areas on the checklist that follows. The skills you use with people, things, and information can be described in three broad groups: personal skills, experience skills, and knowledge skills. A helpful way for you to begin to identify your skills in each of the three areas is to complete sentences that begin with "I am," "I can," and "I know." You might say, for example, "I am organized," "I can type," or "I know grammar." "I am" skills describe your personal characteristics, "I can" skills come from your experience, and "I know" skills reflect your knowledge.

As you proceed now to the checklist, you should highlight those skills that apply to you in each group. Add any skills that apply to you but do not appear on the lists. Finally, select three or four skills from each list that you think are your strongest assets.

Checklist of Skills

Personal Skills: How You Interact with Others — "I am…"

Adaptable	Enthusiastic	Outgoing	Tactful
Aggressive	Flexible	Patient	Thorough
Attentive to detail	Friendly	Perceptive	Thoughtful
Calm	Generous	Polite	Trustworthy
Candid	Good-looking	Positive	Vigorous
Careful	Gracious	Practical	Warm
Caring	Hard-working	Precise	*Others:*
Competitive	Honest	Punctual	
Confident	Humorous	Realistic	_____
Cooperative	Imaginative	Reasonable	
Creative	Independent	Reliable	_____
Curious	Industrious	Resourceful	
Dependable	Intelligent	Responsible	_____
Diplomatic	Loyal	Sensitive	
Discreet	Methodical	Sincere	_____
Dynamic	Objective	Sociable	
Efficient	Optimistic	Spontaneous	_____
Energetic	Organized	Stable	

Experience Skills: What You Do Well — "I can…"

Administer	Draw	Mediate	Tabulate
Advise	Edit	Motivate	Team build
Arrange	Evaluate	Navigate	Test
Assign	Examine	Negotiate	Travel
Bargain	Experiment	Paint	Update
Check	Facilitate	Perform	Write
Coach	File	Plan	*Others:*
Collect	Forecast	Prioritize	
Compute	Guide	Problem solve	_____
Coordinate	Help	Promote	
Construct	Identify	Purchase	_____
Dance	Initiate	Reason	
Decide	Interpret	Record	_____
Delegate	Inventory	Restore	
Demonstrate	Lead	Review	_____
Design	Lecture	Screen	
Diagnose	Listen	Serve	_____
Direct	Make	Summarize	
Draft	Map	Supervise	_____

Checklist of Skills

Knowledge Skills: What You Have Learned — "I know…"

Accounting	Decorating	Law	*Others:*
Architecture	Etiquette	Literature	_____
Art	Fashion	Medicine	
Auto mechanics	Film making	Music	_____
Ballet	Financial planning	Political process	
Baseball	First aid	Punctuation	_____
Basketball	Fishing	Secretarial procedures	
Biology	Flower arranging	Sociology	_____
Bookkeeping	Football	Spelling	
Botany	Foreign language	Stage production	_____
Child care	Fund-raising	Statistics	
Community resources	Gardening	Tax law	_____
Cooking	Geography	Teaching	
Computers	Grammar	TV production	_____
Cosmetology	Health care	Word processing	
Current events	History		_____
Customs	Home decorating		

By adulthood, each of us has developed special interests. Your interests evolve as a result of your activities over the course of a lifetime. Interests are those subjects, activities, and relationships that you like and enjoy pursuing. Civil War history, photography, traveling, music, baseball, spending time with your grandchildren, and gourmet cooking are all examples of interests. In the space below, list as many of your interests as you can identify.

Interests

_____

_____

_____

_____

_____

_____

_____

_____

_____

_____

You can use your skills and interests to discover new roles or activities you might like to explore in the future. You will probably find roles that draw on what you are good at (your skills) and what you enjoy (your interests) to be both successful and rewarding. Completing the Pattern of Personal Elements Chart on page 18 can help you to cluster your skills and interests to generate new and exciting roles for your future.

The sample Pattern of Personal Elements Chart on page 17 was completed by LeRoy Charles, a sales manager with teenage children. He enjoys fishing, water sports, computers, painting, and art history. LeRoy is very involved with environmental issues in his community. Some of the skills he has developed on the job and in other past roles include marketing, writing, teaching, learning, researching, communicating, motivating, and guiding. As you will see, he is trying to incorporate his experience and preferences into possible new roles.

Pattern of Personal Elements Chart

Skills	Interests	Future Roles
1. Writing Teaching Researching	1. Fishing Water sports	1. Write a newspaper column about fishing
2. Learning Researching	2. Fishing Environmental issues	2. Take a study trip to the Caribbean to learn about marine life
3. Teaching Guiding Motivating Marketing	3. Computers	3. Become a marketing consultant for SCORE
4. Communicating Guiding Teaching	4. Painting Art History	4. Volunteer as a docent in an art gallery or museum
5.	5.	5.
6.	6.	6.
7.	7.	7.
8.	8.	8.
9.	9.	9.
10.	10.	10.

Personal Planning

Pattern of Personal Elements Chart

Skills	Interests	Future Roles
1.	1.	1.
2.	2.	2.
3.	3.	3.
4.	4.	4.
5.	5.	5.
6.	6.	6.
7.	7.	7.
8.	8.	8.
9.	9.	9.
10.	10.	10.

Personal Planning

Future planning can help you work deferred dreams into everyday reality by recognizing them and plotting them into your goals for the years ahead. The following questions may help you reflect on the exercise you have just completed. The insight you gain will equip you to develop the Action Step and the Master Action Plan later in this unit.

- Have you excluded any possibilities from your chart because "it'll never happen"? Why do you think so? Is making it happen something over which you have any control?

- Do all your entries cluster around one or two interests or skills? Does this focus really represent your preferences, or have you shut down for any reason on more imaginative, expansive choices?

- Have you considered this unit's elements of work, study, community, and leisure in completing the chart? Are all your elements included in your entries? Are all four elements part of your plans for the future as you now see them?

- Do you now see any areas on the chart that you would like to revise? Please go back and do so if this is the case.

The Times of Your Life

Aiming for balance among the major categories of your personal roles is another goal of this unit's assessment step. The two-part pie chart that appears on page 21 allows you to estimate the percentage of time you devote now to the different activities in your life and the percentage you would ideally like to spend in the future in each category. Picturing the reality of how you spend your time in this graphic manner can open your eyes to imbalances in your life that you may not have recognized before.

The sample completed chart shows how a typical participant in Think of Your Future might fill out this assessment tool. Follow this example as you assess your own pattern of time.

You should review and revise this exercise and all other assessment tools periodically over the years. Future planning is a continuous process that must conform to the flow and flux of the planner's life. Change is constant, and keeping plans current is thus an ongoing responsibility.

What Is

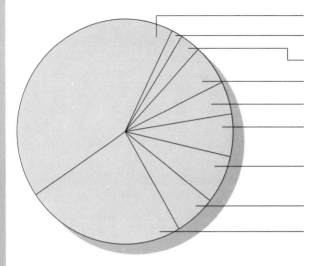

Sleeping and eating	70
Religious activities	3
Outdoor activities	5
Reading, TV, radio	10
Recreation, socializing	8
Home, shopping, repairs	10
Family activities	12
Commuting	10
Work	40
Total. hours	**168**

What Could Be

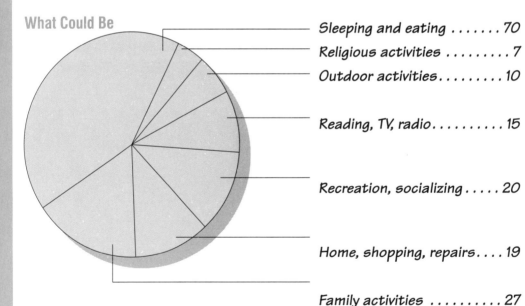

Sleeping and eating	70
Religious activities	7
Outdoor activities	10
Reading, TV, radio	15
Recreation, socializing	20
Home, shopping, repairs	19
Family activities	27
Total. hours	**168**

Pattern of Time

What Is

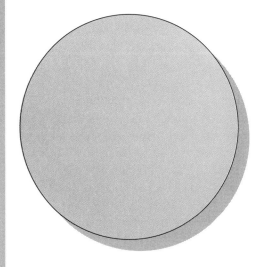

_____
_____
_____
_____
_____
_____
_____
_____
_____
_____

**Total
hours**   _____

What Could Be

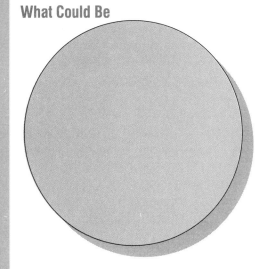

_____
_____
_____
_____
_____
_____
_____
_____
_____
_____

**Total
hours**   _____

Comparing "What Is" and "What Could Be" in your pattern of time provides graphic evidence of how you spend yourself through allotments of time in the present and how you might reassign yourself in the future. The questions that follow may help you understand the lesson of the graphs for your planning activities.

■ Did both you and your spouse or partner complete Pattern of Time graphs? How do they compare? Are they compatible? If they are drastically different from each other, can you live with the results? How?

■ Do your "What Is" and "What Could Be" time allotments differ radically? Is the first list the reality of right now, and the second list the ideal of the distant future? How will you convert from one to the other? Do you need a third, transitional list possibly labeled "On the Way to…"?

■ Have you followed your own dictates in filling in the list? Your time is one of your most precious commodities, and only you know how you want to spend it.

■ How will your "What Could Be" list affect the goals you will determine in your future planning? Do these allotments of time fit in with the other elements of your planning as you see them now?

ALTERNATIVES

The self-assessment you have just conducted should put you in the frame of mind to let your imagination wander across the broad range of possibilities your future may include. Regardless of where you are in the life cycle or in your lifetime of experience, there is no time like the present to reinvent yourself and to seize a new day for yourself. Reality may keep you anchored, but it should not stop you from trying to carve out the best life plan you can conceive. This is what Think of Your Future hopes you will accomplish through your participation in this program.

Education

Lifelong learning, whether in formal programs, from a book, or through your experiences and surroundings, can form a framework for a successful life plan. Remaining open to new information, opinions, and environments reveals an attitude that will be forever youthful, inquisitive, and both interesting and interested. You will want to consider this component of your life balance very carefully.

Nontraditional students form a large part of many college and other educational populations. Continuing education courses, GED programs, vocational and technical education classes, and advanced degree curriculums in numerous subjects all cater to the student whose formal education has been interrupted for one reason or another. Financial assistance can often be obtained for determined students, so you should never let the potential cost of pursuing your educational dream deter you.

Learning in Adulthood

Adults returning to the classroom after intervals of many years report the thrill of the respect that now comes to them from their instructors, who may be younger and less experienced than they are. Teachers in such situations usually perceive themselves as facilitators of learning rather than as disseminators of information.

The whole approach of adult education is to place value on the learner as an integral and vital part of the process of learning. You would no doubt appreciate, as other adult students have, being encouraged to share your experiences, having classes tailored to your needs, and discussing as much with other students as you might once have with your teachers.

Nontraditional College Programs

Community colleges present classes, courses, seminars, conferences, and lectures that are tailored to their local population and generally to the adult student. Many colleges offer degree programs that require little or no time on site at the institution. Most external degree programs grant credit for college-level learning achieved in any setting. The adult learner can also audit college classes, attending the sessions but avoiding the stress of exams, reports, and papers.

The College Level Examination Program (CLEP) offers more than 50 examinations in general and specific subjects that allow persons who pass them to receive college credit without enrolling in or attending the class involved. The opportunity to "CLEP" out of classes is recognized by close to 2,000 colleges and universities. This program is ideal for the adult with a lifetime of experience and a desire for a college degree. The Think of Your Future appendix includes resources that you can contact to find out more about CLEP and the other educational options discussed in this unit.

Continuing Education Units (CEUs), which may be applied to college credit, are awarded for participation in organized continuing education seminars, conferences, and other events. Each unit represents ten hours of instruction in a qualified setting. Sponsors of such events let enrollees know that CEUs are available, and each enrollee then needs to apply for the credit. Many job-related training conferences offer CEU credits.

Staff development training courses put on by employers can also be evaluated as comparable to college-level study and receive college credits. The American Council on Education (ACE) Program on Non-Collegiate Sponsored Instruction administers these evaluations. Educational institutions accept its recommendations at their own discretion.

Elderhostel/Interhostel

Two of the most popular adult education programs are Elderhostel and Interhostel, which offer week-long classes on college and university campuses during the summer months. Elderhostel is available at institutions in all 50 states to persons age 60 and older, and Interhostel offers summer study abroad to individuals age 50 and older.

Courses cover a broad range of subjects and are often supplemented with field trips and social events. Participants live in college dormitories during the experience. The Think of Your Future appendix can guide you to these organizations if you are interested in pursuing these programs.

Other Suggestions

Less formal opportunities are available as well. These include correspondence courses, self-study programs, social/travel vacation schools, and special-interest programs offered by churches, museums, organizations, and community groups. The Think of Your Future appendix includes suggested resources for exploring many of these educational possibilities.

Correspondence courses are offered by all-mail schools or by the extension divisions of large universities, which may grant degrees in this manner. The quality and value of programs available through both sources vary widely, and you should check carefully on any such program you are considering.

Adult learning is also available through telecredit courses, audiotape and videotape instruction, Mind Extension University, and computer networks such as America Online and PC Link that offer classes and workshops. Various computer bulletin boards provide the opportunity for the exchange of information and viewpoints among registered members. Senior Net, a California-based nonprofit organization, works through local groups to develop computer skills in older learners.

Vocational and technical schools provide specialized hands-on training to help students obtain or retain employment, develop skills, and gather information for going into business for themselves. Classes include subjects like nursing, word processing, computer skills, printing, and culinary arts.

Many vocational and technical schools target displaced homemakers — women never in the work force or out for extended periods who, for economic reasons, must now find paid employment. Job-related training classes offered to this clientele are linked directly to opportunities in the work force. The Women Work! program sponsors job-readiness classes, classroom training, counseling, and information and referrals to other community resources.

Work

Working throughout life is an idea that many individuals heartily endorse. Economic realities may require that you stay employed in one capacity or another, but many additional reasons support this decision as a means to remain productive, challenged, and responsible. These intellectual and emotional rewards are available from volunteer positions as well as from paying jobs, and both will be considered in this section.

Reevaluating your employment situation at midlife is an important part of planning for your future. You have already defined your interests and skills. Now you need to assess how they fit with work roles you may already have or may be considering for the years ahead.

This is another part of the "clean slate" exercise, starting at ground zero. You may choose or need to continue in your current job for the indefinite future. Looking at it anew with the information you have gathered on yourself will nevertheless be instructive for the future. If you find that ideally you are better suited to a different line of work or type of organization, you can strive for those changes in the years ahead.

Past and present job situations can help you to determine whether you prefer working in teams or alone, in large or small organizations, and with structured or unstructured assignments. Your family responsibilities, volunteer activities, and leisure pursuits also provide keys to your likes and dislikes in dealing with people and accomplishing tasks and goals. The

Desirable Work Characteristics

Check off those characteristics you find most desirable. Do your potential work options have those characteristics? You may begin to eliminate some of your options if the characteristics of the job do not match the qualities you would like to see in a work role.

People

Individual assignment
- [ ] Alone (mostly)
- [ ] On a team (mostly)
- [ ] Divided between working alone and on a team

Supervision from others
- [ ] Close
- [ ] Moderate
- [ ] Little

Supervising others
- [ ] To a great extent
- [ ] To a moderate extent
- [ ] Very little
- [ ] None at all

Contact with customers/ clients/the public
- [ ] To a great extent
- [ ] To a moderate extent
- [ ] Very little
- [ ] None at all

Type of Organization
- [ ] Profit
- [ ] Nonprofit
- [ ] Deals in products
- [ ] Deals in services
- [ ] Well-established
- [ ] New/high-risk/growth industry
- [ ] Small
- [ ] Large
- [ ] Highly structured
- [ ] Unstructured
- [ ] Guaranteed earnings
- [ ] Commissions or merit bonuses

- [ ] Centralized
- [ ] Decentralized
- [ ] High turnover, good promotion possibilities
- [ ] Stable work force
- [ ] Clear lines of authority
- [ ] Lines of authority shift with new projects
- [ ] Clearly defined responsibilities
- [ ] Flexibility to define one's own work to some degree
- [ ] Self-employed
- [ ] Employed by others
- [ ] Private industry
- [ ] Government
- [ ] Association
- [ ] Educational institution
- [ ] Other

Location of Work
- [ ] Within a mile of home
- [ ] In urban center
- [ ] In suburb
- [ ] In rural area
- [ ] Mostly indoors
- [ ] Mostly outdoors
- [ ] Both indoors and outdoors
- [ ] Work at home
- [ ] Work in office/shop/store/ other
- [ ] Work at desk or station
- [ ] Work in multiple locations
- [ ] Extensive travel
- [ ] Some travel
- [ ] No travel

Number of Hours Per Week
- [ ] 40+ hours a week
- [ ] 30–40 hours
- [ ] 20–29 hours
- [ ] 10–19 hours
- [ ] Fewer than 10 hours

Content and Pace of Work
- [ ] Deal mostly with things
- [ ] Deal mostly with people
- [ ] Deal mostly with data/ information
- [ ] Split between things/data
- [ ] Split between people/data
- [ ] Split between things/people
- [ ] Same work as now
- [ ] Similar work to now
- [ ] Different work from now
- [ ] Service work
- [ ] Manual work
- [ ] Office work
- [ ] Always busy, fast-paced
- [ ] Steady pace
- [ ] Slow pace
- [ ] Mixed pace

Number of Days per Week
- [ ] 5 days a week
- [ ] 4 days a week
- [ ] 3 days a week
- [ ] 2 days a week
- [ ] 1 day a week

checklists on page 25 will help you get your job preferences down on paper.

After you have checked off all the work characteristics that you appreciate in an employment situation, you should list all of the checked items on a separate sheet of paper. This collection of preferences should give you a profile of the kind of work or volunteer setting that is most appropriate for you.

If you are well matched with these characteristics in your current job or voluntary position, the preferences inventory confirms your wisdom! If your present situation varies widely from the description shown in your list, this may explain any dissatisfaction you may have. It would also indicate that a change might be appropriate, either now if possible or through the goals you will be setting for the future.

Flexible Work Options

Flexibility in the work force and the workplace has increased to meet the needs of employers for valuable workers who do not necessarily fit the traditional employee model of the past. Students, parents, and persons with other sources of income may wish to work only part-time and in their own workspace. Employers may need full staffs only during peak periods and other business upswings. Many options exist for tailoring jobs to your own preferences and your employer's needs without compromising either.

Part-time jobs may have fixed schedules to cover specific periods of time or they may focus on a particular task that the worker can do at his or her discretion. Handling the information desk at a museum during Saturday hours and getting a client's tax returns ready by April 15 are examples of the two kinds of part-time work. Many temporary agencies and some employers have job banks for listing part-time jobs and available part-time workers.

Job sharing is a concept in which two workers split the hours, responsibility, and benefits of one full-time job. Many employers need to be shown the extra advantages that come with two workers essentially for the price of one. These include increased productivity and less downtime, less turnover, year-round job coverage, retention of valued employees who don't want to work full-time, reduced training costs, and twice the skills, experience, and ideas usually found in one full-time staff person.

Temporary work through an agency that provides full- and part-time workers for special projects or crunch periods is an excellent way to test different work environments to see if they meet your needs. It also gives you additional training and up-to-date work experience. Some employers hire temporary workers directly from a pool of their former employees or approved contract workers.

Flextime programs require that all workers be on the job for certain core hours each day but allow individuals to arrange the rest of their work hours to suit themselves.

Flexiplace programs enable employees to work partly or entirely at home, frequently using computers to communicate with their offices or plants.

Sabbaticals, paid or unpaid leave from jobs for up to a year, may be available to some midlife workers. If used productively to plan aggressively for the future by updating or learning job skills, developing personal interests, and preventing burnout, such changes of pace can be tremendously helpful.

Phased retirement may be of interest to you if you plan to take your pension benefits and eventually explore other options in your life. Under this arrangement, you can gradually reduce the hours you work over a year or two and still receive full benefits. Your pension benefits may be decreased as a result of lowered income during your last two years of employment, however.

Mentoring programs that pair experienced workers with less experienced employees are an especially effective way of using the phased retirement period. The younger worker, the older worker, and the employer all benefit when skills and responsibilities are passed on in an orderly transition of this kind.

The Midlife Job Search

Flexible options and nontraditional job descriptions may not be your primary concern at this time. You may simply want or need to find employment.

Corporate reorganizations and relocations, changing career paths, and personal financial situations have brought many midlife and older persons face-to-face with a situation they thought they had left behind them — looking for a job. At the same time, many women in midlife are entering the work force for the first time as a result of divorce, widowhood, family economic pressures, or simple desire for paid employment.

Finding the right volunteer slot for yourself involves basically the same approach as finding the right job. Both role searches require the same strategies that will be covered here briefly.

The Think of Your Work Future program and materials, sponsored and distributed across the country by AARP, offer detailed assistance in defining and seeking the job that is right for you. Local organizations that specialize in matching midlife job seekers with available jobs and with peer support groups may be of great help in your community. Colleges and other educational institutions often present job-coaching seminars that guide participants, largely mature first-time job seekers, through each step of the job-search process. Your own independent research at your neighborhood library and bookstore will also yield helpful guidance and information on finding a job and making it yours.

Collecting Job-Search Information

You have already identified the interests and skills that you bring to your job search and hope to have mirrored in your ideal job. You have also reviewed the nature and dimensions of your ideal employer. Now you need to locate available positions.

Information can come from three main sources: observing, reading, and talking with others. Expand your local networks as you seek information, considering how educational, civic, religious, government, and professional groups can help you. Get up-to-date information on all of your top job possibilities before you discard any of them. Identify potential barriers to your employment, and ask others to help you find innovative ways around them.

If you are new to the job-search process, you may want to plan and conduct several practice interviews. This is an easy, practical, and no-pressure way to gain interview experience. You select an individual who knows something about a field or company you may be interested in and ask if you can talk with them about it. This kind of research interview gives you valuable facts and insights about a particular job, employer, or industry and helps you refine your choice of job options.

Communicating About Yourself

Conveying a positive attitude about your skills and experiences in your written job-search material is one of the best ways to communicate effectively about yourself. Describe yourself in your resume so potential employers can see clearly that you have the abilities and expertise they need. Be responsible for the accuracy of your resume, cover letter, application form, or other written communications. Seek current advice on appropriate formats for your materials. Ask others to review your work for content, consistency, and eye appeal.

The Job Interview

The positive attitude you displayed in your written communications must now be maintained through your in-person contacts with your potential employer. You should spend time preparing and practicing for the employment interview. Learning background information about the company or organization will help you ask intelligent questions during the interview as well as give informed answers. Practicing for the interview by role-playing with family members or friends can help you improve your confidence and your ability to sell yourself during the interview.

You should always respond to the interviewer's queries in terms of what you can do rather than what you cannot do. Present your skills and interests clearly so the employer can see what you have to offer the hiring organization. Emphasize your positive work ethic. Be honest about your strengths and accomplishments but tend to modesty over arrogance. Never lie or brag. Let the interviewer know you are willing and able to do a good job.

Take responsibility after the interview, beginning with thanking the interviewer as you leave for speaking with you. Send a thank-you letter also. Make some notes for yourself about your performance during the interview. Contact the interviewer when you have been told the organization will be making its decision.

Homemakers in the Job Market

Women who have been career mothers and homemakers often approach the job search with fear and anxiety because they believe they have no work experience to present to potential employers. In reality, such women have developed management skills by being leaders in their family systems. If they have worked as volunteer program coordinators, administrators, or fund-raisers, they have acquired additional skills that can be transferred to paid employment.

If a prospective employer is to know what you do well, you must be able to convert your experience as family organizer, manager, supervisor, problem-solver, and trainer into language that is recognizable in the work force. Giving titles to what you may see as everyday skills allows an employer to see your potential.

Programs that work specifically with women entering or reentering the job market after long absences focus directly on these concerns. Both the American Red Cross and the Association of Junior Leagues have publications that address the issue of identifying the skills acquired through volunteer service. Further information appears in the Think of Your Future appendix.

Self-Employment

Owning your own business and being your own boss may be a dream you have had for years. Midlife planning for the future may include this possibility, and midlife pension benefits may provide a financial framework within which it might become reality.

Before you take this step, think long and hard, do careful research, and get advice from individuals who have first-hand knowledge of what you are contemplating. The Service Corps of Retired Executives (SCORE), a program of the Small Business Administration, offers the guidance of experienced retired executives in various fields to entrepreneurs and small business owners in related areas. Local chambers of commerce and financial institutions sometimes offer planning assistance as well.

Some entrepreneurial ventures are considerably more risky than others. Franchising and other businesses that require large investments of capital to get them off the ground are clearly more dangerous financially than consulting and other personal services. Fast-food restaurants, video stores, car washes, motels, and other national franchising concerns typically sell you the right to run an outlet for their product or service in a particular area. In return for your investment, which can be sizable, they provide the name, products, methods, advertising, training, and management advice. Extensive research should go into investigating any franchise you are considering, and an attorney should advise you on legal aspects of any such enterprise.

Real estate sales and businesses like accounting, editing, and repair services that you can run from your home office represent risks essentially only of time spent without compensation. You should attempt to start up such ventures while you are still employed full-time in a salaried position to test their viability. You will want to take note of zoning, licensing, and other restrictions that may apply to working out of your home. A certified public accountant can advise you on legitimate tax deductions and benefits of home-based businesses.

Any successful business has five basic ingredients. You will want to consider how your proposed effort stands up to these criteria:

- A good idea; a needed product or service;
- A good location (for a retail business);
- Good management skills, including record-keeping, cost control, cash flow management, marketing and distribution, and interpersonal aptitude;
- Financial stability; and

■ A practical, well-thought-out business plan for at least the first three years of operation.

You will also want to determine if you have the personal qualities and resources that will help you succeed in your own business. These are as follows:

■ Good personal health, high energy level, willingness to work hard over extended periods;

■ Ability to make informed decisions quickly and stick to them;

■ Willingness to take responsibility for what goes wrong as well as what goes right;

■ Orientation to wise risk taking;

■ Ability to manage crises in a calm, poised, and clearheaded manner;

■ Objectivity about yourself, your business, and other people;

■ Balanced perspective between detail orientation and being able to see the big picture; and

■ Support of family and friends and willingness to let those affected by your business decisions participate in your plans.

Volunteering

Your interest in giving something back to your community and to society at large may increase in midlife as other pressures of family and livelihood start to ease. On the other hand, you may have spent many years as an active volunteer and now want to enter the paid work force or follow your own personal agenda. Volunteering is a part of most persons' lives at one time or another and should be considered as part of planning for the future.

You should approach volunteer roles with the same care you take in choosing work-force positions. Matching your interests and skills to responsibilities you take on voluntarily will increase both your effectiveness in the role and your satisfaction in taking it on. The Think of Your Future appendix includes resources for identifying volunteer opportunities.

Everyday kindnesses performed in the name of friendship or neighborliness can be described as informal volunteering. Checking on a frail or ill friend or neighbor, teaching the boy next door how to bat a ball, and tutoring an acquaintance in a subject you know well are all ways to share yourself with others.

Educational Opportunities. Adult literacy is a cause that draws many midlife individuals into volunteering. Teaching adults to read is a tremendously satisfying experience and a desperately needed service that now has the commitment of many communities and organizations. Reading and writing services for blind or other persons with limitations are also needed.

Schools at all levels can always use volunteers for one-on-one interaction with students with special needs, for teaching specialty subjects, and for helping with transportation and tutoring. Big brother and big sister programs match adults with young people whose own families may need help in rearing them.

Cultural Opportunities. Museums, art centers, theater groups, orchestras, public radio and television stations, and opera and ballet companies all depend on volunteer assistance to operate. Important positions include fund-raisers, guides and ushers, announcers, stage managers, costume designers, docents and instructors, and other creative roles.

Health-related Opportunities. All hospitals use volunteer workers as receptionists, gift shop attendants, file clerks, nurse's aides, and companions to patients. A volunteer director usually trains the volunteer force and places members where they are needed in the hospital.

Hospice programs, nursing homes, telephone hot lines, mental health associations, emergency rescue squads, and the American Red Cross need volunteer help as well. Organizations that raise money to combat and treat AIDS, Alzheimer's disease, cancer, child abuse, schizophrenia, and many other physical, social, and mental illnesses all depend on volunteers to help in their efforts.

Services to Older Adults. Many local organizations that provide services to frail or isolated elderly persons rely on volunteers for the bulk of their outreach activities. Meals on Wheels, phone-link programs, adult day care, and regular home visits are some of the services that volunteers provide to help clients stay in their own homes rather than move to supervised housing.

Lobbying for the rights of older adults is another activity that midlife volunteers may want to pursue. AARP, the Gray Panthers, and many state and local groups provide materials, focus, and activities that help in this effort.

Political and Civic Opportunities. Volunteers can work for good government in many ways. Nonpartisan groups, like the League of Women Voters, and local political party affiliates both need volunteers to help with the stimulating and strenuous work of local, state, and national election campaigns. Civic organizations ranging from the chamber of commerce to specific environmental or consumer groups all provide a significant amount of fund-raising and other services to community programs. Volunteers are the backbone of these efforts.

Government-Sponsored Opportunities. The federal government sponsors several volunteer programs, some especially geared to midlife and older participants. The Action agency administers VISTA (Volunteers in Service to America), RSVP (Retired Senior Volunteer Program), the Foster Grandparents Program, and the Senior Companions Program. Volunteers in these programs may receive small stipends.

The National Park Service has volunteer openings, as does the Department of Veterans Affairs. Volunteers for SCORE/ACE (Service Corps of Retired Executives/Active Corps of Executives) use their skills to help individuals who are starting their own businesses.

International openings for volunteers exist as well. The Peace Corps is eager to recruit midlife and older Americans who are willing to share their skills and experience overseas. VITA (Volunteers in Technical Assistance) is a private, nonprofit organization that brings technical assistance to persons and groups in more than a hundred developing countries. The International Executive Service Corps offers business counseling in other countries in a program similar to that offered here by SCORE.

Leisure

Leisure roles may represent the one area of future planning for which you need little guidance. You may already have a long list of what you want to do when you "have a little time." You may also be the kind of person who has let your responsibilities take over your life and is unfamiliar with the concept of leisure time. Regardless of where you are in the spectrum of attitudes about leisure, you should address it as you Think of Your Future.

Your interests and skills will naturally incline you toward certain leisure pursuits. You may prefer rigorous physical activities like hiking, biking, or landscaping over contemplative choices like reading, writing, and painting. You may choose your solitude over group activities. Travel to you may mean going to the beach rather than going to Europe.

If you are planning your future with your spouse or partner, this could be an especially sensitive area to negotiate between you. This is exactly why you need to address the issue in your plans for the future. Unpleasant surprises can ruin the most idyllic of plans. If you know that you and your spouse or partner are on different wave lengths, you can cover these variances in your long-term planning by allowing each of you separate time and space.

RESPONSIBILITY

After assessing your interests and skills and considering the alternative ways you can use your time and energy in the future, you may be somewhat more comfortable about focusing entirely on yourself. This focus now needs to move into choices and decisions about the roles you see yourself taking on or maintaining in the years ahead.

You may have learned a good deal about yourself through this unit, and some of it may have surprised you. Let your thoughts continue to flow as you brainstorm about what you would really like to do with the rest of your personal life. Let fantasy contribute to your ideas along with reality as you formulate your plan. As you work, remember that no plan is set in concrete, that periodic review and revision are essential to any workable agenda, and that no one has the insight to decide now what you will be doing in twenty or thirty years.

Good luck with the Action Step that lies ahead! You may want to use the completed Action Step on the next page as a model for your own decisions. This sample represents the choices made by the typical Think of Your Future participant you met several pages ago. Then proceed to your own Action Step.

Personal Planning

Action Step

List any and all roles you might choose to pursue in the future. Remember your interests and skills as you compile the list. Think of choices in the suggested education, work, and leisure categories. Include volunteering as a role that spans all three categories. Use verbs — action words — to describe your new or revised roles.

When you believe your list is complete for now, rank your role choices in the right-hand column according to their importance to you, with number 1 being the most important. Use a second sheet of paper to continue your list if needed.

Actions Regarding Roles	Rank by Importance
Volunteer to work part time in art museum or gallery	2
Take a bicycle tour of Holland	3
Become a marketing consultant for SCORE/ACE	5
Write a newspaper column on fishing	1
Take Elderhostel or Earthwatch program in Caribbean to study marine life	4

Personal Planning

Action Step

List any and all roles you might choose to pursue in the future. Remember your interests and skills as you compile the list. Think of choices in the suggested education, work, and leisure categories. Include volunteering as a role that spans all three categories. Use verbs — action words — to describe your new or revised roles.

When you believe your list is complete for now, rank your role choices in the right-hand column according to their importance to you, with number 1 being the most important. Use a second sheet of paper to continue your list if needed.

Actions Regarding Roles	Rank by Importance

THE AARP APPROACH
PLANNING

You have now come to the final step in planning for your personal future, plotting out the specific actions you will take to meet the actions you have listed on your Action Step. Your Master Action Plan is the final product of this life component unit. It functions as your "to do" list for meeting your role goals.

You should list each of your Actions Regarding Roles from your Action Step as a Goal Statement on your MAP. Then follow through with the logical sequence of events that will result in fulfillment of each goal. You can review the sample Master Action Plan completed by the typical Think of Your Future participant to guide you in completing your own MAP.

Master Action Plan

Goal Statement: Write a newspaper column on fishing

Actions	Resources	Time Frame	By Whom?
1. Write 3–4 sample articles/columns	Library; other fishing enthusiasts	4 months	Self
2. Develop list of topics for future articles/columns	Library; other fishing enthusiasts	5 months	Self
3. Identify publications that might be interested in a fishing column	Library; fishing or leisure clubs/organizations	5 months	Self
4. Contact features or sports editor at each publication	Self	6 months	Self

Goal Statement: Volunteer to work in art museum or gallery

Actions	Resources	Time Frame	By Whom?
1. Take an art history class	Community college	4 months	Self
2. Contact museum volunteer administrator	Museum directory; volunteer referral organization	1 month	Self
3. Read books on art and art appreciation	Library; bookstore	Ongoing	Self
4. Take docent training	Museum	2 months	Self
5. Improve public speaking skills	Community college; library	4 months	Self

Personal Planning

Health
Planning

Health Planning

*G*ood health is life's only unmixed blessing. Being physically fit and medically sound has no downside at any point in life. You are fortunate to live in a time when health and fitness are receiving considerable emphasis throughout all sectors of society. Wellness coordinators make up a new employment category at many large organizations. Books and magazines, videotapes, health clubs, health products, fitness equipment, seminars, and workshops all advance the cause of getting you to take charge of your physical and emotional well-being.

Today's adults generally are healthier and more active than previous generations. If you are among them, congratulations! If you have some catching up to do, jump on board!

Your health is determined by the interaction of physical, emotional, and psychological factors, many of which you can control or influence. You can increase your chances of having good health through proper nutrition, exercise, rest, and a positive outlook on life. Most of today's health problems have their origins in matters of lifestyle — poor diet, lack of exercise, smoking, inappropriate reactions to stress, and misuse of drugs and alcohol.

A good health and fitness program does not have to be complicated or expensive. The best program is one that becomes part of your everyday life. You can make positive moves to change habits and revise routines at any point in your life with beneficial results for your general health and well-being.

This unit raises issues for you to consider in developing your health and fitness plan and provides information and resources to help you realize that plan. Remember that you are in charge of your health and fitness, just as you are in charge of other aspects of your life. Many professionals, organizations, programs, and publications can help you reach your goal for a healthful lifestyle now and in the future. Nevertheless, the one with the ultimate responsibility for your health is you.

Unit Objectives

■ **Assessment:** To assess the current state of your health, review your relative fitness in terms of lifestyle and medical history, and suggest changes you might want to make in the future

■ **Alternatives:** To consider various approaches to improving your health and fitness

■ **Responsibility:** To make decisions about your health and fitness that maximize your potential for a long, robust, and satisfying life

■ **Planning:** To make specific plans to put your health and fitness decisions into practice in ways that are practical, achievable, and affordable

What Do You Think?

The following questions raise some important health and fitness issues that you will want to consider now and review again periodically in the years ahead. You are encouraged to discuss them with family, friends, or other individuals in your support network. Group seminars based on Think of Your Future will use the questions as workshop discussion topics.

1. How can you reduce and manage the daily stress in your life?

2. What community resources are available to help you in a medical emergency? What emergencies of this kind can individuals prepare themselves to handle? How can you prepare yourself for such emergencies?

3. What are some simple adjustments that you can make in your eating habits to ensure good nutrition and improve your overall health?

4. What internal and external factors can affect personal health?

5. What actions should you consider in setting up a program to protect or improve your physical and mental health?

6. What is rhythmic exercise? Why is it important? Which sports and other activities provide continuous, rhythmic exercise?

We have the privilege of knowing more about healthful living than any generation before us. With this knowledge, we also have the responsibility to act on what we have learned to improve our own and our families' health and well-being. Be your own best advocate in every aspect of life. Nowhere is this self-sufficiency more urgent than with your health.

Increasing age does not automatically bring increasing infirmity or advancing disability. Individuals can and do live long and fully functional lives. The more you know about health and fitness, the better equipped you will be to lead yourself and the persons who are dear to you to improved physical, mental, and emotional health and fitness.

New information is available on the connection between mind and body, on the effect that your attitudes and emotions can have on your body. Researchers continue to discover how your lifestyle influences your health and fitness. You can keep yourself up to date on these matters simply by learning what publications, organizations, and individuals committed to health and fitness are reporting.

Preventive self-care includes being aware of your body and recognizing the early warning signs of potentially serious health problems. This unit of Think of Your Future includes basic information on illnesses and conditions that can occur at any point in the life cycle, but become more common as we grow older. You can reduce your risk of illness if you practice care and follow preventive measures.

Heart Disease

Coronary artery disease is the most common form of heart disease. It results from narrowing and blockage of arteries supplying the heart muscle. Symptoms, including shortness of breath, pain, weakness, and fatigue, usually do not occur until the disease is advanced. Preventing heart disease involves controlling the following risk factors:

- High blood pressure (hypertension). This condition is easy to diagnose. Make it a point to check your blood pressure regularly and report changes to your health care provider.
- Overweight. Studies have shown that significantly overweight middle-aged men have three times more risk of fatal heart attack than their thinner counterparts.
- Cigarette smoking. Heart attack risk increases directly with the number of cigarettes smoked.
- Lack of exercise. Inactive people have a higher risk of fatal heart attack than those who exercise.
- High cholesterol. If your cholesterol levels are not within normal range, your doctor will probably prescribe a diet low in fats — especially saturated fats — to help prevent clogged arteries.

Stroke

A stroke, or cerebrovascular accident, results when the blood supply to the brain is cut off, causing paralysis and sometimes death. Strokes are associated with many of the same risk factors as coronary artery disease.

Cancer

An abnormal growth of cells that invades and destroys normal body cells, cancer can spread quickly and be fatal if not detected early. With early detection, many forms of the disease can be arrested before they spread. The American Cancer Society lists seven danger signals for cancer. If any of these symptoms lasts more than two weeks, you should see your doctor.

1. Unusual bleeding or discharge.
2. A lump or thickening in the breast or elsewhere.
3. A sore that does not heal.
4. Change in bowel or bladder habits.
5. Persistent hoarseness or cough.
6. Indigestion or difficulty in swallowing.
7. Change in a wart or mole.

Breast Cancer

Breast cancer is the most common cancer in women. If detected early and treated, this serious disease does not have to be fatal. The keys to early detection are regular breast self-examination and mammograms.

The American Cancer Society has a free, waterproof card to place in your shower that will show you how to examine your breasts. Call 1-800-ACS-2345 to request the breast cancer self-examination card.

A mammogram is an X-ray procedure that can detect minute changes in the breast. All women over the age of 35 should have a baseline mammogram done for comparison with future mammograms. If your doctor does not recommend the procedure, you should bring up the subject. It can save your life.

The National Cancer Institute recommends that women have a mammogram every year or every other year, depending on their risk of developing breast cancer. After a woman has reached 50, she should have a mammogram annually. Women who have had breast cancer before

Safeguards Against Cancer

The American Cancer Society suggests these positive ways to detect different forms of cancer. Each individual needs to accept responsibility for his or her own health and act upon these suggestions.

Site	Action
Breasts	Monthly self-examination
Uterus	Pap test regularly
Prostate Gland	Rectal exam annually after 40
Lungs	Don't smoke cigarettes
Skin	Avoid excessive exposure to sun
Colon-rectum	Proctoscopic exam annually, especially after 40
Mouth	Exams regularly
Whole Body	Regular health checkup

or whose mothers or sisters have had it are far more likely than other women to develop breast cancer. These individuals should be especially diligent in early detection activities.

Many women fear mammograms because they have heard that the procedure is painful. In the hands of a skilled technician, a mammogram can be painless. The brief compression of the breast may be uncomfortable, but it is nothing to fear.

Some communities now offer low-cost screenings to low-income women. If lack of money or insurance is preventing you from having a mammogram done, ask your doctor whether such a service is available in your community. If you participate in an employer's group health plan, ask if the plan covers mammograms.

Menopause

Menopause, which is a natural step in a woman's life cycle, is often viewed as a disease and shrouded in the mystery our society tends to associate with sex and reproduction. Learning about menopause, especially before you experience it, can alleviate your concerns and worries.

Menopause marks the end of a woman's childbearing years. The menstrual cycle stops completely and with it, ovulation, the process that occurs each month as the mature egg passes from the ovaries to the uterus.

The menstrual cycle is triggered and regulated by two hormones, estrogen and progesterone. As a woman grows older, the body decreases the amount of estrogen it produces. When this happens, menstrual periods become irregular and eventually stop altogether. Because the cycle of irregular periods may go on for a few years before menopause, it is important to understand that you can still conceive children.

Many menopausal women experience hot flashes and vaginal dryness. Hot flashes appear without warning, causing the upper body to feel uncomfortably warm even in a cool setting. Many women whose menopausal symptoms are extreme or uncomfortable benefit from estrogen replacement therapy, also known as ERT. Doctors prescribe low dosages of the hormone estrogen, supplementing what the body no longer makes. It is most useful in treating hot flashes, vaginal irritation, and osteoporosis.

ERT, like any drug therapy, is not appropriate for every woman. Some women experience discomforting side effects. Discuss ERT therapy with your doctor and be sure to understand its benefits and risks.

Osteoporosis

Osteoporosis is a degenerative disease that involves the loss of normal bone density, mass, and strength. Its bone-thinning characteristic is responsible for the loss of height, stooped posture, and broken hips often seen in older women. Although women are four times more likely than men to develop the disease, men also suffer from osteoporosis.

Bone mass measurement, a simple, painless test that measures bone thickness with small amounts of radiation, can determine whether you have or are at risk of developing the condition. If your bone mass is low, your doctor can prescribe a program of treatment and monitor it with further measurements.

Osteoporosis can be prevented by consuming adequate amounts of calcium and by exercising regularly. The recommended daily amount of calcium for women after menopause is 1,500 milligrams, or the equivalent of six glasses of milk. You can also obtain calcium from yogurt, cheese, fish canned with bones, broccoli, collard greens, and calcium supplements.

Male Menopause

Men do not lose their reproductive ability in midlife as women do. They nevertheless do enter into a new stage of life that in many ways complements the experience of women. Physically, they may notice a gradual decrease in muscle mass and strength. They may experience psychological symptoms like lethargy, depression, mood swings, and irritability. Their sexuality may suffer from diminished interest and ability. At the same time, they may become more capable of real emotional closeness with their spouse, partner, or other important persons than at any time in their lives.

Prostate Problems

The prostate is a walnut-sized gland found only in men. The prostate, which produces semen, is located below the bladder, surrounding the urinary tube. Prostate enlargement may be the most common health problem of older men, and causes difficulty in urination. Prostate cancer is the most common cancer found in men. After age 50, an annual prostate exam is recommended.

Alzheimer's Disease

Public awareness of Alzheimer's disease has brought this form of memory loss to the front of everyone's consciousness. If you have noticed memory lapses or forgetfulness in yourself, you may have feared that you were developing this serious condition. Just as most skin lumps are not cancer, however, most slips of memory are not Alzheimer's disease.

Three kinds of memory lapse or memory loss are associated with age. The normal forgetfulness that may frustrate you when names, addresses, or dates are slow in coming is part of the normal aging process and does not necessarily worsen over time. Memory loss can also result from disorders or conditions like depression or malnutrition. This kind of memory loss can be reversed if the underlying condition is diagnosed and treated.

Alzheimer's disease is the most common form of the third kind of memory loss, which is a disease of the brain and not a normal part of the aging process. Alzheimer's is progressive and irreversible and includes a general decline in intellectual abilities and often-bizarre changes in behavior.

AIDS

Acquired Immune Deficiency Syndrome (AIDS) is becoming a fact of life for persons in all sectors and age groups of society. This deadly disease, in which the human immunodeficiency virus (HIV) effectively destroys the body's immune system, spares no family, community, or race. Persons in midlife may be infected themselves or be the spouse, partner, parent, grandparent, or caregiver of a person with AIDS.

Prevention begins with learning the facts. AIDS is spread from person to person through the exchange of bodily fluids, such as semen and blood. Most commonly, the virus is spread by sexual contact or by sharing drug needles and syringes with an infected person. Otherwise, AIDS is not easy to catch. Despite what many believe, AIDS is not spread by mosquito bites, using a public telephone or restroom, being coughed or sneezed on by an infected person, or touching someone with the disease.

The responsibility for preventing the spread of AIDS rests with each individual's behavior (for example, choosing to use condoms when sexually involved with someone other than a mutually faithful, uninfected partner).

Many HIV-positive adults and their caregivers or families feel isolated. Fear surrounding public disclosure about HIV/AIDS remains a painful issue for affected loved ones as well as for victims of the disease. Grief in nontraditional families may not be recognized or respected because society often ignores or excludes these loyalties.

Support groups and information are important to anyone battling any aspect of this tragic epidemic.

Depression

Everyone feels "down in the dumps" or "blue" from time to time. That is the human condition. When these feelings persist over long periods of time or are combined with difficulties in concentrating, sleeping and eating disorders, feelings of worthlessness, and other telltale symptoms, something else is at work.

Major depressive disorder, or clinical depression, is a common and treatable illness that can affect anyone. More than 11 million people each year in this country suffer from depression. This is a medical disorder that day after day affects your thoughts, feelings, physical health, and behaviors.

Some of the recognizable symptoms of depression are:

■ Change in eating, sleeping, or sexual habits;

■ Inability to concentrate or difficulty in making decisions;

■ Withdrawal from social contact;

■ Preoccupation with "aches and pains";

■ Persistent sadness or hopelessness; frequent crying for no apparent reason;

■ General irritability;

■ Thoughts of death or suicide, suicide attempts; and

■ Decreased energy or fatigue.

If you or a loved one appear unable to shake feelings of sadness and hopelessness over an extended period, you should arrange a visit to your doctor, clinic, or health maintenance organization. These health care providers can find out if your depression has a physical cause, treat it, and possibly refer you to a mental health specialist. Antidepressant medications, psychotherapy, or a combination of the two are most frequently prescribed for victims of depression. Some of the many resources available in this area are listed in the Think of Your Future appendix.

Alcohol and Nutrition

Moderate drinking (one or two drinks a day) may aid digestion, relieve stress, and stimulate the coronary arteries. Nevertheless, as people grow older, their bodies change the way they metabolize alcohol. The same amount of alcohol that was tolerable in youth may become a problem in later life.

Besides damaging the liver, brain, and heart, excessive drinking may lead to malnutrition. Alcohol contains no nutrients, and heavy drinkers often skimp on meals.

Another potential problem comes from mixing alcohol with certain medications. Check with your doctor about whether you can drink alcoholic beverages while on medication.

Wear and Repair

Throughout life, some of your body tissues and cells are continually rebuilt and renewed. Nutrition, rest, exercise, and stress influence the balance your body maintains between wearing down and rebuilding body tissues. As you grow older, your eyes, ears, and teeth change. These changes are normal, and you adapt to them. But some vision, hearing, and dental problems need treatment or correction, and others can be lessened or avoided.

Eyes

Cataracts, a cloudiness in the eye lens that interferes with vision, may develop quickly or over a number of years. Usual signs are hazy vision, double vision, or difficulty seeing at night. At first, special eyeglasses may help, but surgery is needed when the lens becomes opaque.

Glaucoma, loss of vision associated with increased pressure inside the eye, can go unnoticed and can lead to blindness if not treated. When detected and treated promptly, glaucoma need not cause serious vision loss.

Ears

Your ears control your balance as well as your ability to hear. Both faculties may be affected by aging. Almost everyone experiences some degree of hearing loss with age. Certain workers — tractor operators, drillers, factory workers, and aircraft personnel, among others — run a higher risk of hearing loss.

Depending on the type of dysfunction, surgery or a hearing aid may be helpful. A hearing aid must be prescribed and adjusted by a specialist. Buying a hearing device "over the counter" or through a mail-order business is at best a waste of money, but could cause serious hearing damage.

Teeth

Periodontal (gum) disease is easy to control if detected early. Pyorrhea, the most common form of this disease, starts with inflamed gums and occasional bleeding. Gums then begin to recede, and roots are exposed. To help prevent pyorrhea, use dental floss daily and have plaque (tartar) removed by your dental hygienist every four to six months.

ASSESSMENT

What Would You Do?

The case studies that follow describe situations that persons at midlife might confront as they try to plan for the future. These individuals are attempting to make certain health and fitness decisions for the years ahead.

What would you do if you were in their positions? None of the cases may reflect on your health and fitness situation, but looking in on other persons' dilemmas may shed light on your own plans.

Barry Roberts

Barry Roberts, a computer manager with a large corporation, has for years been known as the brawn of his extended family. His physical strength is almost legendary, and everyone who has heavy boxes or furniture to move seems to call on him. Even though he has worked behind a desk since his graduation from college, Barry's greatest pleasure comes from working on his house and yard. He is looking forward to building a vacation home for his family when his schedule permits.

While putting away the lawn mower recently, Barry felt a sharp pain in his back. By the end of that weekend, he could not stand upright and was in agonizing pain. Although Barry "hates" doctors, his wife insisted that she take him to an orthopedic specialist and Barry was too miserable to protest.

Painkillers and other medications, traction, and physical therapy have now reduced Barry's discomfort to occasional pain. The doctor has suggested back surgery, and friends say that Barry will never again have a strong back. Barry has become depressed over the apparent loss of his ability to do what he loves most.

What are Barry's options?

_____

_____

_____

_____

What are the advantages of each option?

_____

_____

What are the disadvantages of each option?

_____

_____

What would be your recommendation to Barry? Why?

_____

_____

Health Planning

Ann Rosenberg

Ann Rosenberg's adult children are thrilled that she finally seems ready to get her life back together after the death of their father. Ann had had little time to devote to her own fitness as she nursed her husband through a long illness. Because their children all live several hundred miles away, Ann had been his sole caregiver for many months.

Now Ann's doctor is urging her to lose some of the extra weight she put on during that trying time. He has suggested she start an exercise program to help with the weight loss. Ann thinks she will join a Weight Watchers group in her city, but she is not sure what to do about the exercise. She knows that walking is a good place to start, but the weather seldom is ideal for outside activity and the threat of street crime frightens her.

What are Ann's options?

_____

_____

_____

_____

What are the advantages of each option?

_____

_____

What are the disadvantages of each option?

_____

_____

What would be your recommendation to Ann? Why?

_____

_____

Leanna and Ron Phillips

Leanna and Ron Phillips married in their middle thirties and had three children over the next several years. Now their children are typical teens, full of energy, playing sports, eating fast food, and skipping meals. Meanwhile, Leanna has discovered that she has high cholesterol, and Ron is concerned about the history of early heart disease in his family. Their doctors have given them information on low-fat foods and animal-product substitutes.

Leanna and Ron realize they need to make some revisions in their family diet but know that their teens will have little interest in oat bran, turkey burgers, and skim milk. They also question whether such a restricted, "heart-safe" diet is really necessary or healthful for youngsters in their growth years.

What are the Phillips' options?

_____

_____

_____

What are the advantages of each option?

_____

_____

What are the disadvantages of each option?

_____

_____

What would you advise Leanna and Ron to do? Why?

_____

_____

Health Planning

CASE STUDY

Laura Chung

Laura Chung travels regularly in her job as a meeting planner for a national organization. Her children and grandchildren are located all over the country, and she often combines visits with them with her business trips. Sometimes her retired husband travels with her or meets her en route. Life at this point is tremendously satisfying.

In recent months, Laura has felt unusually "down," as if a dark cloud is hanging over her. She can find no explanation in her life for her feelings of depression, but she realizes that it is starting to affect her productivity at work and her relationships with her family and friends.

At the same time, Laura's monthly cycle has become increasingly irregular. She often finds herself sweating profusely when others in the room are turning up the heat. She suspects that menopause may be on the way, but she has not mentioned it to anyone. Her mother never talked about such things, she has no sisters, and her friends are of varying ages.

What are Laura's options?

_____

_____

_____

_____

What are the advantages of each option?

_____

_____

What are the disadvantages of each option?

_____

_____

What would you advise Laura to do? Why?

_____

_____

Planning for the future regarding your health and fitness means that you must look realistically at some of your lifestyle patterns. As you complete the following checklists, you should try to be honest with yourself in your answers. These reviews will help you realize where change is indicated in the habits that affect your health and fitness.

How Does Your Nutrition Measure Up?

Ask yourself these questions to see if you eat a balanced diet each day.

_Do I..._

- drink milk or consume 2–3 servings of dairy products daily?
- consume 2–3 servings of meat, fish, poultry, eggs, or other protein foods such as dried beans or peas daily?
- eat a citrus fruit daily?
- eat 2–4 servings of fruit daily?
- eat a leafy green or deep yellow vegetable each day?
- eat 3–5 servings of vegetables each day?
- consume at least 6 servings of enriched or whole-grain breads or cereal each day?

If you are eating a balanced diet, you should have answered yes to each question. If you answered no to any of the questions, you should add that type of food to your diet.

Health and Fitness Checklist

The 15 questions presented here address different aspects of your life that have a bearing on your overall health and fitness. Answer "yes" or "no" to each query. When you have completed your answers, go back and rank the No responses in order of their importance to your future planning, with "1" being the most important need. You will be able to refer back to these judgments later in this unit when you complete the Action Step and the Master Action Plan.

	Yes	No	Ranking
1. Do you incorporate regular screening exams into your medical and dental care?	____	____	____
2. When you wake in the morning, do you feel rested and ready to face the day?	____	____	____
3. Do you include a planned exercise program in your daily/weekly activities?	____	____	____
4. Are you watching the cholesterol, fat, and calorie content of foods you eat these days?	____	____	____
5. Do you incorporate stress reduction techniques into your daily activities?	____	____	____
6. If you cut back on your work schedule, do you have a plan for what you would do with your time?	____	____	____
7. Are you able to laugh at yourself?	____	____	____
8. Do you feel good about yourself most of the time?	____	____	____
9. Do you feel you have a purpose in your life to work toward?	____	____	____
10. Do you feel you are in control of your life?	____	____	____
11. Do you have hobbies that give you pleasure, relaxation, or a sense of accomplishment?	____	____	____
12. Are you active in your local church, community, or political activities?	____	____	____
13. Do you have close friends or confidants?	____	____	____
14. Are you involved in support groups or organizations?	____	____	____
15. Are periods of relaxation incorporated into your daily routine?	____	____	____

Health Planning

ALTERNATIVES

In assessing your current lifestyle and health and fitness habits, you may have confronted ways in which you are sabotaging your future well-being. Turning an unhealthy life or habit around is possible at any point in the life cycle. The choice is yours! The time can be now!

Exercise

A key ingredient in healthy living is exercise or physical activity. Increased physical activity increases bone mineral content, reduces the risk of osteoporotic fractures, helps maintain appropriate body weight, and increases longevity.

If you are over 40 and haven't been exercising, your first step before starting a program is to see your doctor for a medical evaluation and guidance. Then look into fitness programs in your community. Clinics, senior centers, your local Y, and other community groups often offer low-cost or free programs. These groups also have specialists who can help tailor a program to fit your specific needs.

The best exercises are rhythmic, continuous, and vigorous. They stimulate the heart, blood vessels, and lungs. Some examples are brisk walking, bicycling, swimming, and dancing. For those in good condition, jogging may be added to the list. Jogging, however, can strain the knees, ankles, and Achilles tendon if overdone or done incorrectly.

If exercise is to be truly beneficial to your circulatory system, it must be:

- At least 20 to 30 minutes in duration, excluding warm-up and cool-down.

- Frequent — three times a week, preferably on alternate days.

- Gradual and progressive — start by pushing the body just beyond the point of comfort, but not to the point of fatigue.

Burning Calories Through Exercise

The average adult burns between 1,700 and 4,500 calories a day, depending upon the amount and kind of exercise involved. Active persons such as manual workers and athletes may consume as many as 6,000 calories a day and yet not gain weight.

Probable Calorie Expenditure per Hour for a 150-Pound Person

Bowling	190	Swimming ($1\frac{1}{4}$ mph)	300
Bicycling ($5\frac{1}{2}$ mph)	210	Badminton	350
Walking ($2\frac{1}{5}$ mph)	210	Square dancing	350
Gardening	220	Volleyball	350
Canoeing ($2\frac{1}{2}$ mph)	230	Table tennis	360
Golf	250	Wood chopping or sawing	400
Lawn mowing (power mower)	250	Tennis	420
Lawn mowing (hand mower)	270	Aerobic dancing	445
Row boating ($2\frac{1}{2}$ mph)	300	Jogging	665

This chart was prepared by Robert E. Johnson, M.D., Ph.D., and colleagues at the Department of Physiology and Biophysics at the University of Illinois, with additions by the Center for Science in the Public Interest. It is reprinted with their permission.

- Intense — it should increase your pulse rate, make you breathe deeply and perspire.

- Ongoing — benefits are cumulative and quickly lost. If you become bored with one kind of exercise, switch to another activity.

Include warm-up and cool-down periods in your exercise program. These periods, five to ten minutes before and after strenuous exercise, allow the body to prepare for and recover from the exercise. Light calisthenics, stretching, slow-paced walking or jogging, and using an exercise bike are good for this purpose.

If you hate the idea of exercise, think in terms of activity — keep moving. Find every opportunity to walk, bend, and stretch. Incorporate exercise into your daily routine, for example, by walking more. Get off the bus or subway one or two stops early and walk. If you work in an office, walk at lunch time; invite a co-worker to join you. Take the stairs instead of the elevator. If you can, do some bending or stretching exercises at your desk.

Danger signs: If any of the following symptoms occurs while exercising, stop immediately and check with your doctor: tightness or pain in the chest, light-headedness, severe breathlessness, loss of muscle control, or nausea.

Nutrition

The benefits of good nutrition go beyond weight control. Good eating habits will help you look and feel better, produce more energy with which to enjoy life, and offer protection against a number of serious conditions and diseases.

A good rule for getting the required nutrients is to eat the number of servings in each food group recommended by the U.S.

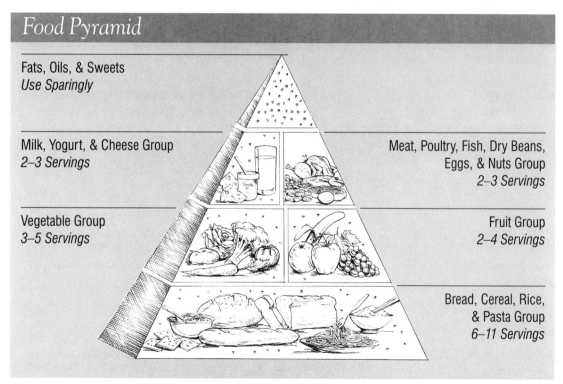

Food Pyramid

Fats, Oils, & Sweets
Use Sparingly

Milk, Yogurt, & Cheese Group
2–3 Servings

Meat, Poultry, Fish, Dry Beans, Eggs, & Nuts Group
2–3 Servings

Vegetable Group
3–5 Servings

Fruit Group
2–4 Servings

Bread, Cereal, Rice, & Pasta Group
6–11 Servings

Departments of Agriculture and Health and Human Services. Breads, cereals, rice, and pasta constitute the most important food group in the current federal nutrition guidelines. These guidelines are illustrated in the Food Guide Pyramid that is shown on the previous page.

Nutritionists recommend a balanced diet that includes 55–58 percent carbohydrates found in whole-grain breads and cereals, peas, and beans. Complex carbohydrates are broken down more slowly by the body than simple carbohydrates, like sugar or honey, and provide sustained energy.

Complex carbohydrates are a good source of protein, fiber, vitamins, and minerals. They are also filling and often inexpensive. In selecting breads and cereals at the store, be sure to read the labels and watch for high levels of sodium and sugar. Avoid the coated cereals and instant hot cereals that contain a lot of sugar. If you are eating a well-balanced diet, you probably don't need the fortified cereals with added vitamins.

Meat, poultry, fish, and beans provide the greatest source of protein. You need only 12 percent of your calories from protein. Protein is found in dairy products, meat, fish, poultry, eggs, nuts, beans, and peas. To make healthful choices from this group, keep in mind that red meats are higher in saturated fats. Processed meats (such as hot dogs and bacon) and lunch meats (such as salami and bologna) are both high in fats and sodium. In general, poultry and fish are lower in calories and fat. Broiling, baking, poaching, or microwaving are fat-free ways to cook that can keep calories down. Removing the extra fat and skin on meats before cooking will also reduce calories and the amount of saturated fat in your diet.

Using beans and nuts gives you the bonus of protein, carbohydrates, and fiber plus adding calories to your diet. They're inexpensive substitutes for meats.

Many experts question the value of vitamin and mineral supplements unless they are prescribed. Your body uses vitamins from food to maintain proper health, appetite, and resistance to infection. It eliminates excessive amounts of vitamin C and vitamins of the B complex, but it stores vitamins A and D in the liver and other organs. More than the recommended daily amount of some vitamins may have harmful effects.

One way to increase the nutritional value you get for your money and to plan well-balanced meals is to examine the nutritional label found on most food containers. The label lists ingredients in order of decreasing amounts. The label will often list food additives also. These range from staples such as salt and sugar to substances that retard spoilage, enhance flavor, or add color. Some additives are potentially harmful. Nitrites, for example, enhance the color and flavor of many cured meats and prevent the formation of deadly botulism toxins. Under laboratory

Ten Ideas for Healthy Snacking

1. Plain popcorn, without added butter or oil
2. Whole-grain crackers
3. Unsalted pretzels
4. Low-fat yogurt
5. Low-fat cheese and spreads
6. Unsweetened fruit juices
7. Tomato juice
8. Slices of fruit with peel (for more fiber)
9. Raw vegetable strips and pieces
10. Sparkling water flavored with a slice of lemon or lime

conditions, however, they have been shown to cause cancer in rats. The federal government has reduced the amount of nitrites permitted in meats and continues to monitor their use.

Food labels also provide the number of calories per serving; the number of grams of protein, fat, and carbohydrates per serving; and the number of milligrams of sodium per serving. Also listed are the percentages of the U.S. Recommended Daily Allowance (RDA) of seven major vitamins and minerals. Nutritional labeling is especially important for dieters and for persons who must limit their intake of certain substances, such as sodium or cholesterol.

Convenience foods can provide the nutrients essential to your diet if chosen carefully. They should be supplemented with fresh fruits and vegetables. Remember, it pays to check the package's nutrition label. Frozen foods can be equal in value to fresh foods, which lose nutrients if they are overcooked, stored at the wrong temperature, or kept too long.

A balanced diet should contain fiber or roughage. Evidence suggests that fiber reduces the risk of heart disease and cancer. To ensure enough fiber in your diet, eat whole-grain breads and cereals, fresh fruit, and vegetables.

Concern about the link between high cholesterol levels and heart disease has led people to eat less animal fat (found in butter, eggs, and red meat). People of all ages would do well to cut down on several other substances, too, such as salt, sugar, and caffeine.

Tips for Improving Your Diet

For a diet low in fat:

- Eat fruits and vegetables, fish, poultry (without the skin), dry beans, and peas to obtain protein, rather than red meat.
- If you eat red meat, switch to lean cuts of red meat and trim off excess fat.
- Eat moderate amounts of eggs, at most three to four per week.
- Switch to skim and low-fat milk for cooking and drinking.
- Limit your intake of butter, cream, hydrogenated margarines, shortenings, cheese, coconut oil, and foods made from these products.
- Broil, bake, boil, steam, roast, or microwave foods rather than frying them.

For a diet low in sodium:

- Cook without adding salt.
- Season food with lemon, spices, and herbs instead of salt.
- Learn to enjoy the natural, unsalted flavors of food.
- Add no salt to food at the table.
- Limit intake of salty foods such as canned soups, potato chips, pretzels, salted nuts, popcorn, cheese, pickled foods, cured meats, and condiments such as soy sauce, steak sauce, barbecue sauce, catsup, and garlic salt.
- Choose unsalted snack foods such as unsalted nuts, fresh fruits, and vegetables.
- Read food labels for the salt content, including monosodium glutamate, and avoid products with high levels.

For a diet low in sugar:

- Use less of all sugars — white sugar, brown sugar, raw sugar, honey, and syrups.
- Eat fresh vegetables and fruits, plain yogurt, and whole-grain crackers for snacks rather than candy, ice cream, cakes, and cookies.
- Drink fruit juice or water rather than soft drinks.
- Use no sugar in tea and coffee.
- Eat fresh fruits or fruits canned without syrup.
- Cut down on the use of sweeteners in your favorite recipes.
- Read food labels for sugar content, including dextrose, fructose, and corn syrup.

For a diet low in caffeine:

- Substitute herbal or decaffeinated teas and decaffeinated coffees for regular tea and coffee.
- Check labels for caffeine, and substitute fruit juice, bottled water, or caffeine-free soft drinks for those with caffeine.
- Cut down on chocolate.

Losing Weight

Maintaining the weight that is ideal for your body is an important part of a healthful lifestyle. But what is your ideal weight? Your height, body frame, eating habits, general health, and age all affect your ideal weight. As those factors change, so can your ideal weight. For example, new evidence from the National Institute on Aging indicates that "the healthiest weight seems to rise with age." A woman who is five-foot-six and who weighs 120 at age 20 could have a healthy weight of 150 at age 50. Discuss your weight

with your doctor before beginning any kind of diet.

Whether you have forty pounds to lose or five, don't expect to take weight off overnight. Crash diets and diets that focus on one type of food can be dangerous. For maximum results, it is best to combine dieting with exercise. Anyone with more than ten pounds to lose or just beginning an exercise program should see his or her physician first.

To lose weight and keep it off, you will need to proceed slowly and steadily. Expect to lose one or two pounds a week. Your diet should be well-balanced and nutritious. Select foods from each of the five major food groups, cut down on portions, restrict your intake of sweets and alcohol, and exercise as appropriate to your age and condition.

Once you have lost the desired number of pounds, you will need to continue to modify your eating habits through your life as well as to continue a regular exercise program. Self-help groups like Weight Watchers have aided many men and women in achieving permanent weight loss.

Cooking for One

At some point in your adult life, you may be living alone. This can pose special nutrition problems, especially if you have been used to cooking and eating with several family members or others who share your household. The preparation and enjoyment of meals are social occasions to many in our culture. The suggestions that follow may help you to anticipate and prepare for such an adjustment if you need to.

- Establish a routine for your meals that suits you. Make your meals pleasant — set the table, sit down, take your time eating, listen to music, or read a favorite book.

- Establish a routine for food shopping to avoid daily impulse buying. Don't rely on frozen foods for all of your meals.
- Prepare larger-than-usual quantities of favorite dishes and freeze the extras for future meals.
- Look for meals-for-one cookbooks and experiment with their suggestions.
- Plan inexpensive meals that you can prepare for company, or have guests bring some part of the meal so that you can have people over on a regular basis.
- Go out to eat once in a while, either by yourself or with family or friends.
- Remember, your welfare is worth the effort. Don't shortchange yourself.

Dealing with Stress

Stress has been defined as "the body's response to any demand made upon it." The causes of stress can be positive as well as negative.

People differ widely in their ability to tolerate stress. Some people seem to thrive on it. Others can become ill. Unrelieved stress can result in lack of concentration, irritability, fatigue, loss of appetite, chronic anxiety, and depression. If unchecked, it can also lead to ulcers, hypertension, heart attack, or stroke. The important thing is for you to determine the level of stress at which you function best and discover how you can cope with stress when it goes beyond that point.

Ways to Beat Stress

Here are some proven techniques for dealing with stress in daily living:

- Recognize stress. It's all right to admit you feel stressed.
- Identify the cause of the stress. Withdraw for a while every day to talk to yourself about the day's stress-producing problems.
- Take action. Decide what you want out of the situation, set realistic goals, then act to achieve them. Indecision is one of the worst stress producers.
- Accept the fact that you cannot control every situation.
- Seek advice. Sharing problems with others, one on one or in a group, can help you find new ways of coping. Seek counsel from someone you can talk to honestly.
- Exercise. Take a walk, play tennis, ride your bike, exercise in your home or office.
- Rest. Fatigue makes even small problems loom large. You will deal with the causes of stress better if you are well-rested. Mind-relaxing techniques, including music, yoga, and hypnosis, can be helpful in this regard.
- Avoid self-medication and potentially abusive substances. Caffeine, nicotine, alcohol, medicines, and food only appear to relieve the symptoms of stress. In reality, they can aggravate your symptoms.
- Laugh more. Humor is perhaps the best stress reducer.

Your Health Care Team

You will want to have your health care team in place before you need them. Chief among your health care providers is your internist or general practitioner. Your team should also include professionals in specialty areas, such as your dentist, optometrist or ophthalmologist, gynecologist, podiatrist, hearing specialist, chiropractor, or nutritionist.

If you are looking for a new doctor in any area, ask for referrals from your current physician or from friends or family members whose judgment you trust. Public libraries, particularly in metropolitan areas, offer reference directories in which you can check the credentials and backgrounds of any doctors you are considering adding to your list of health care providers.

If your health care team does consist of several different health care professionals, it is vitally important that you educate yourself about which one is the best provider for a particular service. Also, find out which services and procedures by which providers are covered by your health insurance.

You are responsible for getting the health care you need. The way to do this is to become informed about your body so that you can better determine when you should consult with your physician. Learn to listen to your body so you can recognize any changes or early warning signs of potentially serious health problems.

Become an informed and assertive health care consumer. Before consulting a member of your health care team, prepare yourself. Be ready to describe your symptoms accurately. Know when you first noticed each symptom and how often and under what conditions it recurs. Bring a list of all medications you are taking. If you have any doubts about treatments or procedures, let your health care provider know. Ask about alternative treatments, side effects of drugs and procedures, and costs.

Write down in advance all the questions you want answered and insist that they be answered fully and in a way you can understand. If you find that you are unable to remember a lot of what the doctor says, ask if you can record the answers to your questions. You should get a second opinion

if you have any doubts about a diagnosis or proposed procedure. Many insurance providers in fact require a second opinion before surgery or certain procedures.

Keep your complete medical history and a list of medications you are taking in an easily accessible place. For people living alone, it is particularly important to have this information handy. Tell a close friend or family member where it can be located in an emergency.

The Physical Examination

How often you have a physical examination should be determined by you and your doctor based on your medical history and present condition. To provide the best advice and treatment, your doctor will need to obtain baseline data on you for later comparisons.

When you undergo a complete medical screening, your doctor will examine your lymph nodes, veins, joints, and reflexes. You will also be tested for arteriosclerosis, high blood pressure, diabetes, and possibly other conditions. Your doctor will check your lungs, liver, and spleen and will take an electrocardiogram to detect changes in your heart. Simple tests can identify bladder and kidney conditions as well as tumors. Regular physical examinations often detect trouble that, if left untreated, could become serious.

Your doctor should ask about your personal habits (smoking, drinking, eating, etc.) and about any unusual symptoms. Be frank. Tell your doctor about any pills or medication you are taking, including aspirin, tranquilizers, and sleeping tablets. Even the most common drugs, such as aspirin, can alter the potency of other drugs.

After reviewing your case history and the reports from your various tests, your doctor will discuss the findings with you and probably make some recommendations.

Health Care Costs

The cost of medical care is increasing at almost twice the general rate of inflation. As a consumer of health care services, you need to take every measure possible to keep your own health care costs down without shortchanging yourself as to the quality and extent of the care you receive. The tips that follow are intended to help you do your part to control your own and overall costs.

- First and foremost, take care of yourself. "Listen" to your body. Recognize early-warning signs and have them checked promptly.

- Take advantage of non-hospital health care facilities and programs such as free community clinics, health fairs, freestanding emergency clinics, and same-day surgery centers.

- Take advantage of any free testing procedures offered by your employer or a community agency or group. Free testing is often available for blood pressure, diabetes, and colo-rectal cancer.

- Comparison shop for doctors' fees and services.

- Comparison shop for drugs and medications. Compare prescription drugs and their generic counterparts. Discuss with your doctor any generic alternatives to prescription drugs. Also compare prices for nonprescription drugs and products.

- Get second opinions for non-emergency surgery and other major procedures. Medicare and a majority of private health insurers now pay for second opinions.

- Schedule non-emergency hospital surgery and procedures for weekdays, not weekends.

- Examine all bills thoroughly. Be sure you understand everything on them. Learn what your rights of appeal are.

- Analyze your health insurance policies to see if you are underinsured, overinsured, or have overlapping coverage. Medicare, on average, pays for about 40 percent of a program participant's health care expenses. The remainder must come from employer and pension plans, supplemental health insurance, and the participant's pocketbook.

- Consider signing up with a health maintenance organization (HMO). These prepaid health plans provide both office visits and hospitalization for a fixed monthly fee.

- Keep all receipts for medical expenses, including transportation to and from doctors' offices and hospitals, medicines, eyeglasses, orthopedic shoes, and other items, for income tax purposes.

- Look into long-term-care insurance, a concept that helps meet the costs of a nursing home, should you or your spouse ever need such care. The earlier such insurance is taken out, the lower the annual premiums will be.

Prepare for Emergencies

First aid action often saves a life in an emergency. When a person's heart stops beating, a technique called cardiopulmonary resuscitation (CPR) may keep the person alive. The American Red Cross, the American Heart Association, and many local hospitals offer CPR training to the public. Call any of these groups for information on how you can become better equipped to deal with emergencies.

Many large communities have paramedic units, which are often attached to police or fire departments. Paramedics are especially trained to treat seriously injured persons or heart attack victims. Find out what other emergency facilities and services your community has and post their phone numbers near your telephone.

Medic Alert is an organization that provides a system of emergency medical identification for persons with certain chronic medical conditions. Members of Medic Alert wear a necklace or bracelet, or carry a card in their wallet, with their personal medical information on it. This information can save the life of a person who is unconscious or who for some reason cannot explain his or her condition. Such persons could die or suffer permanent injury if they do not receive special care or treatment or if they are given medicine to which they are allergic.

Long-Term Care

Long-term care refers to a comprehensive range of medical, personal, and social services designed to meet the needs of chronically ill and disabled persons. These services can be delivered in the recipient's home, in a community-based program such as an adult day care center, or in a nursing home.

You may believe that long-term care is only a distant, barely conceivable possibility. Yet adults of all ages do suffer disabling strokes, survive horrendous accidents, and develop crippling and incapacitating illnesses. Parents, other family members, or friends may need your advice and assistance in securing long-term care. For many reasons, it is important that you become knowledgeable about this aspect of health care.

Long-term care differs from acute care. Acute care is provided in a hospital and is usually short-term and aimed toward recuperation. Long-term care pertains to persons needing continued support because of chronic, degenerative illnesses or disabilities. This support may include help with housework, shopping, transportation, personal care such as bathing or dressing, rehabilitative care such as that following a stroke, or intensive, long-term, skilled nursing care.

Medicare is not intended to cover long-term care. Medicaid requires that a person deplete assets and savings, with the exception of the person's home, to receive benefits. Some insurance companies are now offering long-term care insurance to help with the catastrophic costs of such assistance. The Think of Your Future appendix lists some resources on this topic.

Caregiving

If you are taking care of a seriously ill or disabled relative or friend, you may be physically and emotionally exhausted yourself. If you are holding down a full-time job at the same time, you may wonder how you even get through the day. Locating appropriate services, identifying and understanding problems, and being there for your loved one can take all the time you have to give.

Resources are available to help ease your burden, and you should take advantage of them. Community organizations, state and local government agencies, and even your employer can be of assistance. The Think of Your Future appendix will guide you in the direction of getting support for yourself and for the person whose care you are supervising or providing.

RESPONSIBILITY

Comparing your health and fitness habits with the norms that constitute the recommended healthful lifestyle may have been an eye-opener. Ideally, this unit has reinforced practices that you already know about and are following. In either case, the next step is up to you!

Good health is yours to pursue at any point in life. It is never too late — or too soon — to change to a more healthful lifestyle. The Health and Fitness Checklist that you completed in the Assessment section has given you some idea of what your priorities are in this area. Review them now, and add any new thoughts that may have occurred to you while you were going through this unit.

Planning your health and fitness for the future is the same as any other proposed long-term schedule. It needs to be kept up-to-date through periodic comparisons with what is possible and what is necessary in the years ahead.

Begin this ongoing planning process now by completing the Action Step that represents your intentions at this time. You may want to use the completed Action Step as a model for your own decisions.

Health Planning

Action Step

List any and all health and fitness actions you might choose to pursue in the future. These can include lifestyle changes as well as other positive moves to get your physical, mental, and emotional health and well-being under control. The Health and Fitness Checklist you completed in the Assessment section will provide you with starting ideas. Use verbs — action words — to describe your health and fitness choices.

When you believe your list is complete for now, rank your health and fitness choices in the right-hand column according to their importance to you, with number 1 being the most important. Use a second sheet of paper to continue your list if needed.

Health and Fitness Actions	Rank by Importance
Start a regular exercise program	2
Stop smoking	4
Cut back on fats in my daily diet	5
Learn to control/reduce stress in my life	6
Find an internist or general practitioner with whom I feel comfortable	1
Get a physical exam	3
See a podiatrist about my bunion	7
Join a health club or aerobics class	8

Health Planning

Action Step

List any and all health and fitness actions you might choose to pursue in the future. These can include lifestyle changes as well as other positive moves to get your physical, mental, and emotional health and well-being under control. The Health and Fitness Checklist you completed in the Assessment section will provide you with starting ideas. Use verbs — action words — to describe your health and fitness choices.

When you believe your list is complete for now, rank your health and fitness choices in the right-hand column according to their importance to you, with number 1 being the most important. Use a second sheet of paper to continue your list if needed.

Health and Fitness Actions	Rank by Importance

You have now come to the final step in planning for your health and fitness in the future. On the Master Action Plan, the final product of this life component unit, you will plot out the specific actions you will take to meet the goals you have listed on your Action Step. This Master Action Plan functions as your "to do" list for meeting your health and fitness goals.

You should list each of your Health and Fitness Actions from your Action Step as a Goal Statement on your MAP. Then follow through with the logical sequence of events that will result in fulfilling each goal. Use the sample Master Action Plan as a guide in completing your own MAP.

Health Planning

Master Action Plan

Goal Statement: Find an internist/GP appropriate for me

Actions	Resources	Time Frame	By Whom?
1. Get referrals from others who have regular doctors	Friends, family, neighbors	2 weeks	Self
2. Check with local hospital physician referral service	Local hospital	2 weeks	Self
3. Research backgrounds of physicians whose names I collect	Local directory of physicians (at bookstore, library); local health consumer groups	1 month	Self
4. Make appointments with doctors I would like to interview	Telephone; physicians' receptionists	2 months	Self
5. Prepare questions I would like answered	Self	1 week	Self
6. Interview prospective health care providers	Self; physicians	2 months	Self
7. Select physician with whom I feel most confident, compatible, and comfortable	Self	1 week	Self

Goal Statement: Start a regular exercise program

Actions	Resources	Time Frame	By Whom?
1. Read up on what I should do	Bookstores, library for books & magazines on fitness	2 weeks	Self
2. Talk with others who exercise regularly	Friends, family, neighbors	2 weeks	Self
3. Get a physical to see what kind of exercise would be best for the shape I'm in	Internist whom I will be identifying soon	1 month (if I can get appt.)	Self
4. Start program modestly by taking daily walks in the neighborhood (safe approach till doctor gives OK)	Self	2 weeks	Self

Social
Planning

Social Planning

Rarely do we consider planning when we think of our friendships and relationships. Relationships enrich and enlarge our lives and are vital to our sense of well-being. It is precisely because of their importance in our lives that social planning must be part of your planning for your future.

Positive relationships with family members and friends can enrich and enlarge your life at any stage. Social networks affect you at work, at play, at home, in your community, in your chosen field or pastimes.

Your relationships and social networks expand and contract as your lifestyle changes. The types of relationships that you desire are also likely to change with you. Your attitudes toward people, relationships, friendships, sharing, companionship, and spontaneity all come into play in determining the scope of your social support system. Taking an objective look at your social resources, while different from examining other aspects of your life, can and should be done.

Unit Objectives

■ **Assessment:** To assess your current social networks and their importance in your life, determine how they might be improved in the future, and speculate on how you might accomplish this improvement

■ **Alternatives:** To consider alternatives to your present interpersonal relationships that take into account the ongoing change that is a part of life

■ **Responsibility:** To make decisions about your social interactions with family members and friends that demonstrate an active approach to your life in the years ahead

■ **Planning:** To make specific plans for implementing your decisions about relationships with family members and with current and future friends

What Do You Think?

The questions that follow are designed to increase your awareness of the social aspects of your life and of the many components that contribute to successful and satisfying interpersonal relationships. The first group of questions is appropriate for workshop discussion within a group planning seminar. The second set is individual in nature and better suited to personal reflection or discussion with family, friends, or other members of your support system.

For Group Discussion:

1. Do you have family members whom you consider good friends? What qualities in a family member would lead you to regard that person as your friend? Are these qualities different from those you would look for in any friend? How can you make new friends in retirement?

2. What are the essential ingredients of good communication? What skills does a successful communicator demonstrate? How can these skills be learned or acquired?

3. How are family members and friends important to one's quality of life? How might group activities and individual interests substitute for close personal relationships?

4. How can a person prepare for such eventualities as children leaving home or the loss of a spouse or partner through death, divorce, or alienation?

5. What issues should you resolve before having a parent, adult child, or someone else move in with you?

For Personal Reflection:

6. Consider your current social networks — on the job, in the neighborhood, in volunteer activities, at school. What is the balance in these relationships between friends and acquaintances? Is this the balance you are comfortable with and want to maintain? If not, how could you work to change it?

7. What kinds of changes have you experienced in your life? Have you thought ahead to how you would deal with dramatic change in your important interpersonal relationships?

8. Do you typically initiate new friendships? Do you seek out new activities and relationships and actively work to maintain established ones? Do you think both parties need to work to keep a relationship alive?

For Your Information

Your personal well-being and satisfaction are derived primarily from your sense of yourself and your contentment with who you are. However, friends, family, and other people in your social network all contribute to your general well-being. Rich interpersonal relationships enable you to share your joys and triumphs with those who sincerely rejoice in your good fortune. More important, perhaps, friendships can support you in your disappointments and can cushion you from some of life's harsher blows.

Opportunities for friendship abound in daily life. Traveling to work on a bus or in a car pool, delegating assignments or receiving jobs, taking a coffee break or eating lunch, arranging for dishwasher repairs or buying a newspaper, playing tennis or doing grocery shopping — all involve contact and communication with other individuals.

Whether casual contacts develop into actual relationships depends on timing, circumstances, luck, and the parties involved. You can, nevertheless, increase the chances of expanding your social network by actively pursuing relationships with individuals who strike a responsive chord in you.

Your sense of personal well-being and satisfaction generally develops out of your comfort with the people who share or in some way affect your life. You don't need hundreds of friends and family members to be happy, but you do need to relate in a positive manner to the individuals who are a part of your life. Feeling good about yourself is the first step toward achieving this kind of contentment. You must first love and appreciate yourself before you can project these feelings into relationships with others.

Your physical and mental health can benefit significantly from a strong social support system. Social isolation is seen as a powerful indicator of premature death as well as harmful effects of stress. Well-developed social networks serve as buffers against stress, loss, disappointment, and loneliness.

Forming and Maintaining Friendships

Opportunities to focus on friendships, to nurture relationships, may increase over the course of your life. As the responsibilities of work, raising children, and establishing a home begin to diminish, you may finally have the time and the desire to concentrate on a fundamental necessity of daily life — the people with whom you share your life. These relationships include those between you and your spouse or partner, your parents, siblings, your children, other relatives, your friends, and associates.

For many adults, the demands of earning a living and meeting other obligations can get in the way of maintaining these essential connections with other people. You may regret having let some friendships drift or fade, or wish that you had found more time to nurture relationships with family and friends. Planning for your future can help you get back in touch with the people and the experiences that really make a difference in your life.

The self-assessment that is a natural part of life is just as important if you have remained single, have had no children or have had them later in life than your contemporaries, or are still immersed in the thrust of upward mobility on the job.

Changing Relationships

Relationships change over the course of one's life. Births and deaths, marriages and divorces, relocations and reassignments, changing circumstances and modifying interests all affect the flow of friendships and relationships in anyone's life over the years. Family members can be among your closest friends, but even these relationships feel the effects of geographical distance, being at different points in your lives, and competing friendships with other individuals. Your work associates may be close friends now, but will such friendships survive if one of you changes jobs?

Telephone calls and letters to the friend or relative who moves away, suggestions for lunch or a movie to the former co-worker who changes jobs, and friendly greetings to the neighbors coming out the front door all send the message that you are interested in being a friend. This proactive approach works equally well in making new friends and in mending or reviving old friendships

that may have been neglected or forgotten in the rush of keeping up or getting ahead.

Loss of Relationships

When someone you love dies, the emotional loss can be devastating. The disintegration of a relationship through divorce or other breakup can cause you much the same kind of grief.

Mourning is essential to healing and is an intensely personal process. It is important to recognize that individuals grieve in different ways and that no one can set the pace or pattern of another person's grief. Time does gradually make loss bearable, and social support can lessen some of the pain. The Think of Your Future appendix includes publications, organizations, and other resources that are available to the newly widowed, divorced, and other persons coping with loss.

Social Regrouping

While the loss of a loved one can intensify the need for friendship and support, you need not wait until you suffer such a loss to begin focusing your attention and efforts on your social support system. As you consider your existing relationships and think about the kinds of friendships you would like to have in the future, remember that relationships are two-way affairs that require the active participation of both parties in order to flourish.

You can only be responsible for the role you will play in your relationships. This entails taking an active part in the pursuit of new relationships as well as in the maintenance of existing ones. It may also mean that you must carefully consider your ongoing relationships in terms of the demands they make of you and what they give you in return. You may need to sever some ties.

ASSESSMENT

Assessing your personal relationships and friendships may bring you to a new level of understanding. You may never have considered why certain persons are your friends or how you could improve family relationships or how you might pursue a new friendship. You may have simply accepted the fact and the fabric of your social network, without realizing how you shaped this network that is now yours to deal with.

You cannot choose your relatives. Your family is a permanent fact of your life. Families frequently have well-established patterns of behavior that can be difficult to alter. Patterns of behavior and ways of communicating within a family are often firmly entrenched. If you are dissatisfied with any of your familial relationships, you may want to begin thinking about how you can change them. The only place to implement change is in your own actions. Examine how your own behavior maintains the status quo. Hopefully, changing the way you act with others will in turn change the way they respond to you.

What Would You Do?

The case studies that follow are intended to help you focus on the real situations in your social network that you may want to work on during your participation in Think of Your Future. None of the cases may reflect your life situation, but brainstorming options and solutions to the challenges that face other persons can bring unexpected clarity to your own plans for the years ahead. What would you do if you were in their positions? If you are reviewing Think of Your Future on your own, you may want to discuss these cases with close friends or family members. Group settings for future planning will use the studies for workshop sessions.

Social Planning

Carl Costas

Carl Costas has been divorced from the mother of his three teenaged sons for several years. During that time, he has been working overseas and has had little contact with his teens, although he has sent regular support payments to his ex-wife.

Now he is back in the United States and wants to improve his relationships with his children by seeing them regularly. He has suggested taking them to baseball or basketball games, but their only interest seems to be in heavy metal concerts.

What can he do to become a part of his sons' lives again?

_____

_____

_____

_____

Can you think of other activities that might provide opportunities for bonding with his sons?

_____

_____

What are the advantages of each option?

_____

_____

What are the disadvantages of each option?

_____

_____

What would you do in these circumstances? Why?

_____

_____

Mary and Lou Kosnick

Mary and Lou Kosnick are typical of families facing "sandwich generation" issues. The couple's two daughters, Jessica and Hope, are now in high school. Jessica is preparing to go away to college in the fall. Both daughters have after-school jobs to help pay for their college tuition and expenses.

Mrs. Kosnick's 80-year-old mother, a recent widow, lives about three hours away from the Kosnicks in the long-time family home. The grandmother is self-sufficient at this point, but Mary and Lou have suggested that she consider moving in with them when Jessica starts college. She could sleep in Jessica's old room.

Mary is a little apprehensive about working full time and caring for her mother at the same time, but she hopes she can share some of the caregiving responsibilities with Lou and the girls. In any case, she would feel better having her mother close by.

What are the Kosnicks' options?

_____

_____

_____

What are the advantages of each option?

_____

What are the disadvantages of each option?

_____

_____

What do you think they should do? Why?

_____

_____

Social Planning

Annabelle Morse and Louis DeMarco

Annabelle Morse and Louis DeMarco, both widowed and both in their sixties, have known each other for years as members of the same church. After spending time together last year on a church-sponsored trip to Ireland, they started dating and are now thinking about getting married.

Each of them has several adult children and numerous grandchildren. Neither of them has discussed the couple's romantic involvement with any of their family members, and they honestly do not know how their children will react. They are both financially independent at the present time, but Ms. Morse is concerned about how remarriage might affect her Social Security survivor benefits.

What are the options available to Annabelle and Louis?

_____

_____

_____

_____

What are the advantages of each option?

_____

_____

What are the disadvantages of each option?

_____

_____

What do you think they should do? Why?

_____

_____

_____

Jane Adachi

Jane Adachi had been a successful interior designer with an East Coast department store for more than twenty years. She enjoyed her job and her social life, much of it spent with Karen Elgar, a chef and Jane's closest friend since their college days together. When Karen suggested that both of them strike out in a new direction, Jane thought for a while and then agreed to move to the West Coast with the adventurous Karen. Their ultimate plan in their new location was to open a restaurant together.

Jane got a job with a private design firm, and Karen joined a prestigious catering organization. They rented a comfortable apartment together and proceeded to get used to their new city. Within six months of their arrival, however, Karen met the man of her dreams, married him, and became pregnant. Although Jane is happy for Karen, she feels deserted, alone, and at loose ends in a place she really doesn't call home.

What are Jane's options?

_____

_____

_____

_____

What are the advantages of each option?

_____

_____

What are the disadvantages of each option?

_____

_____

What would be your recommendation to Jane? Why?

_____

_____

Ben and Sarah Callahan

Ben Callahan has always been very supportive of his wife's interests and activities. Now Sarah Callahan has received an important promotion in the job she started two years ago and travels much of the time. Ben's own job is less demanding than it was earlier in his career, and he finds that he has more spare time than he did before Sarah went back to work.

Ben misses having Sarah around and the life they used to share. At the same time, he knows how much Sarah loves her job and how long she waited to be able to pursue her dreams. He is trying to figure out how he can make himself feel better about the situation without alarming Sarah.

What are Ben's options?

_____

_____

_____

_____

What are the advantages of each option?

_____

_____

What are the disadvantages of each option?

_____

_____

What would be your recommendation to Ben? Why?

_____

_____

ALTERNATIVES

Interpersonal relationships take many routes throughout life, but the middle years introduce a variety of new paths that you may not have explored to date. In planning for your future, you may want to consider these alternative patterns of friendship and relating that the years ahead may bring.

Marriage and Partnership

The passage of time brings moments of truth to marriages and other partnerships. When the parties involved are reassessing all aspects of their lives, they naturally regard their primary relationship with discerning eyes. Some marriages end in divorce after such scrutiny, but even more unions are revitalized and renewed. Stopping to remember all the positive reasons you and your spouse or partner are together can be a life-affirming process.

Marriages and other partnerships may be affected by the pressures of job responsibilities, child rearing, and the routine of daily life. When children reach adulthood and other pressures ease, spouses and partners are often free to explore their relationship. What they find may be a pleasant surprise — that what drew them together years ago is still alive and begging for attention.

Spouses and partners who respect each other's individuality and allow each other space to have a life outside the partnership increase their chances for continued happiness. Trust between spouses or partners encourages each party to have friends and activities outside the marriage or partnership. No one person should be counted on to fulfill all of the needs and expectations of another. Long-term commitments get into trouble when either party expects the other to fill such a role.

It is important to keep in mind that relationships are never static. The changes that life brings can strain or enhance a relationship. For example, many women come into their own in terms of their careers in midlife at the same time that their mates may be slowing down or wanting to do something other than work every day. Flexibility, fair-mindedness, and open communication are essential to maintaining balance in such an arrangement. Couples often get bogged down in their daily routines and neglect to make time for one another. The following tips are intended to help you reopen the lines of communication and improve your relationship in the process.

- Plan for the future together. Be mutually supportive. Reaffirm your love and respect for each other.

- Manage and plan your finances as a team. Establish goals, select advisers, determine allocation of assets, and draw up separate wills together.

- Encourage the development of mutual and individual friendships throughout your life together.

- Develop new activities and routines to replace those that no longer pertain to your lifestyle. At the same time, keep yourself open to spontaneous suggestions for new adventures.

- Respect each other's privacy, space, and time.

- Renegotiate your marriage arrangements. Exchange and share roles.

- Keep up your appearance.

- Communicate. Make time to talk, and listen carefully. Be sure you understand, with acceptance and empathy, what the other person is saying.

- Recommit yourselves periodically to your relationship and to everything it means to both of you.

Sexuality Through the Years

Popular perceptions in society and the media are finally catching up with what many people already know — that sexuality remains an important part of your life as long as you live. Couples have an ongoing opportunity to renew this aspect of their relationships, taking into account the physical changes that do occur with the passage of time but that need not diminish enjoyment or caring between partners.

The emotional intensity that can be found in a solid relationship can compensate for any lessening of physical prowess. This kind of deepening warmth can lead to greater intimacy and tenderness than had been experienced earlier in the union. Open discussion between spouses or partners about each other's needs and expectations is critical to such closeness.

Divorce

Divorce after many years of marriage can be particularly painful and complicated. With a couple's financial worth probably at its peak and social and family patterns firmly entrenched, a marital split in the middle years rocks every aspect of the partners' lives. Individuals who have maintained a life and a livelihood apart from their marriage will have an easier time making the transition to single life than will those, most often women, who derived their identity primarily from their marriage.

After dealing with the emotional trauma of divorce, newly single persons may need to reassess their identities, their support systems, and their activities. However justified anger and bitterness over the divorce may be, individuals need to work through these feelings to move on in their lives.

Organized support groups that provide emotional support and practical advice are available to help separated and divorced persons build new lives for themselves. Such organizations can be found within your own community or region. The Think of Your Future appendix contains information to help you locate one.

Widowhood

A very difficult change in relationships occurs when a spouse or partner dies. The chance of a woman being widowed is far greater than it is for a man, and women are more likely than men to remain single after being widowed or divorced. Therefore, it is very important for women to make sure they are informed and prepared for whatever the future brings.

Planning together for the future, both for the years together and for the time after one partner dies, can help ensure peace of mind for both members of a couple and a positive future for the one who survives. Become familiar with your own and your spouse or partner's wills, insurance policies, investments, real estate holdings, retirement benefits, the location of vital documents, and the names of professional advisors such as your lawyer, banker, and stockbroker. The Financial Planning and Legal and Estate Planning units of Think of Your Future present specific details of such long-term planning.

The emotional shock and grief of losing one's spouse or partner cannot be overestimated. A social support network of family members and friends that has been cultivated over the years can provide tremendous comfort and assistance to the person who has been left alone by such a tragedy. Counseling and support groups for newly widowed individuals also offer valuable companionship and other services, often provided by volunteers who have themselves been widowed. The Think of Your Future appendix includes guidance on these resources.

The Single Life

Close to half of all persons age 65 and older in this country have never been married or are single because of divorce or the death of a spouse. Planning for the future alone is very different from the experience shared by spouses or partners who chart out the years ahead together. The importance of a social support network of friends is especially critical to the well-being of single persons.

Dating

A person who is single again for the first time in many years because of divorce or widowhood may feel somewhat awkward about getting back into circulation. If you are newly single, you are reentering the dating game at a time when health and other concerns have brought about a conservative and cautious approach to dating and sexual intimacy in all age groups.

How can you find other single individuals to date? Singles dances, bars, clubs, parties, advertisements, and dating services are all available, but they are not necessarily the answer for everyone.

A logical first step is to find and make new friends who didn't know you as a member of a couple and who can appreciate you solely on your own merits, interests, and enthusiasm. Engaging in activities that you really enjoy will also put you in touch with like-minded individuals who may become close friends or dating prospects. Getting out and getting involved will demonstrate that you are an interesting person who will draw other interesting people to you.

Remarriage

Remarrying or making a similar commitment can provide the spouses or partners with companionship, affection, and mutual security at a time in life when this reinforcement is especially needed. If you are considering such a step, you will want to look frankly and openly at the issues of sex and intimacy, money, and children from previous marriages or liaisons.

Sexual expectations can vary widely between couples of any age. Discussing this important matter before you make any commitments can save you and a prospective mate from embarrassment, misunderstanding, disappointment, or divorce later on.

Some individuals contemplating remarriage have adult children who do not take kindly to their parents' new relationship. This disapproval may come out of a misplaced sense of loyalty to the other, uninvolved parent or the misconceived notion that romance and intimacy are only for the young. Such concerns can also mask the younger generation's fear of losing parental affection, assets, and inheritance.

Unromantic though it may be, marriage has a business side that is best addressed before the wedding ceremony rather than after it. Remarriage can involve children from previous marriages on both sides, multiple homes, investments, and personal belongings. A thoughtfully prepared prenuptial agreement spells out exactly who owns what going into the marriage and who will own what if the marriage is dissolved by death or divorce. The Legal and Estate Planning unit of Think of Your Future presents detailed information regarding these agreements.

Following are some guidelines to help you determine whether you are ready to remarry. A "no" answer to even one question should lead you to resolve that issue before making a serious marital commitment.

- Have you been widowed or divorced at least two years?
- Have you built a sustaining and full life for yourself alone?
- Are you happy with your life?
- Have you known your potential spouse at least six months, and do you feel you know each other well?
- Are you both willing, where it is appropriate, to give up your present homes and make a new life together in a new housing arrangement?
- Will your joint incomes support you both in the styles to which you are accustomed?
- Are you both well-adjusted individuals?
- Have you agreed on your hopes and dreams for the future and on a basic life plan for your years together?
- Do your children, close friends, and family members support your decision to remarry? If not, how can you address their disapproval?
- Can you talk comfortably together about your previous mate without making comparisons?

Intergenerational Families

Many persons attempting to make their own plans for the future find themselves caught between their aging parents, who are trying to maintain their independence, and their teenaged children, who are trying to gain their independence. Some members of this aptly titled "sandwich generation" host their adult children as well, members of the rebound generation who have returned home to get a second wind before rejoining the work force.

Combining all these forces in harmony under one roof can be a challenge. Members of the oldest generation want to preserve their self-sufficient lifestyle as long as possible and generally want to avoid being burdens to their adult children. The youngest generation may feel crowded out by the addition of another layer of authority at the top. The group in the middle, which carries most of the responsibility for all three generations, can feel overwhelmed, overworked, and overloaded.

Sharing a home among generations in this manner can work if the arrangement is negotiated and carefully planned beforehand. If mutual benefits for all concerned can be structured into the ground rules of joint living situations, the arrangement will be viewed as an asset rather than a burden.

Many persons find themselves with significant caregiving responsibilities for elderly parents at the same time that they are trying to give full time and attention to their jobs. Juggling the demands of both is difficult and sometimes impossible. Common sense and a realistic outlook must prevail in such situations. One person cannot do everything, and sharing caregiving duties with other family members or delegating them to paid help may be the sensible approach.

If you find yourself in the position of having no time for yourself or for your spouse or partner, you need to regroup and do some quiet thinking about what is important in your life. You do not have to do everything that everyone else wants or expects you to do. Perhaps you need to learn to say "no" to parents, to children, to friends, to organizations. Life is too short to try to please everyone else before you take time for you.

Children, Grandchildren, and Other Joys

Members of your family can be your dearest friends, your strongest allies, and your greatest resources. Such relationships do not develop overnight, but if you have cherished and cultivated the idea of family for most of your adult life, you should be reaping significant benefits. The addition of grandchildren to the mix is an especially satisfying development that will keep you young in spirit and fresh in outlook.

If you have no children or grandchildren of your own, or if they live too far away for frequent visits, seek out friends in younger generations. The benefits for everyone involved can exceed your expectations.

THE AARP APPROACH
RESPONSIBILITY

Making decisions that will bolster your social support network is a considerably less precise endeavor than strengthening your pension plan or selecting an agreeable location for future housing. Relationships are ongoing projects that must be nurtured. Still, improving your social support network shows that you are not willing to let other people and external events determine your well-being and personal satisfaction.

Record your relationship decisions now on the Action Step in this section. You may want to use the completed Action Step on the next page as a model to stimulate your own thinking. You can then go on to your own Action Step.

Action Step

On the Action Step, list any and all interpersonal relationships you have chosen to work on in the future. Remember that these decisions represent attitudes toward these persons or situations that you plan to pursue over the long term. Use verbs — action words — to describe your new or revised approaches to elements of your social support network.

When you believe your list is complete for the time being, rank your decisions in the right-hand column according to their importance to you, with number 1 being the most important. Use a second sheet of paper to continue your list if needed.

Relationship Actions	Rank by Importance
Renew contact with college roommate	7
Find family I stayed with during Peace Corps service in India	8
Make peace with the brother who stole my business idea	6
Make friends with someone who appreciates Chinese food and old movies	4
Try to recapture the magic of those early years with my spouse	1
Work at enjoying my own company	2
Eliminate negative people from my social network	3
Accept the fact that my mother never initiates phone calls, and call her regularly	5

Social Planning

Action Step

On the Action Step, list any and all interpersonal relationships you have chosen to work on in the future. Remember that these decisions represent attitudes toward these persons or situations that you plan to pursue over the long term. Use verbs — action words — to describe your new or revised approaches to elements of your social support network.

When you believe your list is complete for the time being, rank your decisions in the right-hand column according to their importance to you, with number 1 being the most important. Use a second sheet of paper to continue your list if needed.

Relationship Actions	Rank by Importance

PLANNING

The final step in planning your approach to relationships in the future involves plotting out the specific actions you will take to initiate the goals you have listed on your Action Step. Your Master Action Plan is the final product of this unit. It functions as your "to do" list for meeting your social network agenda.

You should list each of your Relationship Actions from your Action Step as a Goal Statement on your MAP. Then follow through with the logical sequence of events that will help you achieve each goal. You can review the sample Master Action Plan to help you complete your own MAP.

Master Action Plan

Goal Statement: *Recapture magic of early years with spouse*

Actions	Resources	Time Frame	By Whom?
1. Talk with spouse about goal	Memories, mutual respect	Ongoing, start now	Both
2. Look at old pictures	Family albums	2 weeks	Both
3. Play old music, dance together	Old records, record player	Ongoing, once a week	Both
4. Ask each other for dates	Movies/dining section of newspaper, imagination	Ongoing, once a week	Both
5. Plan trip together	Books, travel agent, friends, magazines	6 months – 1 year	Both

Goal Statement: *Work at enjoying own company*

Actions	Resources	Time Frame	By Whom?
1. Take long walks	Self, walking shoes	Ongoing, every day, start now	Self
2. Read good books	Bookstores, library	Ongoing, start now	Self
3. Do needlepoint	Yarn store, catalog	Ongoing, start now	Self
4. Plant a garden	Local nursery, seed catalogs	Ongoing, every spring	Self

Housing Planning

Housing Planning

Our notions of home tend to change as our reality of family adjusts in midlife. The traditional pattern of family life has typically found husband and wife alone again together after children have moved on to establish their own homes. Today, diversity rather than tradition is the norm in family arrangements.

Single-parent families abound. People are marrying later and more often or not at all. Children are being born to parents in their late thirties, forties, and beyond. Single persons are establishing homesteads together, adult children are returning to their parents' homes, and multigenerational and multifamily households are not unusual. Each of these situations has implications for future planning.

Decisions about where you will live in the future — the geographic location and type of housing — relate directly to the lifestyle you have chosen or accepted. You have already reviewed personal, health, and social aspects of your life and developed a profile of your individual lifestyle. In the units that follow, you will look seriously at your financial ability to maintain this lifestyle in the years ahead. Now you can progress to the life component at hand — housing and location.

Unit Objectives

■ **Assesment:** To assess your current housing and location in terms of how they will continue to support your individual lifestyle in the future

■ **Alternatives:** To consider alternatives to your present housing and location that might better meet your needs in the future, including but not limited to modifications in your current situation

■ **Responsibility:** To make decisions about your housing and location in the years ahead that could enhance the quality of your life

■ **Planning:** To make specific plans for implementing your decisions about housing and location, at the same time remaining open to periodic review and revision of such plans

What Do You Think?

The questions that follow are intended to stimulate reflection on and awareness of some of the issues involved in considering housing and location decisions at midlife and beyond. You are encouraged to discuss them with family, friends, or other members of your support network if you are studying Think of Your Future on your own. Group seminars in future planning will use the questions as workshop discussion topics.

1. Can you adapt your current housing to fit changing circumstances, e.g., children moving out, children moving back, your retirement, elderly parents moving in, widowhood? (You may find Your Checklist for Age-Proofing a Home on page 108 a useful tool in assessing your home's adaptability.)

2. How does your current community meet your needs and desires for cultural and educational opportunities, leisure and sporting activities, employment options, climate, social services? What kind of ties do you have to the area in which you now live?

3. What are the advantages of home ownership over other housing options? What are the disadvantages?

4. What housing alternatives for elderly or disabled individuals are available in your community? What community resources and services can you obtain for your elderly or disabled relatives or for yourself as you grow older?

5. Why would you move to a new home or a different community? Why would you choose not to relocate in either way?

6. What relationship issues and what financial matters need to be addressed when you are considering sharing your

housing with elderly parents, adult children, close friends, or students or other tenants?

For Your Information

Housing and location decisions in midlife depend on two areas of consideration: financial resources and lifestyle preferences. Each topic is covered in further detail elsewhere in this Think of Your Future workbook, but a brief discussion of how each impacts your decisions about housing and relocation is presented here.

Financial Considerations

Housing is a major component of everyone's budget. Persons buying a home expend a slightly larger percentage of their monthly income on housing than renters do, but homeowners are often rewarded with equity and with income tax advantages. Homeownership has traditionally been an important goal of adulthood. By the age of 65, three times as many people own their homes as rent them.

When persons in midlife begin to plan for the future, the home they own may prove to be their largest financial asset to apply toward the future. Those who purchased their homes before housing prices skyrocketed in the 1980s have probably accumulated considerable equity (the difference between the market value of a property and the amount still owed on it). Some homeowners will not have realized much or any profit on their home. These two groups of individuals will clearly be facing two different versions of future planning if they anticipated their home equity as a major financial resource.

Having equity in a home does not in itself guarantee financial security in one's middle and later years. The homeowner needs to gain access to these funds, either by selling the home and taking out the profits or by refinancing the house through some kind of home equity conversion mortgage.

Reverse mortgages, which allow the homeowners to remain in the house and draw out part of their equity each month for living expenses, have come into the financial market relatively recently and are increasing in popularity in most states. The money that is drawn out on a monthly basis is repaid when the house is eventually sold. Reverse mortgages, utilized principally by older homeowners, have definite risks and should be assumed only with professional legal and financial advice. If the homeowner lives longer than the term of the loan, or if the value of the house declines below the amount of collateral required by the loan, foreclosure or other forced sale of the property could occur.

Will you be able to afford the type of housing and geographic location you select for your future? An honest appraisal of expected income in the years to come is critical to making any decisions about this life component. If the family homestead will be too large and too expensive to maintain on future adjusted earnings, alternative routes need to be explored. Should the house be sold and the equity received used to purchase a smaller, more manageable home? Should part of the building be converted to an apartment and rented out? Should the homeowner offer to share space and expenses with friends or family members? Such questions are better addressed before the need to do so arises.

Lifestyle Considerations

There are predictions that mature lifestyles will soon glow with renewed vigor and fresh approaches. Retirement communities will specialize in sports and athletics or health and fitness or time-sharing with other communities or gardening or high-tech devices. Futuristic though these ideas may appear, they illustrate the fact that housing and location can reflect the lifestyles of those who choose them.

In making midlife projections on your housing and location needs and interests in the future, you need to consider your preferred or inevitable lifestyle. Proximity to friends and family, access to community resources and activities, health concerns, and the opportunity for work, study, or entertainment pursuits all help move you toward decisions on where you will live and how you will live.

Flexibility is an important element in these decisions. While retaining home ownership in the middle years may be practical and highly desirable, such responsibility may weigh heavily on those in the extremes of old age. Your home choices should enhance and support your lifestyles at all stages of maturity, and you should be adaptable to revising your plans if they become cumbersome.

Some future planners want to move to a new town, a different part of the country, even a different country. They may want a warmer or cooler climate, to be near friends or family, or to settle in a favorite place they have visited. It is a good idea to make a longer-than-vacation visit to a possible permanent residence before you make a definitive decision to move.

Others have deep roots in their communities and elect to maintain the sanctuary of their present location. Community services are continually expanding to help older adults stay in their original homes as long as possible. Meals on Wheels, Friendly Visitor, home health and personal care, home maintenance services, and telephone monitoring networks are examples of local resources of this kind.

Older women are especially likely to live alone, to have lower incomes than their male counterparts, and to have caregiving responsibilities for elderly parents or other relatives. Their longer life expectancy tends eventually to leave them alone, often in public housing or nursing homes, and vulnerable to debilitating chronic conditions that require outside assistance.

The Think of Your Future appendix includes a guide to community resources that may be available in your area. This information can be confirmed by consulting your telephone book or local advocacy groups for aging or disabled persons. A list of state agencies on aging appears in the appendix as well.

Making the Decision

The basic decision in planning where you will live in the future is whether to stay where you are or move to a different home or location that you believe will improve your quality of life. Several different decisions may occur as your life progresses. Although most people prefer to stay in their present homes, some do move to other locales or to other homes in the same area — though the type of housing they choose may be different. Even when their present home becomes unsuitable for the needs of their later years, most individuals choose to remain in the same state, if not the same neighborhood.

Selecting a new location requires time, effort, careful research, discussion, and first-hand exposure to the area before any long-term commitment is made. Using vacation time to test the new environment and renting housing before purchasing a new residence are both wise strategic moves when you are contemplating relocation. Year-round living in an area may not be the same as vacationing there, especially when the climate varies widely from what you are used to. This is an important point to remember.

You should review four major categories before arriving at a decision on housing and location for the future:

- ■ **Your personal situation:** age, health, marital and family status, number and ages of children or other dependents, potential changes in situation (dependent elderly parents, grown children, health condition, widowhood, etc.);

- ■ **Condition of your present home:** state of repair, upkeep and maintenance costs, neighborhood and community resources, proximity to family and friends, suitability for lifestyle and meaningful involvements;

- ■ **Available alternatives:** repairing or modifying your current home to reverse negative factors, moving to new home or location, moving to different type of housing (rental vs. purchase, apartment vs. single-family home, etc.); and

- ■ **Costs of decision:** financial expense of moving or staying put, emotional costs of leaving familiar surroundings or remaining in less-than-satisfactory environment, social toll taken on family and close friends — effects of your decision on those who live with you or are close to you.

What Would You Do?

The case studies that follow depict situations that persons at midlife might confront as they approach future planning. Making decisions about housing and location that support one's chosen or accepted lifestyle is the focus of these examples.

None of the cases may reflect your life situation, but brainstorming options and solutions to the challenges that face other persons can bring unexpected clarity to your own plans for the years ahead. What would you do if you were in their positions? If you are reviewing Think of Your Future on your own, you may want to discuss these cases with close friends or family members. Group settings for future planning will use the studies for workshop sessions.

CASE STUDY

Mary Brady

Mary is a single woman in her late fifties. She works for a trade association in a large city and expects to continue working as long as she is able and interested in her job. Mary has never married or had children, but she maintains a lively relationship with her sisters and brothers and their children.

Managers of the building in which Mary has rented her comfortable apartment for many years have just announced that they will be converting their units to condominiums. The current occupant of each apartment will receive the first opportunity to purchase it and will be able to do so at a price below that to be offered to the general public.

Mary is tempted by the idea of finally becoming a homeowner, but she doesn't want to eventually burden her nieces and nephews with having to dispose of her property. Based on what you know about Mary's situation, what would you advise her to do?

_____

_____

_____

What are Mary's options? (Remember that flexibility is the key to successful future planning!)

_____

What are the advantages of each option?

_____

What are the disadvantages of each option?

_____

What would be your recommendation to Mary? Why?

_____

_____

CASE STUDY

Dave Estrada

Dave is a 52-year-old divorced father of four who suffered a stroke a year ago that has led to his retirement from the Air Force Reserve and from his administrative position with the state government. He has a mortgage on the two-story house where two of his children have been staying during his time in a rehabilitation hospital.

Dave will be released from rehab soon and needs to decide where he will live. His physical mobility is limited, and he needs assistance in daily living. Dave has invested much of himself in his home and likes having the space for his children and their friends to visit. The social worker at the hospital has told him about several continuing care communities in the area and has offered to take Dave to visit them.

Dave will be receiving disability and retirement income, but the amounts have not yet been determined. His savings are negligible. Based on what you know about Dave's situation, what would you recommend he do?

_____

_____

_____

_____

What are Dave's options?

_____

What are the advantages of each option?

_____

What are the disadvantages of each option?

_____

What would you suggest to Dave? Why?

_____

_____

CASE STUDY
Jim and Jane Dahlgren

Jim and Jane are 60 and 52, respectively. Their three children are 10, 12, and 14. Jim works for a major corporation, and Jane is a self-employed landscape architect. They realize that Jim will probably have retired from his regular job by the time all three children are going through college. He is thinking about joining Jane in her business after he retires.

Jim and Jane's current home is becoming too crowded for their family's needs, and they are considering a move, probably within the metropolitan area where they now live. Several neighboring states have good state university systems, but the cost of living is as high as it is in their present location.

Jim and Jane want to provide for their family and to fully nourish their own enthusiasm for life. Based on what you know about the Dahlgrens, what would you suggest they do?

_____

_____

_____

_____

What are Jim and Jane's options?

_____

_____

What are the advantages of each option?

_____

_____

What are the disadvantages of each option?

_____

_____

What would you recommend? Why?

_____

_____

CASE STUDY
Margaret and Ed Hanson

Margaret and Ed are about to retire. They have enjoyed going to Florida every winter for their vacation because they love warmer weather. Although they will miss the friends they have in their hometown, they have developed a new circle of friends in Florida.

Margaret has a serious health problem. This has affected her ability to keep up their home. Consequently, they are considering purchasing a unit in a continuing care community in Florida. They have looked at several but have not decided what they should do.

Based on what you know about their situation, what would you recommend?

_____

_____

_____

_____

What are their options?

_____

_____

What are the advantages of each option?

_____

_____

What are the disadvantages of each option?

_____

_____

What would be your recommendation? Why?

_____

_____

The next case study, Annette Browning, and the assessment tools that follow it will help you determine the adequacy of your current housing for present or long-term planning purposes. Begin with the Move or Stay Put Checklist to determine if you want to remain where you are or move to new housing. In her case, Annette Browning determined that staying put was the better solution. The Summary of Move or Stay Put Checklist helped her begin to identify ways she would modify her home to accommodate her future needs.

If you decide that the better solution for you is to move to a new home, a second case study, Charles and Jane Houghton, guides you through further assessments. After uncovering many negatives about their current home on their Move or Stay Put Checklist assessment, the Houghtons went on to complete the Housing Factors Checklist, which helped them focus on what was most important to them when relocating. The additional assessment tools and readings may also help you simplify planning for moving to a new home.

Annette Browning

Annette is a 45-year-old recent divorcee with three teenage children. She received the family home as part of her divorce settlement. She currently has three years left to pay on the mortgage. The home appears to be worth about the same as the average home in her community and is in a good area for appreciating in value over the long term. Currently, she receives child support from her ex-husband, which she uses to help her with mortgage payments and household expenses. Fortunately, she will have the mortgage paid off by the time she no longer receives that support.

She is trying to begin her future planning. Her concern is that she will not be able to afford to stay in her home the rest of her life. She is aware that once she no longer has the child support from her ex-husband, she may not have the financial resources to make a change, if that is the best alternative for her. Therefore, she is carefully considering her alternatives for her late life now, while she has options.

Annette first evaluated the status of her current home, completing the Move or Stay Put Checklist. This tool indicated to her that she can comfortably stay in her current housing with some changes. Next, she summarized those negative factors and determined how she can change them to positives on the Summary of Move or Stay Put Checklist. She is now ready to state her planning goals for her future housing.

Annette Browning's Move or Stay Put Checklist

Annette Browning completed the Move or Stay Put Checklist and noted her findings on the Summary of Move or Stay Put Checklist that follows.

Complete the following questions by checking "yes" or "no." Add up your score to determine whether you should stay where you are or whether you should consider moving.

Yes	No	Factors
X		1. Are you happy and comfortable where you live now?
X		2. Have you adjusted to the climate and temperature?
	X	3. Is your house paid for, and are expenses under control?
	X	4. Are general maintenance expenses manageable?
X		5. Is your housing in good repair, or can it be fixed up easily?
X		6. Is your house easy to clean and maintain?
	X	7. Is the yard small enough to care for easily?
X		8. Are you friendly with your neighbors and proud of the area?
X		9. Can you travel without fear of vandalism to your home while you are away?
X		10. Is local transportation adequate for all your needs?
X		11. Are your relatives near? Can you visit often?
X		12. Are there opportunities for you to be active in social, civic, and/or community organizations?
X		13. Are you near places of worship? recreation?
X		14. Are you near shops and stores?
X		15. Is the community stable and safe, and is it likely to remain so?
X		16. Are there job and/or volunteer opportunities in your community that match your interests, values, and skills?
X		17. Do you have a reliable and well-staffed hospital in the area?
X		18. Is the economy stable or growing in your community (an important influence on property values)?
X		19. Are property values stable or on the increase in your neighborhood?
	X	20. Is the size of the house appropriate for your family size?

__16__ × **5 =** __80__   **Total Score** (Allowing 5 points for each "yes" answer)

Scoring: 90 – 100 points   Stay where you are!

75 – 85   You present home and community are adequate.

60 – 70   Some alterations to your present home could be enough to make it adequate.

55 or less   Search for a site or housing that can provide more "yes" answers. (Scores in this range indicate that your home is more of a "hassle" than a "castle.")

Based on the number of "yes" answers, you and Annette Browning should be able to predict her decision.

Annette Browning's Summary of Move or Stay Put Checklist

Annette found that her home was basically satisfactory, with two exceptions. The house and yard were too large for her now that her children have moved away from home and too expensive for her to maintain on her own. She did some creative thinking and completed her summary as follows.

"No" Factors	Potential Solutions

Expenses —
    Mortgage
    Maintenance
	Solutions =
	    Pay off mortgage early.
	    Rent part of house for additional income and help with maintenance (but check on costs of converting to an apartment).

Size — too large
    Yard too big
    House too big for only me
	Solutions =
	    Convert children's wing into apartment.
	    Rent apartment to young person or person who could help with yard maintenance for a reduced rent.

	Solutions =
	Solutions =
	Solutions =

Annette decided she was able to alter the negative factors enough to make it worthwhile for her to stay in her current home. She concluded her assessment by adding to her Action Step the following Housing Actions:

1) pay off her mortgage and 2) convert an area of her home to a rental apartment.

Now you can move on to your own Move or Stay Put Checklist on the next page.

Your Move or Stay Put Checklist

Following Annette Browning's example, assess the status of your current housing situation. Complete the following questions by checking "yes" or "no." Add up your score to determine whether you should stay where you are or whether you should consider moving.

Yes	No	Factors
		1. Are you happy and comfortable where you live now?
		2. Have you adjusted to the climate and temperature?
		3. Is your house paid for, and are expenses under control?
		4. Are general maintenance expenses manageable?
		5. Is your housing in good repair, or can it be fixed up easily?
		6. Is your house easy to clean and maintain?
		7. Is the yard small enough to care for easily?
		8. Are you friendly with your neighbors and proud of the area?
		9. Can you travel without fear of vandalism to your home while you are away?
		10. Is local transportation adequate for all your needs?
		11. Are your relatives near? Can you visit often?
		12. Are there opportunities for you to be active in social, civic, and/or community organizations?
		13. Are you near places of worship? recreation?
		14. Are you near shops and stores?
		15. Is the community stable and safe, and is it likely to remain so?
		16. Are there job and/or volunteer opportunities in your community that match your interests, values, and skills?
		17. Do you have a reliable and well-staffed hospital in the area?
		18. Is the economy stable or growing in your community (an important influence on property values)?
		19. Are property values stable or on the increase in your neighborhood?
		20. Is the size of the house appropriate for your family size?

_____ × **5** = **Total Score** (Allowing 5 points for each "yes" answer)

Scoring:

90 – 100 points	Stay where you are!
75 – 85	You present home and community are adequate.
60 – 70	Some alterations to your present home could be enough to make it adequate.
55 or less	Search for a site or housing that can provide more "yes" answers. (Scores in this range indicate that your home is more of a "hassle" than a "castle.")

Your Summary of Move or Stay Put Checklist

Note the factors you determined were negative about your current housing under the "No" column. Then list possible solutions that could change that negative factor to a positive one. Note if there are some things that you can't change without moving, like location.

"No" Factors	Potential Solutions
	Solutions =
	Solutions =
	Solutions =
	Solutions =
	Solutions =
	Solutions =

If you are able to improve your current housing or it is adequate as it is now, you are ready to list your goals for future housing and plan the action steps necessary to achieve them.

If moving to different housing appears to be the better alternative for you, continue with the next set of assessments, Or Move to a New Situation.

Or Move to a New Situation

Staying where we are is not always appropriate or financially feasible. Some people will find so many "no" answers on their Move or Stay Put Checklist (scores 60 or below) that moving is the best choice. Some of the "no" answers may be so permanent and important that it is worth moving in order to improve them.

Moving is a complex decision, because so many factors are involved in selecting different housing. Some elements may be more important to you than others, and these should be the basis for your decisions. Use the Housing Factors Checklist to determine the factors most important to you in deciding where to move.

It may be useful to study the case of Charles and Jane Houghton.

CASE STUDY

Charles and Jane Houghton

Charles and Jane Houghton, a midwestern couple ages 60 and 55, respectively, are planning to retire in five years. They completed their Move or Stay Put Checklist and discovered very little about their present location to encourage them to stay put (they scored only a 45 rating on their current housing). Their house was too large for them, now that their children had grown and moved to several different southwestern states. They had few opportunities to enjoy their hobby, golf, because of the expense and climate in their metropolitan area. Finally, they were concerned about living in and maintaining a two-story house when they become less mobile.

They decided that they should begin to explore alternatives and perhaps even vacation in some of the areas that they want to consider seriously. They saw this as a way of being comfortable with a decision to move when they retire in five years. Finally, they summarized their factors on the Summary of Housing Factors Assessment to help them focus their plans. They used this summary to help them formalize their goals and plan the action steps necessary to achieve them.

Complete the same process for yourself after reading Charles and Jane's example.

The Houghtons' Housing Factors Checklist

Check "yes" or "no" if the following factors are important to you when selecting a new housing choice.

Yes	No	Location Factors
X		1. Geography/Climate — Sunbelt, change of seasons, or same climate as now
	X	2. Geography/Topography — water, plains, mountains, etc.
	X	3. Geography/Environments — rural, city, or metropolitan area
X		4. Proximity to family
X		5. Proximity to friends
X		6. Proximity to desired leisure activities (fishing, golf, mountain climbing, etc.)
X		7. Proximity to health care
	X	8. Proximity to public transportation
	X	9. Proximity to work/volunteer activities
	X	10. Proximity to present location (but improved housing/services/access to friends, family, or activities)
X		11. Environmental considerations: quality of air, water; conservation of natural resources
X		12. Public safety, fire protection

Yes	No	Financial Factors
X		1. Desire to own (and resulting advantages/disadvantages)
	X	2. Desire to rent (and resulting advantages/disadvantages)
X		3. Initial cost of home
X		4. Cost of living (taxes, food costs, utilities)
X		5. Maintenance costs
	X	6. Services and amenities included in monthly fees or initial costs
	X	7. Subsidized housing (government HUD projects, community housing for older adults, etc.)

Yes	No	Housing Types (see alternatives for description)
X		1. Single-family home
	X	2. Mobile home
X		3. Multiple-family house — (shared house, duplex, or townhouse)
	X	4. Apartment — small garden apartment complex, condominium
	X	5. Accessory apartment (attached to single-family home)
	X	6. Apartment — large apartment complex, condominium complex (generally high-rise)
	X	7. Assisted living apartment (food, health care, and/or personal care services included in rental agreement)
	X	8. Continuing care community (insurance for life care typically including food, health care, personal care, transportation, recreation, and other amenities in purchase agreement)

The Houghtons' Summary of Housing Factors Assessment

Here the Houghtons summarized the factors they decided were most important in selecting new housing alternatives. They reviewed their answers on the Housing Factors Checklist and transferred them here in order of priority.

Most Important	Location	Close to family
	Financial	Initial cost of house
	Type of Housing	

Moderately Important	Location	Proximity to leisure
	Financial	Cost of living
	Type of Housing	

Only Minor Importance	Location	Close to friends
	Financial	
	Type of Housing	Single-family home

Your Housing Factors Checklist

Check "yes" or "no" if the following factors are important to you when making a new housing choice.

Yes   No   *Location Factors*

1. Geography/Climate — Sunbelt, change of seasons, or same climate as now
2. Geography/Topography — water, plains, mountains, etc.
3. Geography/Environments — rural, city, or metropolitan area
4. Proximity to family
5. Proximity to friends
6. Proximity to desired leisure activities (fishing, golf, mountain climbing, etc.)
7. Proximity to health care
8. Proximity to public transportation
9. Proximity to work/volunteer activities
10. Proximity to present location (but improved housing/services/access to friends, family, or activities)
11. Environmental considerations: quality of air, water; conservation of natural resources
12. Public safety, fire protection

Financial Factors

1. Desire to own (and resulting advantages/disadvantages)
2. Desire to rent (and resulting advantages/disadvantages)
3. Initial cost of home
4. Cost of living (taxes, food costs, utilities)
5. Maintenance costs
6. Services and amenities included in monthly fees or initial costs
7. Subsidized housing (government HUD projects, community housing for older adults, etc.)

Housing Types (see alternatives for description)

1. Single-family home
2. Mobile home
3. Multiple-family house — (shared house, duplex, or townhouse)
4. Apartment — small garden apartment complex, condominium
5. Accessory apartment (attached to single-family home)
6. Apartment — large apartment complex, condominium complex (generally high-rise)
7. Assisted living apartment (food, health care, and/or personal care services included in rental agreement)
8. Continuing care community (insurance for life care typically including food, health care, personal care, transportation, recreation, and other amenities in purchase agreement)

Your Summary of Housing Factors Assessment

Here you should summarize the factors you decided were most important in selecting new housing alternatives. Review your answers on the Housing Factors Checklist and transfer them here in order of priority.

Most Important   Location   _____

                          Financial   _____

                          Type of Housing   _____

Moderately Important   Location   _____

                          Financial   _____

                          Type of Housing   _____

Only Minor Importance   Location   _____

                          Financial   _____

                          Type of Housing   _____

Your Lifestyle

As added preparation for housing and location decisions, you may want to complete this quick study of how the type of home you choose and its location may affect your lifestyle. If you have a spouse or partner, it is important that both of you explore and try to reconcile your differing priorities.

One couple listed the geographical area and type of housing each prefers and their reasons. Here are their separate lists.

Partner One

1. *Move to the suburbs*
2. *Small town*
3. *Good golfing*
4. *Small house/mobile home*
5. *Good friends nearby*

Partner Two

1. *Stay in the city*
2. *Many friends in town*
3. *Married children nearby*
4. *Yard for gardening*
5. *Can convert house to two-family to rent*

Have you and your spouse or partner prepared similar lists of your own? Try it now! Record your individual housing objectives in the following column. If you are single, use only the lower panel.

Partner One

1. _____
2. _____
3. _____
4. _____
5. _____

Partner Two

1. _____
2. _____
3. _____
4. _____
5. _____

Now combine your two lists into one, making a longer list if necessary. You may find that differences or conflicts between your lists resolve themselves as you accumulate more data and experience. If not, how can the two of you work to resolve your differences?

1. _____
2. _____
3. _____
4. _____
5. _____
6. _____
7. _____

Since you won't be making these decisions for a few years, take the time to explore each of the geographical areas or types of housing during your vacations. Remember, although you should explore alternatives and try out "dream" sites, the vast majority of individuals decide to remain in their present homes or stay in the same general area.

ALTERNATIVES

If your assessments have led you to consider moving, it should be useful for you to consider some alternatives you may not have thought about seriously for both the near and the distant future.

Housing Options

The housing market includes all manner of alternatives. Descriptions of some of the more common types of housing follow here along with useful pointers related to the particular type of housing.

Single-Family Homes. Single-family units include the familiar homestead in the general community or in a retirement community, or a vacation or second home that eventually becomes a retirement home. Average costs of single-family homes vary considerably depending on area of the country and rural versus urban location. Issues for single-family homes are renting versus buying; new versus older home; and location, location, location.

Mobile Homes. Manufactured (or mobile) homes offer an economical, low-maintenance housing alternative. Since 1976, federal construction standards require that units be stronger, safer, more energy-efficient, and better built than formerly.

Multiple-Family House. Multiple-unit housing includes apartments, duplexes, townhouses, condominiums, and cooperatives that are owned rather than rented.

Duplexes can be attractive alternatives to a single family home because you can live in one side and rent out the other side for additional income and certain tax deductions. Check with people who have tried this arrangement for additional pros and cons.

Townhouse/co-op/condominiums are generally smaller than single-family homes but are owned rather than rented. The major advantage is freedom from many outdoor maintenance chores, although owners pay for the service through a monthly maintenance fee.

Rental Apartments. Apartments can vary between small, garden apartments with some outdoor space to large high-rise buildings. Typically, maintenance is provided as part of the cost of renting. There is adjustment, however, for those who are used to the privacy of a single-family home or for those who like outdoor activities. Sometimes, large apartment complexes have recreational amenities like gardens, pools, tennis courts, and so on, to attract people who still want some outdoor freedom.

Senior Housing. As you plan for both the immediate future and many years ahead, you will find that several types of housing are specifically designed for older adults. They vary in the amount of supportive services offered, and in whether the property and service are provided for a rental charge or for an entry fee and monthly charge.

Assisted Living Apartments (also known as congregate housing facilities) traditionally have been operated by government agencies or nonprofit groups, but now are operated increasingly by for-profit sponsors. They usually provide room, meals in a central dining room, transportation, and social and recreational programs. The services of health professionals, housekeepers, and personal assistants may also be available, although this varies considerably.

Accessory Apartments are independent living units added on to or carved out of single-family homes. Zoning regulations generally are strict regarding such apartments, but in some communities the restrictions are being relaxed.

ECHO Housing (Elder Cottage Housing Opportunity) is a small, free-standing, energy-efficient, barrier-free unit that is installed adjacent to an existing single-family home. ECHO units provide comfortable, efficient housing for older relatives, and their proximity to the main house encourages day-to-day support that benefits both households. When no longer needed, the ECHO unit can be easily removed. ECHO housing is inexpensive but subject to very strict zoning laws.

Shared Housing occurs when an elderly person moves into someone else's home, or another person(s) moves in with the elderly person. Often this arrangement is intergenerational, so that the younger person receives the benefit of rent reductions and the older person receives much-needed companionship, home maintenance services, or transportation services.

Board and Care Homes are usually privately operated facilities that provide a room, meals, and some personal care services such as help with bathing, dressing, and taking medications. No health care is provided.

Nursing Home Care offers higher levels of personal and health care than typical in the assisted living housing arrangements. This type of housing is appropriate only for those who are chronically ill or who cannot take care of themselves. Skilled nursing facilities, the highest level of care outside an acute care hospital, offer 24-hour nursing care.

Continuing Care Communities. This type of housing, specifically designed for older or disabled adults, is an increasingly available and popular choice, particularly for those in extreme old age. Most offer lifetime housing and a range of health care similar to that in nursing homes, social activities, and other services. They emphasize independent living in rooms, apartments, or individual cottages as long as possible. If the time comes when extended or extensive nursing care is necessary, nursing home care is also available.

Moving Issues

If your future housing and location considerations convince you that you should move, either now or sometime in the near future, it will pay to take your time and evaluate the short- and long-term financial ramifications of each of several alternatives.

■ **Consider the Tax Breaks in Selling Your Home.**

Caution: Tax laws change frequently. These opportunities are current as of this writing, but you need to keep yourself informed if you are considering using these options.

Option 1: If you sell your home outright and buy or build and occupy the new house within two years of the sale of your old house, and if the price is the same as or more than that of the old house, you have no tax to pay on the profit of the sale of the old house.

Option 2: If you sell your home outright and buy a house that costs less than the old house or rent a new house and invest the cash from the sale, you may be entitled to a once-in-a-lifetime exclusion of up to $125,000 on the profit from the sale of that house. To qualify for this exclusion you must be age 55 or older, have used the home as your principal residence three of the last five years, and not be married to someone who has already used this exclusion. This tax break can be complex, and you should check with a qualified tax consultant for details.

■ **Consider the Degree of Commitment in Renting Your Home.**

Option 3: If you decide to relocate to a new home, selling your current home but renting the new one may give you the flexibility to invest the cash from the sale in a liquid investment while trying out the new location without a long-term or major financial commitment.

Option 4: If you decide to relocate to a new home, renting out your old home and renting a new one may be the safest and surest method of trying out the new location. This option keeps you from having to make a large financial commitment that will be difficult to get out of should you decide to move back home.

■ **Consider the Financial Merits of Renting or Selling Your Old Home.**

The following form can help you determine how much it costs you to live in your present home.

Present Home (Monthly)

Mortgage payment $ _____ × 12 = $ _____

Property taxes _____ _____

Property insurance _____ _____

Maintenance and repairs

   Electricity _____ × 12 = _____

   Gas or fuel oil _____ × 12 = _____

   Other costs _____ = _____

Total Carrying Costs $ _____ $ _____

Estimate the price you might get for your house if you sell it (a good guess will do, based on similar houses that have sold recently in your neighborhood).

If You Sell

Estimated selling price $ _____

(Subtract):

   Commission _____

   Miscellaneous costs of selling _____

   Balance of mortgage _____

   Potential taxes owed _____

   Other costs _____

   Total costs $ _____

Net Benefit (Selling price minus total costs): $ _____

Estimate how much rental income your home might bring in (based on rents being charged for similar homes in your area). Use only eleven months to allow for some vacancy time.

If You Rent to Others

Income   (Monthly)

   Monthly rental payment _____ × 11 = $ _____

Expenses

   Mortgage payments $ _____

   Property taxes _____

   Maintenance and repairs _____

   Liability insurance _____

   Management fee or
     collection expenses _____

   Other costs _____

   Total Expenses $ _____

Net Cost or Profit (income less total expenses) $ _____

Professional Help to Sell Your Home

To sell a home most effectively, make use of professionals — the real estate agent, the lawyer, and the tax adviser. Each can play an important role.

The *real estate agent* can help negotiate the best price and can assist in finding financing. It can be worth an investment of your time to look for a reliable and reputable agent. Ask for and check personal references. Know that a listing agreement, which most agents will ask you to sign, can require you to pay a commission under a variety of circumstances and commits you to that agent for a set period of time. If time is of no concern to you, you might want to try to sell your house on your own.

The *lawyer* can help you understand the listing agreement with the real estate agent and can also advise you with respect to a contract to sell the property. A contract to sell real estate can be very involved, and legal help is advisable before you sign any documents. Neither the real estate agent nor the escrow agent is the proper person to give you legal advice.

The *tax adviser* can play a most important role, for the sale of your home can have complex tax implications (see earlier, Consider the Tax Breaks). If you sell your home at a profit, that profit can be taxed unless you reinvest in a home within two years that costs as much as the home you sold, or if you are age 55 or older and elect to use your once-in-a-lifetime $125,000 exclusion. The tax adviser can help you determine which might be best for you and the implications, if any, of renting out your home instead of selling it.

Home Equity Options

Reverse mortgages represent one of several means available to homeowners to gain access to the equity in their homes in most states. The loan is paid to the homeowner in monthly payments, with the amount of the loan determined by the amount of home equity borrowed against, the interest rate, and the length of the loan. These funds are repaid at a scheduled time or, under some arrangements, when the homeowner dies or sells the home. A variation on the reverse mortgage is a line of credit that the homeowner has access to based on the equity in the home. The amount used does not have to be repaid until the homeowner dies or sells the home.

In a **sale/leaseback arrangement**, the owner sells the property, often at slightly below the market rate, to an investor. The owner retains the right to live in the house as a renter for life. The investor pays the owner in monthly installments over an agreed upon period and also covers the obligations of homeownership such as insurance, taxes, and repairs. Frequently, the investor will purchase a deferred-payment annuity to provide the former owner with continued monthly income once the house has been paid off by the investor.

Homeowner equity accounts are, in effect, a second mortgage in the form of a revolving line of credit. They are offered by brokerage houses, finance companies, and banks, which will provide a line of credit up to 80 percent of the unmortgaged value of a home. The homeowner draws on the line of credit, by using a credit card or checks provided by the lender. Most homeowner equity accounts have a variable interest rate, plus an origination fee and an annual service fee.

Researching a New Area

Write to the local chamber of commerce. Mention specifically that you are considering moving to that area. Ask for information about:

- Cultural and educational centers, public school facilities
- Health facilities
- Radio and TV (cable) reception
- Local public transportation
- Airport and train facilities
- Churches, synagogues, other religious organizations
- Business and industry
- Civic groups, social clubs and organizations
- Community resources
- Shopping

Subscribe to the weekly or Sunday newspaper to find out about local business, crime, social life, cost of living, real estate, etc.

Write to the U. S. Department of Housing and Urban Development Information Center for housing information (see the appendix for this address).

Inquire at your religious, fraternal, social, or professional organizations to learn if they operate in the new locale. If so, ask for a contact person to talk to personally about the quality of life, housing alternatives, etc.

Write to the state's tourist center or bureau for information about recreation and travel centers, areas of interest in the general area.

Contact any personal acquaintances living in the area to get different viewpoints on lifestyle questions you may have.

Stop and Think

Your Checklist for Age-Proofing a Home

Following the Houghtons' example, check "yes" or "no" if the following factors are important to you in your housing and location planning for the future.

Yes   No

Levels
1. All rooms on the first floor or
2. A bathroom, kitchen, bedroom, and laundry facilities on the first floor

Entrances
1. Well-lighted with no steps; protected against weather
2. Secure locks on doors that can be opened quickly from inside

Steps
1. Have sturdy handrails
2. Well-lighted but glare-free
3. Have nonslip surfaces

Doors
1. 36 inches wide for wheelchair accessibility
2. Handles or levers easy to grasp
3. No thresholds or tracks to trip over

Halls
1. 48 inches wide for possible wheelchair use

Windows
1. Large, easy to open, with secure locks
2. Low enough to see outside from chair or bed

Floors
1. Coverings free of holes, tears, or barriers
2. Nonslip surfaces
3. Rugs and mats are nonskid or fastened to floor

Lighting
1. Lots of glare-free light
2. Switches at top and bottom of stairs
3. Night-light between bedroom and bath and in every hallway

Bathroom
1. Seat, grab bars, and nonslip floor in shower or tub
2. Grab bars next to toilet
3. Shower doors of safety glass, easy to open
4. Easy to turn faucets

Kitchen
1. Fire extinguisher/smoke alarm
2. Burners on stove that turn on/off safely

THE AARP APPROACH
RESPONSIBILITY

Decision Time

Decisions as complicated and as important as where you want to live in the more long-term future are difficult to make. The Assessment section has helped you examine your current situation and your preferred housing factors for future housing. The discussion of Alternatives has raised ideas and possibly new issues for you.

Based on the exercises you completed and your consideration of alternatives and costs, what decisions have you made about where you will live in the future? If you are still uncertain, what information do you need to help you decide? What stands between you and making your decision a reality? How can you avoid or remove these obstacles?

Action Step

Example

In the space below, state what decisions you have made concerning your housing plans for the future. List three to five things you need to do to achieve your housing objectives. These actions will become a part of your Master Action Plan.

My Housing Decision: *We will sell our current home and move to the Southwest. Our new home will be nearer to our children and provide us access to golf and the other leisure activities we enjoy.*

Housing Actions	Rank by Importance
Vacation in the Southwest	1
Plan long-term visits to our top relocation sites	4
Make necessary repairs to current home before selling	3
Purchase single-family retirement home	2

Action Step

In the space below, state what decisions you have made concerning your housing plans for the future. List three to five things you need to do to achieve your housing objectives. These actions will become a part of your Master Action Plan.

My Housing Decision:

Housing Actions	Rank by Importance

PLANNING

The last step in the AARP Approach and your final product of this unit is your Master Action Plan. Simply put, your MAP is your "to do" list stated in clear, realistic, and measurable actions. Transfer the housing action statements you wrote on page 111 to your MAP.

Translate these goals into specific steps you would need to act upon in order to achieve the goal. Remember to use action verbs — things you do. Beside each Housing Action, list potential resources that could help you accomplish the step and, finally, assign the persons who are responsible for accomplishing the step and the time frame they have to get it done. Brainstorm and list possible resources for helping you take the actions. Then give yourself, or the person you assign the task, a time frame for completing the job.

Circumstances change over time, which may cause you to take another path toward reaching your future goals. Go back to your MAP periodically and make any revisions or updates necessary to keep your plan current and vital. Keep track of your planning progress on your Master Action Plan by marking off the planning steps as you complete them.

Before you begin this definitive activity, you may find it helpful to look at the example on page 113 completed by Charles and Jane Houghton.

Master Action Plan

Example

Goal Statement: *Vacation in the Southwest*

Actions	Resources	Time Frame	By Whom?
1. Get information on areas: Nevada, California, New Mexico, Arizona	State tourist boards; chambers of commerce; library	4 months	Jane
2. Get additional information on costs	Real estate agents; library	6 months	Jane
3. Select areas of interest and plan to vacation in all these in next 3 years (N.B. Go at different times of year to test seasonal differences in Southwest)	Travel books and magazines; golf magazines; golf and resort directories; friends, family	Next 3 years	Both of us

Goal Statement: *Purchase single-family retirement home*

Actions	Resources	Time Frame	By Whom?
1. Decide on desired floor plan	Homes and architecture books and magazines; own experience with past homes	1 year	Both of us
2. Talk to realtor about market value of current home	Real estate agent; tax assessments	6 months	Charles
3. Look at housing in areas when vacationing	Local newspapers, housing guides; real estate agents	Over next 3 years	Both of us
4. Explore renting at first (perhaps with option to buy) if cannot find ideal home	Local newspapers, housing guides; real estate agents	3 years	Both of us

Income
Planning

Income Planning

Financial considerations are the primary focal point of planning for the future. All the dreams and fantasies in the world will remain just that if you are not able to afford them. The protection that you, your employer, and the government have built up on your behalf will need to be carefully evaluated in terms of their ability to support you in the years ahead. Flexibility must go hand in hand with realism. Setting goals and reviewing and revising them regularly is the key to sensible and productive planning.

Unit Objectives

- **Assessment:** To assess your current and anticipated sources of income as they relate to your plans for your future

- **Alternatives:** To consider alternatives and modifications to your sources of income that are likely to maintain or improve your economic stability in the future

- **Responsibility:** To make decisions about your sources of income that will enable you to pursue your chosen or accepted goals

- **Planning:** To make specific plans to follow through on your decisions regarding income, remembering to remain flexible and to consult those who share your personal financial life

What Do You Think?

The questions that follow will help you get started on the sometimes difficult but critically important issue of financial planning for the future. You are encouraged to discuss these thoughts about income production with your spouse or partner, other family members and friends, and anyone else in your network of trust.

1. If you suddenly won the lottery or otherwise came into unexpected wealth, what would you do with the money and with your life? How could these dreams be pursued on a lesser scale with the more realistic assets you have at your disposal?

2. Will you need to work as long and as much as you can in your middle and later years to maintain the lifestyle you want?

3. Do you look forward to a second career? Are your skills, experience, and interests adaptable to such pursuits? How much income could you generate this way?

4. What sources other than working can you think of that would generate income in the future?

For Your Information

Whatever the future promises financially, you need to plan carefully to make sure the lifestyle you envision for your future is one you can afford and continue to support. You will need to evaluate all sources of income, determining which will be temporary and which will be permanent, which will be stable and which will fluctuate, and which will survive the disability or death of a spouse or partner. It is never too early to set goals, make plans, and map out courses of action. This is what Think of Your Future is about!

Think of Your Future is also about flexibility. Nothing stays the same, and nothing is guaranteed, particularly in the financial arena. Inflation, generally figured at 4 to 5 percent annually, can adversely affect both the income and the expense sides of your planning equation. Changing housing needs, declining health, rising or falling interest rates, and increasing or decreasing time spent working, traveling, or caregiving will all have effects on your financial future. You will want to consider several scenarios in your planning and be prepared to regroup and replan when the need arises.

The financial considerations you need to examine will be covered in three sections of this handbook. This section will provide information on income sources, while the next two units will help you analyze expenses and clarify saving and investment options.

Where Will Your Retirement Money Come From?

The predominant goal of financial planning for the years ahead is to have a steady income after you stop working full time. Many sources of retirement income are possible. Most individuals consider the following as their major income-producers if and when they retire from their principal jobs.

1. Social Security retirement benefits
2. Employer-provided benefits
3. Tax-deferred individual retirement plans
4. Employment earnings during retirement
5. Personal savings and investments

Social Security

Most American workers are eligible for Social Security benefits. To receive Social Security, you must have worked in a covered occupation and paid Social Security taxes for at least 10 years (or 40 quarters) over the course of your lifetime.

Social Security can make an important contribution to your financial well-being during retirement, but it was never intended to serve as the sole source of your retirement income. It is meant to supplement your pension, savings, and investments.

Many retirees erroneously think receiving Social Security is a relatively simple matter. Once you stop working, the government automatically sends you checks each month. Social Security is much more complex than that, and considerable planning is necessary to make sure you receive what you are entitled to.

Your first step is to visit your local Social Security office and obtain the most up-to-date literature on benefits. In addition to retirement benefits, the Social Security Administration provides benefits for disabled workers, for the survivors of a deceased worker, and for dependents of a retired or disabled worker. Medicare is also available to those 65 and older and to long-term disabled persons.

The Social Security office will provide you with an inquiry card, "Request for Statement of Earnings." By completing and submitting that card to the Social Security Administration, you will get a statement of the Social Security earnings that have been credited to your Social Security number. It is wise to periodically check on the accuracy of these amounts. The office can also give you estimates as to the amount of Social Security benefits you will be entitled to receive upon retirement, but it will not be able to give you more specific amounts until you are at least 60 or within a few months of actual retirement.

In addition to inquiring about your retirement benefits, you should definitely contact your Social Security office if:

■ A worker in your family dies;

■ You are disabled before age 65;

■ You are age 62 or older and plan to retire soon;

■ You are near age 60 and a surviving spouse; or

■ You are within three months of age 65 and can enroll in Medicare, even if you do not plan to retire.

Social Security benefits are not paid automatically. You must file for them on prescribed forms, with specific documentation and — for some claims — within certain time limits. Survivor benefits in particular are often left unclaimed because the survivors are not aware they are available.

Social Security Retirement Benefits. If you are eligible for Social Security, your benefit amount at retirement will be based on your earnings averaged over your entire working career.

When you receive retirement benefits, some members of your family also can receive benefits. Eligible family members include the following:

■ Your spouse age 62 or older;

■ Your spouse under age 62, if she or he is taking care of your child who is under age 16 or disabled;

■ Your former spouse age 62 or older and unmarried, if the marriage lasted at least 10 years;

■ Children up to age 18;

■ Children age 18–19, if they are full-time elementary or secondary school students; and

■ Children over age 18, if they are disabled.

The full benefit for a spouse is one-half (50 percent) of the retired worker's full benefit. If you are eligible for both your own retirement benefits and benefits as a spouse, you will receive the higher of the two benefits. You will not receive both.

If you have children eligible for Social Security, each will receive up to one-half of your full benefit. There is a limit to the amount of money that can be paid to a family. If the total benefits due your spouse and children exceed this limit, their benefits will be reduced proportionately. Your benefit will not be affected.

A Special Note to Divorced Persons. If you were married to your spouse for at least 10 years, you may be eligible for a benefit based on your former spouse's earnings, even if those earnings were during a period you were not married. This benefit — no more than half your former spouse's benefit — is paid to you separately. To be eligible for this benefit, you must meet the following requirements:

■ You must be at least 62 years old;

- You must be unmarried at the time of application;
- Your former spouse must be at least 62 years old and qualify for Social Security by having sufficient quarters of coverage (QCs) or be receiving disability benefits; and
- You are not eligible for a benefit based on your own wage record that is equal to or greater than one-half of your former spouse's full benefits.

If your former spouse is eligible for benefits but not actually receiving them yet, you can still qualify if you have been divorced at least two years, unless you were receiving benefits before the divorce.

Even if you have lost track of your ex-spouse and don't know whether he or she has retired, whether he or she is still alive, or what his or her Social Security number is, you should apply for benefits, if you think you might be eligible. The Social Security Administration can help you locate the necessary information.

If you are divorced and your former spouse dies, you may be eligible for benefits if you meet all of the following requirements:

- Your former spouse was fully insured for Social Security benefits and was married to you for at least 10 years;
- You are unmarried or you remarried after the age of 60;
- You are at least 60 years old (50 if you are disabled) or you are caring for your former spouse's child who is under age 16 or who was disabled before age 22; and
- You are not eligible for a greater benefit based on your own wage record.

Retirement Age. "Full retirement age" according to Social Security is currently age 65. The benefit amount paid at 65 is considered the full retirement benefit.

Because of longer life expectancies, the full retirement age will be increased in gradual steps until it reaches age 67. This change affects people born in 1938 and later. The table shows full retirement age by year of birth.

Early Retirement. You can begin receiving Social Security benefits as early as age 62. If you take early retirement, your monthly benefits will be reduced, based on the number of months you will receive checks before you reach full retirement age. As a general rule, early retirement will give you

Age to Receive Full Social Security Benefits

Year of Birth	Full Retirement Age	Year of Birth	Full Retirement Age
1937 or earlier	65	1955	66 and 2 months
1938	65 and 2 months	1956	66 and 4 months
1939	65 and 4 months	1957	66 and 6 months
1940	65 and 6 months	1958	66 and 8 months
1941	65 and 8 months	1959	66 and 10 months
1942	65 and 10 months	1960 and later	67
1943–1954	66		

about the same total Social Security benefits over your lifetime, but in smaller amounts, taking into account the longer period you receive them. If your full retirement age is 65, the reduction for starting your Social Security at age 62 is 20 percent. It is reduced 13 1/3 percent at age 63. It is reduced 6 2/3 percent at age 64.

If you were born after 1937, your full retirement age is more than 65. You still will be able to take your retirement benefits at age 62, but the reduction in your benefit amount will be greater than it is for people retiring now.

Sometimes poor health or injury forces people to retire early. If you are unable to continue working because of poor health, consider applying for Social Security disability benefits. The amount of the disability benefit is the same as a full, unreduced retirement benefit.

Delayed Retirement. If you decide to continue working full-time beyond your full retirement age, you can increase your Social Security benefit in two ways. First, higher lifetime earnings result in higher benefits. So if you delay your retirement one year, you add another year of high earnings to your Social Security record.

In addition to the potentially higher earnings, your benefit will increase by a certain percentage. These increases will be added automatically from the time you reach your full retirement age until you start taking your benefits or until you reach age 70. The percentage varies depending on your date of birth. For example, if you were born in 1943 or later, your benefit will be 8 percent higher for each year beyond your full retirement age that you delay signing up for Social Security. Contact your Social Security office for benefit increases for delayed retirement.

Note: If you delay your retirement, be sure to sign up for Medicare three months before you reach age 65.

Cost-of-Living Adjustments. Federal law provides for automatic cost-of-living increases in Social Security benefits. The actual dollar amount received will be adjusted upward for inflation between now and your retirement date. After you start receiving retirement benefits, the amount will go up automatically as the cost of living rises. These increases are effective in December of each year and are reflected in Social Security checks mailed out the following month.

Effect of Work on Social Security Benefits. If you continue working, whether part-time or full-time, once you have begun to receive Social Security benefits, you will lose some or all of your benefits if your income from work exceeds a certain annual amount. If you are under 65, $1 in benefits will be deducted for each $2 in earnings above the limit. If you are 65 through 69, $1 in benefits will be deducted for each $3 in earnings above the limit. The dollar amount of the limit is adjusted each year. Earnings in or after the month you reach age 70 will not affect your Social Security benefits.

If you continue to work once you have started receiving Social Security benefits, you will have to continue paying Social Security taxes on your earnings, as will your employer. The amount of those taxes will, of course, depend on your annual earnings. Your benefits also will be recomputed to account for additional earnings so that your benefits can, in some instances, increase later on.

Taxing Social Security Benefits. If your income exceeds a certain amount once you have started receiving Social Security benefits, a portion of your benefits will be subject to federal income taxes. Income for this purpose includes your Social Security benefits and any tax-exempt interest income. Provisions in the Social Security law strongly influence the feasibility of continuing to work once you have reached the age at which retirement benefits are available. The Assessment exercise "Does It Pay to Work after Retirement?" will help you evaluate the pros and cons of continuing to work.

Employer-Provided Pension Plans

Employer pension plans are those in which your employer (and sometimes you) contribute to your retirement benefits. Under federal law you are guaranteed certain rights, including the right to a simplified explanation of your plan.

A large portion of your retirement income may be from a pension plan. It is important for you to understand how much income you will receive. You will want to visit your employer's benefit office to get answers to some important questions. When will you become vested in your pension plan? What options do you have for receiving your income? What will your beneficiaries receive if something happens to you? What will happen to your health insurance, life insurance, and other employee benefits when you retire?

Defined Benefit Plans. Defined benefit plans are funded by the employer to provide designated benefits. These benefits are often stated as a proportion of your preretirement pay. It commits your employer to giving you a specific amount of money when you reach the retirement age defined in the plan. The amount you will receive may depend on how long you have been a member of the plan, your earnings, or both.

Defined Contribution Plans. Defined contribution plans set certain conditions under which an employer must contribute to each participating employee's retirement account. The individual employer decides what these conditions will be. The amount of money allocated to your account is usually based on your salary and sometimes on your length of service. Your plan may also allow you to contribute voluntarily a certain percentage of your salary. If so, your contributions may be tax-deductible under rules similar to those that apply to IRA contributions.

Defined contribution plans include:

- Money-purchase pension plans, in which your employer promises to set aside a certain amount for you each year, generally a percentage of your earnings.

- Profit-sharing plans, in which the employer's contribution depends on the company's profits reaching a certain level.

- Stock-bonus plans, in which your employer's contribution is used to buy stock in your employer's company for you. The stock is usually held in trust until you retire, when you can receive your shares or sell them at fair market value.

Vesting. Virtually all employer-sponsored retirement plans require that the employee work for a certain number of years to receive certain benefits. This is generally known as the vesting requirement. While the federal pension law does not require that employers offer pensions, nor dictate how much an employer should put into any individual's pension, the law does require all employers offering pensions to choose from specific vesting formulas.

The vesting formula determines at what time you are entitled to the money that has been set aside for your pension. Vesting formulas are either all-at-once or phased-in.

The all-at-once vesting formula will give workers 100 percent vesting after five years of service. The phased-in formula will give an employee 20 percent vesting after three years, then 20 percent per year thereafter, until the employee is fully vested after seven years.

Employers can choose shorter vesting formulas than that, but not longer ones. An example of a phased-in formula: Over the years your employer may have put aside $5,000 toward your pension. If you are 60 percent vested, you would be entitled to 60 percent of the $5,000, or $3,000, should you terminate your employment. That money might not be payable until some later date. Talk with your employer for specifics as they pertain to your individual case.

ASSESSMENT

What Would You Do?

These case studies are of people who, like you, are facing questions about their future income and are not sure of what they need and what they can expect. Each situation has more than one option, but some choices may be wiser than others. If you are going through this workbook at home, you may find it helpful to use the case studies to stimulate discussion between you and other family members or close friends. Which option would be best for you?

Income Planning

John Olson

John Olson has managed to accumulate a
reasonable group of assets. He has money
invested in mutual funds and owns a vacation
home. But he is worried about not having a cash
reserve for emergencies. What should he do?

_____

_____

_____

_____

What are his options?

_____

What are the advantages of each option?

_____

What are the disadvantages of each option?

_____

What would be your recommendation? Why?

_____

Rita and John Blackwell

Rita and John Blackwell both work full-time. John
is vested in his company's pension plan. Rita
works for a small business and does not have a
pension plan. Rita and John want to set up a fund
for her. What should they do?

_____

_____

_____

_____

What are their options?

_____

What are the advantages of each option?

_____

What are the disadvantages of each option?

_____

What would be your recommendation? Why?

_____

Laura Barker

Laura Barker wants to set up an investment program. Her mortgage will be paid in five years. She has a sizable stamp collection. Laura wants to raise some cash to add to the $5,000 she already has for investing. How can she get more money for an investment fund?

_____

_____

_____

_____

What are her options?

_____

_____

What are the advantages of each option?

_____

_____

What are the disadvantages of each option?

_____

_____

What would be your recommendation? Why?

_____

_____

Trudee Shubert

Trudee Shubert is concerned whether her mother, Wilma, age 82, can make ends meet. Wilma owns her own home, but her only source of income is a small Social Security benefit. Wilma has been very ill the past six months, and Medicare pays only about 40 percent of her medical expenses. Trudee would like to help to improve her mother's situation.

What are their options?

_____

_____

_____

What are the advantages of each option?

_____

_____

What are the disadvantages of each option?

_____

_____

What would be your recommendation? Why?

_____

_____

Income Planning

Rick Rivera

Rick Rivera has not worked in one place long enough to qualify for a pension. He is not worried, though, because he thinks Social Security will be enough. His wife, Anna, has seen the problems her parents are facing in retirement because their only source of income is Social Security. Anna would like to help Rick deal with what she considers a major concern.

What are their options?

_____

_____

_____

_____

What are the advantages of each option?

_____

_____

What are the disadvantages of each option?

_____

_____

What would be your recommendation? Why?

_____

_____

Income Planning

Financial Considerations

Financial considerations may be the primary focal point of your retirement plan. The following questions will stimulate your thinking about the financial issues you need to contemplate when planning for your retirement.

	Yes	No	Not Sure
1. Do you know your net worth (assets minus liabilities)?	___	___	___
2. Are you currently employed?	___	___	___
3. Do you know your total annual income and how much you spend annually?	___	___	___
4. Do you have any other source of income if you could not work for pay?	___	___	___
5. Do you know when you will retire?	___	___	___
6. Do you know how much you will spend in a typical month of retirement?	___	___	___
7. Do you have a pension or retirement plan?	___	___	___
8. Does your spouse have one?	___	___	___
9. Will you receive survivor benefits under the pension plan if your spouse dies?	___	___	___
10. Do you have enough savings and investments to supplement your retirement income?	___	___	___
11. Are your savings and investments producing acceptable earnings?	___	___	___
12. Do you have health insurance?	___	___	___
13. If your health insurance is an employee benefit, will it continue after retirement?	___	___	___
14. How much equity do you have in your home?	___	___	___
15. Do you intend to remain in your home after you retire?	___	___	___

Income Planning

Your Retirement Income

In the middle column, check those sources of retirement income from the left column that apply to you. Enter the annual amount expected from each source in the right column. If you do not know the amount now, write in where you will find that information.

Source of Retirement Income (self and spouse)	Check Those that Apply	Income Amount or Information Source
1. Income from work	_____	$ _____
2. Social Security benefits	_____	$ _____
3. Other government income	_____	$ _____
4. Employer pension plan	_____	$ _____
5. Employer profit-sharing plan	_____	$ _____
6. Deferred compensation	_____	$ _____
7. Other employee income	_____	$ _____
8. Government securities	_____	$ _____
9. Corporate securities	_____	$ _____
10. Savings plans	_____	$ _____
11. Other investments	_____	$ _____
12. IRA	_____	$ _____
13. Keogh plan	_____	$ _____
14. Annuities	_____	$ _____
15. Life insurance cash values	_____	$ _____
16. Sale of business	_____	$ _____
17. Sale of other assets	_____	$ _____
18. Other	_____	$ _____

Income Planning

Applying for Social Security Benefits: A Checklist

Timing is important when you apply for Social Security. Apply promptly because many benefits are limited to six months of retroactive payments. It is important to have your records in order so that your application will be fully documented.

Listed below are the records and documents you will need to file for various Social Security benefits. Check the ones you have on hand.

For retirement benefits:

____ Your Social Security card (or record showing your Social Security number)

____ Your spouse's Social Security card (or record showing spouse's Social Security number)

____ Original or certified copy of your birth certificate or other proof of age (e.g., baptismal record)

____ Original or certified copy of your spouse's birth certificate or other proof of age

____ Birth certificate (or adoption order) of each child for whom you are claiming benefits

____ Copies of your income tax withholding statements (W-2 forms) for the past two years

____ Copies of Schedule SE from the last two tax returns, with proof of payment, if you are self-employed

These last two items are important because these earnings will not have been posted yet in Social Security Administration (SSA) records of your earnings. Unless you provide these forms, your last two years' earnings will not be included when the SSA calculates your benefits. Without these forms, it could be as long as 24 months before SSA records show your latest earnings and the SSA can recalculate your benefit rate to include them.

For survivor benefits:

____ Your marriage certificate (and/or divorce papers)

____ Death certificate of your spouse

____ Birth certificates of dependent children

____ Proof that a dependent parent or dependent grandchild was being supported by the worker

For disability benefits:

____ Names, addresses, and telephone numbers of doctors, hospitals, or clinics that treated you

The Social Security Administration advises applicants to apply for benefits *even if these records are not available*. The people in your local Social Security office will tell you about other ways to prove your status when you apply.

Does It Pay to Work after Retirement?

If you continue working once you have started to receive Social Security benefits, you must continue to pay Social Security taxes on your income from work. You may lose some or even all your Social Security benefits, depending on how much you earn. You may have to pay some income taxes on those benefits you do receive. This worksheet is designed to help you decide if it pays to work after retirement.

A. Annual Social Security benefits at age 62 $ _____

                             at age 63 $ _____

                             at age 64 $ _____

                             at age 65 $ _____

B. Amount I can earn from work each year before I start losing
Social Security benefits. $ _____

C. If I earn (your projected earnings), I will lose $ _____ of my
Social Security benefits;

D. Plus, I will pay $ _____ in Social Security taxes.

E. That will leave me with $ _____. Does it pay to work? Are there benefits
beyond the financial rewards?

F. If my earnings from all sources (work, investments, Social Security, pension) push me into
the tax bracket where my Social Security benefits will be subject to income tax, how much
more do I stand to lose? $ _____

Separate fact from fiction. Circle true (T) or false (F) for each item below.

T   F   1. The Employee Retirement Income Security Act of 1974 (ERISA) ensures each employee who participates in a pension plan an adequate retirement income.

T   F   2. The law guarantees a pension to every American worker.

T   F   3. All pensions are insured by the government; you will get exactly what you have been promised.

T   F   4. After you have worked a specified period of time for an employer under a pension plan, ERISA requires that you be given the nonforfeitable right to certain earned benefits.

T   F   5. Your pension will probably be reduced if you retire early.

T   F   6. The law ensures that your spouse will get your full pension when you die.

T   F   7. Employers can fire employees to deprive them of their pensions.

T   F   8. You are entitled to a complete explanation of your pension plan — in easily understood language.

T   F   9. It is your right to know how the money has been and is being invested.

T   F   10. Some pension plans reduce benefits according to your Social Security retirement income.

Answers on page 132.

Answers to "Test Your Pension Knowledge" (page 131)

Check your answers below.

1. False. The 1974 law says nothing about the overall size of a pension. A pension may fail to provide an adequate income, even when added to Social Security payments.

2. False. The law does not require every employer to offer a pension plan.

3. False. Not all pension plans are insured; even a government-insured plan may fail to provide full original benefits in the event an employer cancels the plan.

4. True. This right is called vesting. By law, employer contributions must vest in accordance with a choice from certain schedules set by the government. For example, if your employer chooses a schedule that requires that you be vested after five years of service, then even if you lose your job after five years, you will eventually be entitled to a pension based on the pension plan formula.

5. True. Typically, there is a percentage reduction in benefits for each year a person retires before he or she is 65.

6. False. Most pension plans are required to provide a joint-and-survivor annuity provision. However, when you die your spouse is entitled to receive only a portion — at least half — of your monthly benefits for life. If you elect the joint-and-survivor option, your monthly pension benefit might be lower than with a single life annuity.

7. False. If you think you have been wrongfully denied a pension, you can take legal action. You will, however, need to prove there are no valid reasons for dismissal or for denial of benefits.

8. True. Employers must give each employee a booklet that clearly describes the pension plan and its benefits.

9. True. You have the right to know. If you think your pension money is being invested unwisely, you should contact the Administrator of Pension and Welfare Benefit Programs, U.S. Department of Labor.

10. True. Some plans provide for a Social Security offset by which your Social Security retirement is considered when determining your pension payment. You may be left with little pension, or none at all.

For specific information about your pension benefits, see your employer. If you have questions about provisions of the law, contact a regional office of the Department of Labor.

Get to Know Your Pension Plan

Your pension may be a vital source of income after retirement. Long before you retire, you should be sure you understand fully all aspects of your pension plan.

Can you answer the following questions? Do you know:

	Yes	No
1. If you are covered by a company plan?	___	___
2. If you are vested in the plan?	___	___
3. At what percentage you are vested?	___	___
4. If your benefits are affected if you have a break in service?	___	___
5. When you must apply for benefits?	___	___
6. What pay-out options are offered (i.e., lump-sum or monthly payments)?	___	___
7. If your benefits are guaranteed for life?	___	___
8. If survivor benefit options are available?	___	___
9. If this option can be changed before retirement?	___	___
10. If your monthly benefit amount is affected by choosing a survivor benefit?	___	___
11. What benefits, if any, your beneficiary will receive if you die before retirement?	___	___
12. If your pension is a defined contribution plan or a defined benefit plan?	___	___
13. How the benefits are calculated?	___	___
14. If you have an early retirement option?	___	___
15. If you receive additional benefits in case of disability or death?	___	___
16. If your plan can be changed or discontinued by the company?	___	___
17. If your previously acquired rights can be changed?	___	___
18. If the amount of your benefits depends on investment earnings of the pension fund?	___	___
19. If your company health insurance coverage continues when you retire?	___	___
20. What, if any, other company benefits you will have in retirement?	___	___

Look at your "no" responses. Determine which ones you want to discuss with someone from your benefits office.

Getting Your Pension/Profit Sharing Money: Lump Sum or Annuity?

Your employer should provide you with a "summary plan description" of your pension plan. The description should contain the information you need to fill out this worksheet. If you have questions, see your personnel office or plan administrator. You may also need the help of a tax advisor to complete the worksheet in the most meaningful manner.

1. Current vesting status _____

2. Vesting status at projected retirement age _____

3. If not fully vested at desired retirement age, how many more years
   must you work to become fully vested?_____

4. Do you have a choice between taking a lump sum or an annuity? _____

5. If so, amount of lump sum _____

6. Taxable portion of lump sum _____

7. Projected tax, in year of retirement,
   if you use 10-year averaging (assuming you are eligible) _____

   If you use 5-year averaging _____

8. Net amount of lump sum after income taxes _____

9. Projected annual earnings on amount in item 8 _____

10. Projected annual earnings if full amount of lump sum is invested in IRA rollover account _____

11. Projected income taxes on annual withdrawals from amount in item 10, when withdrawals begin

    _____

12. Projected cash status, five years after retirement, if you have chosen
    the 10-year averaging method _____

    the 5-year averaging method _____

    the IRA rollover method _____

13. Under the annuity option, what are your choices?

	Per month to worker	To spouse*
No survivor benefits	_____	_____
Partial survivor benefits	_____	_____

10-year averaging method   _____   _____

5-year averaging   _____   _____

IRA rollover   _____   _____

After death of working spouse

14. How do your monthly annuity benefits compare with your potential monthly earnings — conservatively projected — from investing lump sum using 10-year averaging method_____

5-year averaging _____

IRA rollover _____

15. Do you feel confident and capable of managing a lump-sum investment prudently?___ Yes   ___ No

16. Would you prefer professional management of your funds, as is available with annuity option, even if it means that the total value of the fund is exhausted when the recipients die?

___ Yes   ___ No

Income Planning

Life Insurance Analysis

The basic purpose of life insurance is to protect your dependents against financial hardship if you were to die prematurely. Another is to provide liquid assets to settle an estate, avoiding the necessity to sell part of the estate. The need for life insurance often diminishes as children grow up and leave home. However, each person's situation is unique.

Before determining your future insurance needs, you first need a clear picture of your current coverage. The sections below will help you analyze your current situation and then determine your future needs. As you do this analysis, be certain to include figures on individual policies as well as any group coverage you may have through your employer, your union, or fraternal associations.

Current Coverage. If exact figures are not available, estimate the face value of your policies to complete the first column; then revise, if necessary, after you have checked your policies.

	Your Coverage Now	Projected Coverage at Age 65
I. Term life insurance — Provides protection for a specific number of years. There is no savings component.	$_____	$_____
II. Whole life insurance — Covers you for your lifetime. Also accumulates savings (cash value). Upon your death, beneficiary gets face value only, not face value plus cash value.	_____	_____
III. Endowment life insurance — Also called retirement income insurance. Provides a larger savings component than whole life. Seldom sold today.	_____	_____
IV. Universal life insurance — Also known as flexible premium, combines term insurance with tax-deferred savings. Premium payments and death benefits can be adjusted periodically. There are many variations of this type of policy.	_____	_____
Total life insurance	$_____	$_____

If you are comparing policies before buying them, record information about policies below.

	Policy A	Policy B	Policy C	Policy D
Company				
Issue date				
Face value				

Owner of policy

Beneficiary

Current cash value

Cash value at age 65

Interest rate for policy loans

Current paid-up value

Paid-up value at age 65

Current extended term value

Extended term value at age 65

Should I Retire Early?

If your employer offers a special early retirement incentive, the most important thing to remember is that accepting does not mean you have to retire from employment altogether. Depending on your skills, interests, abilities, and the job market, it may be possible to accept the retirement incentive and find work elsewhere.

Retiring early may mean smaller pension checks and lower monthly payments from Social Security. If you have a defined benefit plan, your benefit is based on years of service and your salary, so you can lose a significant amount by retiring early. When you retire early, your pension benefits will be smaller because you had lower salaries and worked fewer years. You do not build up any more retirement credits. Your benefit will be based on a lower salary than if you had continued working. An early-out may lower your benefits by 5 to 7 percent for each year you are under full retirement age, usually 65. If you have a defined contribution plan, you can retire early without a penalty, although contributions will cease.

Inflation makes it difficult to maintain your standard of living on a fixed income. Here are some questions to evaluate to decide if you should retire early:

1. Have you been with the company for many years, and are you past 50? If not, the early-out may not be worth considering.

2. You can usually choose to take a reduced pension now or a higher one when you reach normal retirement age. How much will your pension be reduced?

3. What benefits does your early-out retirement package include? Will you be able to continue your health insurance coverage at regular employee rates until you reach age 65, when you become eligible for Medicare benefits?

4. Should you stay or retire? If you stay, it is possible that you risk losing your job and the early retirement benefits you would have received. If you are a couple of years from retirement, you probably have little to lose by retiring early. If you feel you are likely to be discharged, perhaps you should not risk staying on. If you can find another suitable job, you might choose to leave and invest your retirement benefits for the future.

A federal law requires employers to give employees age 40 or older 45 days to decide whether to sign a release in an early retirement offer to more than one person and seven days after signing to revoke it.

Lump-Sum Distributions vs. Annuity Plans. Many retirement plans offer retirees a choice of taking all of the accumulated money in one lump sum or taking one of a variety of annuity plans. With the lump-sum payment, the money is yours to do with as you see fit after payment of taxes. With the annuity plan, you receive a monthly payment. You have a choice of annuity plans. Some terminate on the death of the retiree; some pay a smaller amount per month for the retiree and, upon death, continue payment to a surviving spouse. This decision — lump sum versus annuity — may be the most important one you will ever make with respect to your retirement income.

The choice involves a trade-off. An annuity plan guarantees you a monthly income for the rest of your life. If, on the other hand, you take the lump-sum distribution, your monthly income will depend on the success of your investments. If you invest it wisely and well, you may be able to earn a higher monthly income, plus you have access to the full principal amount. Which would you choose? Much will depend on the availability of conservative investment opportunities at the time you make the decision, plus being ready, willing, and able to manage your lump-sum payment, as opposed to having an annuity company manage it for you.

This does not take into account federal income taxes on either the lump sum or the monthly pay-out plans. Naturally, those would have to be calculated. If you do choose the lump-sum payout, you might be eligible for a favorable tax treatment on that money. If the proceeds that would otherwise be taxable are put into an IRA rollover account, you can postpone the payment of such taxes, and the entire sum can continue to earn interest or dividends on a tax-deferred basis until you withdraw the money.

It might also be possible to take advantage of a technique known as forward averaging. This allows you to pay the taxes due on the lump sum for the year in which you receive it, but at a lower rate than your tax bracket might dictate. If you were at least age 50 on January 1, 1986, you can choose from two different forward-averaging formulas — a five-year plan or a ten-year plan. The advice of a tax counselor is recommended to determine the best choice in your circumstances. Persons under age 50 on January 1, 1986, are limited to the five-year averaging plan.

If you leave your employer before you retire, you may receive a lump-sum distribution from your employer plan. In order to avoid substantial federal taxes, you must arrange for your employer to transfer your distribution directly to another eligible plan or an Individual Retirement Account (IRA). You can no longer take 60 days to deposit (roll over) the distribution. Consult your tax adviser for more information.

Do-It-Yourself Pension Plans

Certain tax-deferred financial products are available that offer you, as an individual, the opportunity to invest in savings for retirement. These include Individual Retirement Accounts (IRAs), 401(k) plans, 403(b) plans, simplified employee pension plans (SEP-IRA), and Keogh plans. You may also have the opportunity to take advantage of a deferred compensation plan or a thrift savings plan.

Individual Retirement Account. The Individual Retirement Account (IRA) is the most common form of tax-deferred retirement plan. The IRA is a personal, rather than company-sponsored, plan. You can contribute as much as $2,000 of earned income to an IRA each year ($2,250 if you

Allowable IRA Deductions

Single Return[1]	Joint Return[1]	Deduction Limit[2]
$25,000	$40,000	100%
26,000	41,000	90
27,000	42,000	80
28,000	43,000	70
29,000	44,000	60
30,000	45,000	50
31,000	46,000	40
32,000	47,000	30
33,000	48,000	20
34,000	49,000	10
35,000	50,000	0

[1]Adjusted gross income
[2]Percentage of allowable IRA Investment

are married and only one spouse works).
Earnings are not taxed until they are
withdrawn.

One of the most publicized aspects of the
1986 Tax Reform Act was the change in the
deductibility of IRA contributions for some
taxpayers. This led many workers to assume
they were no longer eligible for an IRA. But
all or portions of your contribution may be
tax deductible if you or your spouse are not
covered by a pension plan at work or your
adjusted gross income from all sources is less
than $35,000 if your are single and $50,000
if you are married. The chart on the
previous page illustrates your allowable
deduction.

Regardless of whether your IRA
contribution is deductible, the tax-deferred
feature of IRAs makes them more attractive
than most taxable investments. Remember,
though, to keep good records of your annual
contributions. If you have a nondeductible
IRA and file the appropriate tax form, be
sure to save a copy of it and your form 1040
until you have withdrawn all your funds.
You will need to document the years fully
deductible, partially deductible, and
nondeductible contributions were made.
Taxes must eventually be paid on deductible
contributions and IRA earnings. If you
choose not to fund an IRA, due to the
paperwork involved, choose another tax-
deferred product.

Determine when you will need to
withdraw your IRA retirement funds. The
law states that if you withdraw them before
you reach age 59½ you must pay a penalty
equal to 10 percent of the amount
withdrawn. You will also have to pay income
tax on the withdrawn money. In addition,
you are required to begin withdrawing
money from your IRA when you reach the
age of 70½.

401(k) Plan. Employees of for-profit
companies and partnerships are eligible to
contribute pre-tax dollars to a choice of
investment programs. Options may be a
guaranteed fixed account or a variable
account that invests in a variety of stocks
and bonds. It is generally possible to
contribute to both plans and to change your
options at certain times. Your employer also
can contribute a certain amount to your
account, subject to limits of the law. All
contributions and interest or investment
gains are tax-deferred.

403(b) Tax-Deferred Annuity. Employees of
certain nonprofit organizations such as
schools, hospitals, and churches are eligible
to contribute pre-tax dollars to a
guaranteed fixed account or variable
account. All contributions and interest or
investment gains are tax deferred. The
employer cannot make matching
contributions, but this plan allows the
employee to contribute more than is
permitted with a 401(k) plan.

Simplified Employee Pension (SEP).
Simplified Employee Pension plans are tax-
deferred retirement accounts provided by
sole proprietors or small businesses and
corporations that do not have any other
plan. The employer makes contributions to
SEP accounts that are controlled by
employees. By establishing a SEP plan, an
employer is spared the cost and
administrative complexity of a qualified
plan.

SEP plans have a maximum annual
contribution limit. Employees may
contribute up to $2,000 per year. Employers
may contribute up to $30,000 or 15 percent
of the employee's annual compensation.

Keogh Plan. Keogh plans allow self-
employed workers to establish retirement
plans for themselves and their employees
with the same tax advantages available to

corporate employees covered by qualified pension plans. A "profit-sharing defined contribution" Keogh plan is the most flexible. It allows you to decide every year how much you want to contribute. You can even skip a year if your profits are down. The maximum annual contribution is 13.04 percent of your self-employment income up to a maximum contribution of $30,000. The "money-purchase defined contribution" Keogh also has a $30,000 annual limit but allows you to save up to 20 percent of self-employment income. However, you are required to make the same percentage contribution every year.

The "defined-benefit" Keogh plan allows you to save up to 100 percent of your self-employment income. Your contribution amount depends on how large a benefit you want to receive each year after you retire. These plans are attractive to those 50 and over who want to and can afford to build a big retirement fund quickly. It is advisable for people contemplating a Keogh plan to get professional assistance before setting up these plans.

457 Plans. 457 plans are deferred compensation plans available to employees of city or state governments. These plans allow you to defer taxes on both the income you invest and your earnings until some future date. You can set aside up to 25 percent of your *gross* pay from your employer to a maximum of $7,500 per year. Your employer can choose to place your funds in a guaranteed fixed account or into one of several mutual funds that differ in investment objectives.

Starting Your Own Business

If you intend to start your own business, you must undertake some very serious planning. Entering the business world — whether starting from scratch, buying an existing business, or investing in a franchise — can be rigorous and challenging. Starting a new business usually takes more capital than anticipated. You may be risking the depletion of your retirement capital to achieve a hoped-for level of income. And what if that income never materializes? Generally new business ventures do not break even until the third year of operation. Plan to subsidize yourself for that long. Decide whether you want to forgo the interest or dividends you could earn by investing your money in a more secure way.

In short, if you have always longed to be a photographer or chef, repair computers or make pottery, it might make more sense to do that as an employee of another person, at least temporarily, to see if you really do enjoy it. The trial period can save you the potential disaster of losing a large portion of your capital on something that did not work out either financially or psychologically. After the trial period, if you still want to proceed, you can do so with the added assurance of success.

Further advice for those who plan to go into business for themselves after retirement: seek professional assistance. You will need a lawyer to help with leases and contracts; an accountant to determine the financial feasibility of your proposal; a banker to determine how much you can afford to invest; and an insurance agent to guide you through the maze of liability hazards and other business-related risks. Even professional assistance does not guarantee that a business venture will succeed.

Income from Savings and Investments

Savings and investment income represent an important part of your financial profile. The subject is presented in greater detail in the unit on Investments, but its mention here should set the stage for your individual consideration of the topic. With a little thought, you can probably determine whether you are a conservative or an aggressive money manager. You know how much risk you are willing to take, what results you expect, and how much you need to earn or can afford to lose.

Other factors also pertain to your choice of savings and investments. Persons in their forties and early fifties have a longer time to plan, save, and invest than those in their late fifties and sixties. Consequently, younger persons can take greater risks because they have longer to recover from a mistake. Persons reaching retirement age typically concentrate on income-producing securities, predominantly debt instruments like government bonds, high-quality corporate bonds, certificates of deposit, and money market funds.

In your role as purchaser of financial products, you need to be cautious about the pitfalls that lurk in this marketplace. Financial institutions are continually developing new investment products, and salespersons give glowing accounts of their value. The buyer must beware! It is not wise to invest your money unless you know exactly where it is going and how you can get it back, if you can at all.

Dipping into Your Principal

Assume you have $10,000 invested at 7 percent, compounding quarterly. You can withdraw the following monthly amounts for the stated number of years, at the end of which time the $10,000 will be depleted:

Monthly Withdrawal	Length of Time
$116	10 years
89	15 years
77	20 years
70	25 years
59	Indefinitely*

You will be withdrawing interest only.

The following chart can be used to determine how long your retirement savings will last based upon annual payout and assumed interest rates.

Number of Years a Sum of Money Will Last at Specific Withdrawal and Interest Earning Rates

		Earnings Rate of Invested Funds				
		5%	6%	7%	8%	9%
Annual Payout	5%	Forever				
	6%	35 years	Forever			
	7%	24 years	32 years	Forever		
	8%	19 years	22 years	30 years	Forever	
	9%	15 years	18 years	21 years	27 years	Forever
	10%	13 years	14 years	16 years	20 years	25 years
	11%	11 years	12 years	14 years	16 years	19 years
	12%	10 years	11 years	12 years	13 years	15 years

Income from Other Sources

Income from Home Equity. The equity in your home may represent your largest financial asset and an important source of income. Ways of generating that income range from reverse mortgages to sale/leasebacks to outright sale of the property. Renting all or part of your home offers another option for capitalizing on this investment. The previous unit on Housing Planning covers the issue of home equity and its financial aspects.

Income from the Sale of a Business. Methods of figuring how much your business is worth range from rudimentary formulas to detailed evaluations. Any valuation approach you use needs to include your company's tangible operating assets: real estate, buildings, inventory, machinery, and equipment. Manufacturers generally have more of these assets than do service-oriented firms.

Companies for sale are frequently offered at a price that is based on the company's assumed ability to generate enough cash flow to cover the buyer's financing. Sellers project the company's annual net cash flow for the next eight to ten years, find the average, then deduct predicted yearly capital expenditures. The result is the cash flow that will be available for servicing the debt incurred by the new owner.

Most owners enlist the services of a business broker, investment banker, or other qualified intermediary to help them find legitimate candidates for buying their firm. These experts are tied into the marketplace and can expand the list of prospective buyers through their contacts. They also represent the seller at the bargaining table. When selecting an intermediary to help you sell your business, you should base your choice largely on the individual's track record in selling other businesses for close to their expert-estimated value.

Income from Life Insurance Cash Value. If you, at this point in your life, no longer have dependents to protect, you may want to cut back your term life insurance or cash in or borrow against your cash value policy. You may also decide to convert your cash value policy to a paid-up policy or to extended-term insurance. The amount of paid-up insurance or the period of extended-term coverage will vary among different policies. Your particular situation should determine whether you continue life insurance protection, convert a policy to another form, or take the available cash. Deciding what to do about life insurance can be complicated and will be discussed in Personal Financial Planning.

Income from Annuities. Annuities are another source of retirement income. An annuity is a contract issued by a life insurance company that guarantees periodic payments for life or a certain period in exchange for either a lump-sum payment or periodic payments made by the purchaser.

Immediate annuities start benefit payments shortly after purchase. They are bought with a lump sum, such as a pension distribution or an inheritance. Deferred annuities accumulate funds on a tax-deferred basis. They can be bought monthly, through periodic payments or as a single premium deferred annuity. Funds accumulate tax-deferred until retirement and benefit payments start sometime in the future.

Be sure to find out the costs involved in the purchase of a particular annuity product. It pays to comparison shop for an annuity, because there can be substantial differences among contracts. Also check the financial strength of the insurance company.

Income from Nonproductive Assets. Coins, stamps, artwork, furs, jewelry, furniture, precious metals, and other possessions that you no longer want or need can be converted into cash. This approach may be particularly helpful if you are downsizing your household to pursue alternative goals. Prudent investing of the cash received can create a reliable source of income. The services of a professional appraiser should be used for any items that you know have considerable value.

Inheritances. Inheritances are uncertain sources of income, especially if they are payable only on someone's death. If you have reasonable assurance of an inheritance, you can factor it into your financial plan. Discussing the matter with the person from whom you expect to receive the inheritance would be helpful.

A Most Urgent Concern

Financial planning for the future is an activity in your life that must be honestly and straightforwardly shared with your spouse, partner, or other individual who will be personally and financially linked with you for a long time. If one person in a relationship handles all financial matters, and that person is incapacitated or worse, the uninvolved partner can be left in a real quandary, both emotionally and financially.

RESPONSIBILITY

Taking responsibility for your financial future is the only way you can make it conform to your aspirations for your middle and later years. You now have the unique opportunity to restructure your existence based on everything you have learned and experienced up to this time. As the years go on, you will need and want to reconsider and revise your plans, but now is the time to establish your financial foundations, beginning with your sources of income.

You have assessed your current estimates of future income and considered the alternatives you have for supplementing those certain sources. You and your spouse or partner are now coming to decision time, when you need to gather your information, your instincts, your creativity, and your common sense and chart a path to the future. The Action Step that follows here will help you to decide on a specific course of action. You may want to use the completed Action Step as a model for your decisions.

Action Step

On the Action Step, list any and all matters you want to pursue regarding your sources of income for the years ahead. Remember that these activities will provide a baseline for the future you will be able to afford as well as enjoy. Keep in mind also that the decisions involved can and should be reviewed and possibly adapted as needed in the future. Use verbs — action words — to describe what you plan to do in the area of generating and preserving income.

When you believe your list is complete for the time being, rank your decisions in the right-hand column according to their importance to you, with number 1 being the most important. Use a second sheet of paper to continue your list if needed.

Income Actions	Rank by Importance
Find out amount of Social Security benefits I can expect	1
Increase my contributions to the savings plan at work	3
Talk with parents about possible inheritance	7
Set up consultant contacts to get second job going	2
Check into cash values of my insurance policies	5
Consider renting apartment in basement to generate extra income	4
Have coin collection appraised to see if it is worth selling	6

Income Planning

Action Step

Example

On the Action Step, list any and all matters you want to pursue regarding your sources of income for the years ahead. Remember that these activities will provide a baseline for the future you will be able to afford as well as enjoy. Keep in mind also that the decisions involved can and should be reviewed and possibly adapted as needed in the future. Use verbs — action words — to describe what you plan to do in the area of generating and preserving income.

When you believe your list is complete for the time being, rank your decisions in the right-hand column according to their importance to you, with number 1 being the most important. Use a second sheet of paper to continue your list if needed.

Income Actions	Rank by Importance

PLANNING

The last step in the AARP Approach, and your bridge into your financial future, is your Master Action Plan. The MAP documents the step-by-step actions you have decided to take to maintain control over your financial destiny. The first MAP process in the three-phase financial management area involves sources of income.

You should list each of your Income Actions from your Action Step as a Goal Statement on your MAP. Then follow through with the logical steps that will achieve the desired goal. The sample Master Action Plan on the next page may help in this regard.

Income Planning

Master Action Plan

Example

Goal Statement: Find out amount of Social Security benefits I can expect

Actions	Resources	Time Frame	By Whom?
1. Get Social Security Administration (SSA) form to request information needed	Human Resource Dept. at work	1 month	Self
2. Collect information needed to fill out form	Own payroll records, files	1 month	Self
3. Fill out SSA form and mail	SSA form; own records	1 day	Self
4. Review Social Security response when received	Own records; reading on the subject	1 day	Self
5. Verify that this information accurately represents my work history, amount of benefits anticipated			

Goal Statement: Set up consultant contacts regarding second income

Actions	Resources	Time Frame	By Whom?
1. Consider most enjoyable aspects of current job that I would like to retain in future	My own work experience	6 months	Self
2. Consider current contacts who might use my services in these areas	Own experience; contact file	6 months	Self
3. Investigate possible conflict of interest with regular job	Fellow employees; Human Resource Dept. at work	6 months	Self
4. Develop formal or informal proposal re services I plan to offer to clients	Own experience; reference materials; comparable documents	1 month	Self
5. Offer proposal to selected prospective clients; meet if indicated	Prepared proposal; contacts	1 month	Self
6. Start slowly to accept consultant assignments, being careful not to jeopardize principal job	Self	6 months	Self

Investment
Planning

Investment Planning

A sound investment program can make the difference between getting by and living in comfort, between nagging fear and peace of mind in the future. The information included in this unit is intended to help you consider investment possibilities that could add to your future security.

Before you proceed, a few words of caution are in order. First, the investment arena is growing and changing rapidly. New investment opportunities become available almost daily. The value of these opportunities can change rapidly as tax laws and economic conditions change. Thus, this section should be viewed only as a starting point in your reading. Keeping up with changing conditions and new opportunities is essential to being a successful investor.

Second, investing covers a broad spectrum of possibilities, ranging from very safe to very risky. Very risky ventures are better described as ways of speculating rather than of investing. Investing means putting your money to work in ways that make it possible for you to project, with some assurance, how many dollars you will have 5, 10, or 20 years from now. Speculating, on the other hand, means putting your money to work in ways that cannot provide assurance as to how many dollars you will have in years to come; you could end up doubling or tripling your contribution, losing it all, or somewhere in between.

If you do not want to take chances with your retirement fund, you should lean toward investing prudently. Prudence dictates that even willing risk-takers should not speculate until they have first established a well-disciplined investment program. Remember, too, that no investment is entirely risk-free.

Unit Objectives

- **Assessment:** To assess your current and anticipated investments as they relate to your plans for the future

- **Alternatives:** To consider alternatives and modifications to your investment activities that are likely to improve or stabilize your future financial status

- **Responsibility:** To make decisions about your investment activities that will enable you to pursue your goals

- **Planning:** To make specific plans to follow through on your decisions regarding investments, remembering to remain flexible and to consult those who share your personal financial life

What Do You Think?

The questions that follow will help you gain perspective on your general financial position at this time in your life, information that is critical to any investment strategies you pursue. You are encouraged to discuss these matters with your spouse or partner, other family members and friends, or anyone else in your support system that you would like to confide in.

1. Have you saved and invested over the years? Do you have a pension, IRA, 401(k), or Keogh plan or any other predictable income that will influence your planning for the future?

2. Do you have a general idea of your financial assets and liabilities? Can you picture your balance sheet in your mind?

3. How big a role does the equity in your home play in your balance sheet calculations?

4. Do you feel comfortable managing your own assets? Do you understand the stock and bond markets, annuities, and other approaches to investments planning?

For Your Information

Investing means putting your money to work in ways that make it possible for you to reasonably project how many dollars you will earn for future years. Basically two ways exist to put your money to work — lending and buying (debt and equity).

When you lend money, you receive a legal promise of repayment at some future time, plus a promise that you will be paid a fee for the use of your money. This fee, of course, is known as interest. This form of putting your money to work is known as the debt or money market.

When you lend your money to a bank or savings institution, the promise to repay (the debt instrument) may be a certificate of deposit. When you lend money to a corporation, the promise to repay is called a corporate bond (long term) or commercial paper (short term — usually not more than 90 days).

When you lend your money to the federal government, the promise to repay is called a treasury bill, note, or bond (depending on how long the debt is to run). When you lend your money to a state or local government, the promise to repay is called a municipal note or municipal bond, again depending on the maturity of the debt.

The other way to put your money to work is to buy something, hoping that you can later sell the item at a profit. In other words, the buyer takes an ownership position — and equity interest. In addition to a hoped-for profit on a future sale, the investment may generate some income. You may own shares of stock in a successful business that distributes part of its net earnings to you in the form of dividends. Or you may own all or part of a piece of real estate that generates rental income in excess of expenses. Of course, business and real estate ventures can lose money instead, in which case you receive no ongoing income. Many types of equity interests offer no hope of ongoing income: collections such as coins or stamps, precious metals, gemstones, and commodities. You can realize monetary reward only through the profitable sale of these items.

Equity interests such as these represent the speculating approach to the use of money, as they offer no assurance of ongoing income or a profitable sale in the future. You do not know, indeed you cannot know, how many dollars your equity will be worth at any specific time in the future.

Before examining investment alternatives in more detail, we need to explore tax and inflation considerations — critical areas of investment planning. Then we will examine the important investment criteria of liquidity, safety, and yield.

Taxes and Inflation

Investment products should be chosen with your objectives, financial resources, and risk tolerance in mind. Other considerations are your tax bracket and the effect of inflation.

Taxes. When putting your money to work, you naturally want to know how much it will earn. Those earnings are commonly referred to as your yield or return. Just as you must pay taxes on the income you earn from employment, so too must you pay taxes on the income you earn through investments. To know your true (net) investment yield or return, you have to calculate how much those earnings will be taxed (federal, state, and local).

You should investigate the tax implications before you make your investment decisions. For example, assume you are comparing two investment opportunities, A and B. Plan A promises a return of 10 percent per year, while Plan B promises a return of 8 percent per year. Assume that you invested $1,000 in both plans. You earn $100 in Plan A and $80 in Plan B. On the surface, Plan A appears to be the better deal. But if your earnings on Plan A are subject to income tax, while Plan B offers tax-exempt earnings, the picture changes. If you are in the 28 percent tax bracket, for example, for Plan A, 28 percent of those earned dollars would have to go to pay taxes. Consequently, Plan A would yield only $72, compared with $80 in Plan B.

Inflation. It is a fact of life that prices will not stay the same from now until you retire. Because of inflation, a dollar today will not be worth as much in the future. You will find that income generally keeps up with prices. You may recall when gasoline cost less than 50 cents a gallon. The fact that people can still afford to drive shows our ability to adjust to price changes.

Investments must keep up with inflation both before and after retirement. For example, a $5\frac{1}{2}$ percent savings account yields only 3.96 percent after taxes to persons in the 28 percent marginal tax bracket. If the inflation rate is higher, which may be the case, a saver is losing purchasing power. When inflation averages 6 percent, you need $32,000 to purchase what $10,000 did 20 years earlier. This is a significant issue, particularly for persons who plan to retire prior to age 65. The key is to plan for a retirement income that will keep up with, or — better still — stay ahead of, inflation. If your after-tax return on savings and investments exceeds the inflation rate over the long run, you will come out ahead and retain purchasing power.

Taxable Income

Most investment (unearned) income is taxed at the same rate as your income from employment. That includes interest income from savings accounts, income from mutual funds, and income from stock dividends. Congress continually changes the regulations on taxation of capital gains and losses, however. Check the tax regulations when you make investment decisions.

Tax-Deferred Income

When you earn tax-deferred income, you do not have to pay taxes on it in the year in which it was earned. But you will have to pay taxes on it in some future year. In short, the taxation is delayed, or deferred, until later. U.S. savings bonds, IRAs, and tax-deferred retirement plans are probably the best known examples of tax-deferred income. You do not have to pay federal or, in most instances, state taxes on your earnings until you eventually withdraw money from the plan. Tax-deferred annuities are another type of investment that enjoys this favorable tax treatment.

The advantage of tax-deferred income is that you put off paying taxes on it during your high tax-bracket years (while you are still working). You pay taxes on it when you are in lower tax-bracket years (presumably retired). Further, in a tax-deferred plan, all of your earnings keep on working for you, not just a tax-diminished amount.

Tax-Exempt Income

Tax-exempt income is free from taxation permanently. In general, interest earned on tax-exempt municipal bonds is exempt from federal taxes. It may also be exempt from state income taxes if the bond is issued by a governmental unit or agency in your state of residency. Interest earned on U.S. government securities is exempt from state income taxes.

Persons receiving Social Security benefits may find their taxes affected by tax-exempt income. If your combined income from all sources is over $25,000 for single filers or over $32,000 for joint filers, you might have to pay income taxes on part of your Social Security benefits. In determining this possible tax, income from tax-exempt securities must be taken into account. So there can be an indirect tax, although limited, on one's otherwise tax-exempt income.

Tax-Sheltered Income

Tax-sheltered investments have been sharply limited by changes in the tax law. If your adjusted gross income is under $100,000, attractive tax-sheltered benefits can still be found in some investments, such as real estate. You should seek the advice of a capable and trustworthy tax counselor when evaluating any tax implications to your investment plans — particularly in the area of tax-sheltered investments.

Investment Criteria

In addition to tax and inflation considerations, you need to examine other criteria before you make an investment decision. When choosing where to put your money, you will want to consider liquidity, safety of principal, and yield. You will also need to determine the amount of risk you are willing to take.

Liquidity. Liquidity is the ease with which your investment can be converted to cash without loss. You can get your money from a savings account or money market account quickly without penalty. If you cash in a certificate of deposit (CD) prematurely, you will have to pay a penalty for early withdrawal. If you have your money in real estate, you may not be able to find a buyer when you need your money. In general, conservative investments are more liquid, while speculative investments are less liquid.

Safety. With adequate safety of principal, the dollars you invest will remain intact. When you invest a dollar, you will get that dollar back. If you place $1,000 in a certificate of deposit (CD), you will get your $1,000 plus earnings when you withdraw your money. If you place $1,000 into stock, and the price declines, you may not get back all of your initial investment when you withdraw your money.

Investment Yield. The reason you invest is to earn money on your money. Yield is the rate of financial return that you earn from your investment. You want your investment to yield the largest return possible.

Compounding. When compounding, the interest you earn is added to your account. Your balance in your investment has three parts: (1) the initial amount you invest, (2) the interest you earn on your initial balance, and (3) the interest you earn on your interest that you left in your investment. Interest may be compounded annually, quarterly, monthly, weekly, or daily. Greater frequency of compounding speeds up the rate at which your account grows.

Future Value of $1 Invested Once at Various Interest Rates

For Periods of 5 to 35 Years, Interest Compounded Annually

Interest Rate				Years			
	5	10	15	20	25	30	35
4%	1.22	1.48	1.80	2.19	2.67	3.24	4.80
6%	1.34	1.79	2.40	3.21	4.29	5.75	10.29
8%	1.47	2.16	3.17	4.66	6.85	10.06	21.72
10%	1.61	2.59	4.18	6.73	10.84	17.45	45.26
12%	1.76	3.11	5.47	9.65	17.45	29.96	93.05

Compounding makes the most difference when your account is large, when you keep your money in the account a long time, and when you get the highest rate possible.

How your money grows will influence how quickly you can reach your financial goals. The chart on the previous page shows how your money can grow if you make a one-time investment of $1,000 at 8 percent. It will grow to $3,170 in 15 years ($1,000 x 3.17). In 35 years, at 10 percent, it will grow to $45,260 ($1,000 x 45.26). Use this chart to calculate the future value of an investment you plan to make.

Most people save on a regular basis. The chart below can be used to determine how much your savings will be worth when you retire. For example, if you invest $1,000 at the beginning of each year for 30 years at 6 percent interest, you will accumulate $79,060 ($1,000 x 79.06). When you earn 10 percent interest, that investment will accumulate $164,490 ($1,000 x 164.49).

Rule of 72. The Rule of 72 can be used to calculate how long it will take to double your money at various interest rates. To do this, divide 72 by the interest rate. For a 6 percent interest rate, it will take 12 years to double your money. So at 6 percent interest, $1,000 becomes $2,000 in 12 years, $4,000 in 24 years, and $8,000 in 36 years.

To predict how long it would take various inflation rates to halve the purchasing power of your money, divide 72 by the inflation rate. For an 8 percent inflation rate, it would take 9 years to halve the purchasing power of your money. So at 8 percent inflation, $10,000 becomes worth $5,000 in 9 years, $2,500 in 18 years, and $1,250 in 27 years.

Cost of Investing. The return on your investment can be reduced by various charges associated with purchasing, maintaining, and redeeming or selling investments. When selecting investment products, look for investment costs.

Before buying, get disclosures in writing about management fees and commissions. Is there a sales charge, commission, service charge, or annual management fee? How long is the money committed? Find out how you can sell out and what costs will be involved in doing so. Is there a fee or penalty for taking some or all of the money out (minimum balance penalties, withdrawal penalties, or tax penalties)? How long should your money be invested to maximize return? A deal that sounds too good to be true almost always is.

Size of Investment. The amount of money you have to invest at any one time will determine the investment options available to you. If you have only $2,000, you will not

Future Value of $1 Per Year Accumulated at Various Interest Rates

For Periods of 5 to 35 Years, Interest Compounded Annually

Interest Rate	5	10	15	Years 20	25	30	35
4%	5.42	12.01	20.02	29.78	41.65	56.08	95.03
6%	5.64	13.18	23.28	36.79	54.86	79.06	154.80
8%	5.87	14.49	27.15	45.76	71.11	113.28	259.10
10%	6.11	15.94	31.77	57.27	98.35	164.49	442.60
12%	6.35	17.55	37.28	72.05	133.33	241.33	767.10

be able to purchase a Treasury bill of $10,000. However, you could buy a money market fund that invests in Treasury securities. You may be able to make investments in certain minimum amounts. CDs generally have a $500 minimum. Individual Retirement Accounts (IRAs) have an individual maximum of $2,000.

Risk Versus Return

Risk is the possibility of loss from an investment. Return is the potential gain from an investment. The challenge of investing is to weigh the risks of an investment against the potential return. Risk and return are directly related. The more opportunity you have for higher yields, the bigger the risk there is that you may lose your principal dollars.

To reduce the risk in investing, diversify. Spread your money among a variety of investments. Avoid putting all of your money into just one type of stock, bond, mutual fund, annuity, or savings plan. If you concentrate on a particular investment product class, spread your investments

Investment Pyramid

Gems
Collectibles
Commodities
Speculative Stocks
Bonds/Mutual Funds

Growth Mutual Funds
Real Estate
Blue Chip Common Stock

High-Grade Convertible Bonds
High-Grade Preferred Stock
Balanced Mutual Funds

Pension Plans
High-Grade Corporate/Municipal Bonds
or Mutual Funds

Annuities
Equity in Home
U.S. Treasury Bills, Notes, Bonds, Agency Securities
Certificates of Deposit
U.S. Savings Bonds (EE & HH)
Cash Value of Life Insurance
Interest-Bearing Insured Checking Account
Insured Savings Account

among different companies within that industry. Vary maturity by investing so maturity dates will be spread over time, not on the same day or in the same month.

Diversify by region or market sector. Avoid putting all of your money in businesses that rely on the economic prosperity of one region of the country or world, or in businesses concentrating in one industry, such as utilities, health care, transportation, or manufacturing. While one industry may be in a declining period, another may be rising.

Deal with established businesses and professionals whose reputations are known in the community. If the sales representative is not from your local area, investigate the person and company before you buy. Check with your registered stockbroker, banker, lawyer, accountant, or real estate agent. If in doubt, contact your state securities commission office or your local Better Business Bureau to see if the company or individual is properly licensed to do business or has any history of violating the law. Also check with friends or family members.

Be cautious when strangers contact you by phone calls, unannounced visits to your home, or through mailing lists. Get-rich schemes should be the signal of a scam. Question extraordinary returns on your money in short time periods. Avoid high-pressure techniques that require hurried money commitments because "tomorrow will be too late."

Ask the seller to give you written information about the investment, including the prospectus or offering circular and financial statement. Avoid investments where the seller has little or no written information about the company or past performance. Read the materials carefully or get help reading them before you sign a

purchase order to pay for an investment. Ask questions. Check with experts.

Never invest in anything that you do not understand. If in doubt, wait. If something seems uncertain or if your questions are not satisfactorily answered, do not commit your money.

Financial planners often use the concept of the "investment pyramid" at left to describe the risk and return potential of various investments. In general, the higher the rate of return you seek, using investments in the top portion of the pyramid, the more risk you must be willing to assume. The bottom portion of the triangle indicates products where safety of principal is guaranteed or the risk of loss is limited.

ASSESSMENT

What Would You Do?

These case studies follow people who must make financial decisions that will affect their income and thus their lifestyles now and in the future. Each situation has more than one option, but some choices may be financially wiser than others. If you are going through this workbook at home, you may find it helpful to use the case studies to stimulate discussion between you and other family members or close friends. They will also help you develop questions to ask your own financial advisers.

Ralph and Lynn Kieffer

Ralph and Lynn Kieffer are 60 and looking forward to retirement in five years. Ralph has always managed their finances. In addition to some investments, Ralph and Lynn have about $1,500 in a passbook savings account. Their only major debt — their house mortgage — will be paid off in two years. The Kieffers need to buy a car within the next month. They just inherited $10,000 from Lynn's mother. The Kieffers want to invest what money they can for maximum return over the next five years with a minimum risk, keeping an emergency fund of $5,000.

What are Ralph and Lynn's options?

_____

_____

_____

_____

What are the advantages of each option?

_____

_____

What are the disadvantages of each option?

_____

_____

What do you think they should do? Why?

_____

_____

Investment Planning

Emma Mosely

Emma Mosely, who is single, recently was promoted and for the first time in her life can save about $1,500 a year toward her retirement. She works for a small company that does not provide a retirement plan. How can she best put her money to work for the future?

What are Emma's options?

_____

_____

_____

_____

What are the advantages of each option?

_____

_____

What are the disadvantages of each option?

_____

_____

What do you think she should do? Why?

_____

_____

Sam and Janet Novak

Sam Novak will be retiring in a few years. He has been making regular contributions to his employer's 401(k) plan. His wife, Janet, went back to work three years ago to help build their retirement fund. To date, they have put $20,000 of her earnings into a passbook savings account. They want to invest this money for 10 years, then start using it to meet retirement expenses, but they are concerned about the risks involved with different types of investments.

What are Sam and Janet's options?

_____

_____

_____

What are the advantages of each option?

_____

_____

What are the disadvantages of each option?

_____

_____

What do you think they should do? Why?

_____

_____

Investment Planning

Louise Petrillo

Louise Petrillo has no debts but has saved very little for her retirement. She has never really tried to budget her income or expenses. She purchased a whole life insurance policy 20 years ago that costs her $1,200 a year. Although she does not plan to retire for another 10 years, Louise is wondering if she should be putting this money to a different use to maximize her retirement income.

What are Louise's options?

_____

_____

_____

_____

What are the advantages of each option?

_____

_____

What are the disadvantages of each option?

_____

_____

What do you think she should do? Why?

_____

_____

Claire St. Jacques

Claire St. Jacques was widowed recently. With her survivor benefit from her husband's pension and her income from part-time work in a retail store, she meets monthly expenses. She would like to invest the $10,000 from her husband's life insurance to build a nest egg for the future.

What are Claire's options?

_____

_____

_____

_____

What are the advantages of each option?

_____

_____

What are the disadvantages of each option?

_____

_____

What do you think she should do? Why?

_____

_____

Investment Planning

Determining Your Future Financial Needs

To get a true picture of your future needs and determine the best strategies to meet them, use a pen, paper, and calculator to implement the following key steps:

- *Clearly outline your current spending needs and define your financial goals.* How much of your needs and goals will be met from Social Security and pensions? How much from investment income? How much from your investment principal?

- *Estimate carefully the effect of inflation on your retirement income.* Social Security benefits will be adjusted for cost of living increases. You may not be so fortunate with your pension, however, as those benefits are often fixed. Remember, as inflation raises prices, it also tends to increase the return you get on investments.

- *Set aside money to invest and then follow through.* Set aside a fixed amount on a regular basis for your investment program. Know and stay within your "risk zone." Do not invest in anything that leaves you feeling uneasy. An investment that makes you uncomfortable or one that you do not understand is not for you.

- *Diversify your investments and stagger the maturities.* Alternate the maturity dates on your certificates of deposit. Invest so they come due as you need the funds, or so that you will be able to reinvest as good opportunities appear.

- *Review your investments periodically.* While few investments perform well all of the time, you should remove from your portfolio those that are not helping you reach your goals and replace them with others.

- *Be realistic.* Understand that the best way to get rich is slowly and carefully. Very few people ever get rich on a speculative investment.

- *Determine the benefits from a tax-deferred retirement account.* Calculate the benefits you would have from a tax-deferred retirement account such as an IRA, Keogh, or 401(k) plan.

- *Get specific information on lump-sum distributions from pensions and annuities.* They can provide major sources of retirement income. Beware of the tax burdens on these distributions, and, when possible, use an IRA rollover or forward averaging to minimize the tax liability.

- *Seek advice.* The library has many books and periodicals on money management. Also located in libraries are the names of investment advisory services, which are good sources of information about mutual funds, stocks, and bonds. Other sources of information are television shows and newspapers. Stockbrokers, insurance agents, and financial planners can also provide valuable information on investment alternatives.

- *Keep good records.* These are important not only for tax purposes but also to help you to analyze the performance of your investments.

- *Be prepared to change as situations change.* As you achieve some goals and set new ones, be prepared to revise your investment portfolio. Changes in the economy and tax laws may also call for adjustments in your plans.

- *Be sure to make use of your Master Action Plan (MAP) and the financially oriented Action Step and Assessment exercises that follow here.*

The Investment Game

Aunt Mabel just died and left you $100,000. You have managed to resist the temptation to spend it all right now and have decided instead to invest the money for use later — in retirement. How would you invest it and why? Be prepared to discuss your plan.

Investment	Amount	Reason (Growth/Income/Liquidity/Safety/Yield)
Yourself		
Savings accounts		
Money market funds		
U.S. savings bonds		
Corporate bonds		
Municipal bonds		
Preferred stocks		
Common stocks		
Mutual funds		
Real estate		
Annuities		
Precious metals		
Collectibles		
Other		
Other		
Total	$100,000	

Your Investment I.Q.

The checklist below provides a quick review of your current status in the area of investing. Circle your answers to the questions below.

1. Do you know your investment needs?	Yes	No
2. Have you defined your investment goals?	Yes	No
3. Are you striving to meet those goals?	Yes	No
4. Are you knowledgeable about investments?	Yes	No
5. Do you pursue up-to-date investment information?	Yes	No
6. Are you comfortable with your investment choices?	Yes	No
7. Have you reviewed your investments lately?	Yes	No
8. Have you diversified your investments?	Yes	No
9. Do you take advantage of tax-sheltered investments?	Yes	No
10. Do you keep accurate investment records?	Yes	No
11. Do you seek the best professional advice?	Yes	No
12. Have you invested the excess cash from your checking and savings accounts?	Yes	No
13. Are you investing as much as possible?	Yes	No
14. Do you sell unprofitable investments rather than holding them and hoping?	Yes	No
15. Do you reinvest investment gains?	Yes	No

To obtain further help in these areas, continue reading and attending workshops and seminars.

Test Your Knowledge of Investment Strategies

This is an overview to assess your awareness of investment strategy topics. As you proceed through the unit, you will acquire the information needed to discuss these matters. Circle the correct answer.

1. There is a critical difference between investing and speculating.   True   False

2. The market value of a bond will always remain the same.   True   False

3. Tax-deferred income and tax-exempt income are the same.   True   False

4. Series EE Savings Bonds have a fluctuating rate of interest.   True   False

5. Three different calculations of yield are possible on corporate bonds.   True   False

6. All interest earned on municipal bonds is exempt from federal and state income taxes.   True   False

7. Tax-exempt municipal bonds may be a poor idea for some investors.   True   False

8. Zero coupon bonds do not provide a cash flow of interest income to investors.   True   False

9. The types of mutual funds can vary from very safe to quite speculative.   True   False

10. All annuities are alike.   True   False

11. Growth stocks are good choices for the conservative retirement portfolio.   True   False

12. Commodities, precious metals, and gemstones are purely speculative.   True   False

Answers: 1. True   2. False   3. False   4. True   5. True   6. False   7. True   8. True   9. True 10. False   11. False   12. True

ALTERNATIVES

Investing in the Debt ("Money") Market

Savings Plans. The traditional passbook savings account has dwindled in popularity in recent years as time certificates have offered higher returns and more choice to investors. A certificate of deposit (CD) is, in effect, an investment contract for a specific period of time, during which you are promised a guaranteed rate of interest. CDs at federally insured banks, savings institutions, and credit unions offer the extra measure of protection afforded by the respective federal insuring agencies.

Financial institutions can now tailor CDs to fit almost any need. They can be very short term or very long, they can have fixed or fluctuating interest rates, and they can compound with whatever frequency the institution wants to establish. It is therefore important to comparison-shop for the best CD terms available. In addition to shopping for rate, term, and frequency of compounding, you should also determine the penalties set by each institution in the event of an early withdrawal. Find out the interest rate you would have to pay if you wanted to borrow from the institution using your CD as collateral. This may be preferable to cashing in a CD early and paying the penalty.

Money market deposit accounts (MMDA) pay a higher rate of interest than passbook savings. Earnings are tied to current market interest rates and fluctuate. MMDAs require a minimum balance and if your balance drops below the minimum, your interest rate will drop to a lower rate or you will be charged a fee. You also have limited withdrawals and transfers per month.

Several kinds of interest-paying checking accounts are available at most institutions. These should be evaluated as carefully as the longer-term CDs, since the interest rates and minimum deposits required will vary. As a general rule, do not keep any more in your interest-bearing checking account than you need for regular ongoing purposes.

Money Market Mutual Funds. A money market fund is a mutual fund that pools the money from many investors and invests in corporate bonds, municipal bonds, U.S. government bonds, and money market instruments.

Money market funds provide income, liquidity, and a high degree of safety. Once an account is opened, you can add to a money market fund at any time. Interest is paid daily and compounded. You may receive your dividends by check each quarter or month, or you may have them automatically reinvested. Yields are tied to the current cost of money. The yield varies daily, depending on changes in the actual money market securities in which the fund invests. If interest rates rise, so will your earnings. If interest rates go down, so will your earnings.

Money market funds offer liquidity. They are considered safe, because they buy U.S. government-backed debt or that of well-rated corporations. You may transfer into other mutual funds offered by the same advisory service.

Life Insurance Cash Value. Cash value life insurance policies provide death protection and offer a savings opportunity. The cash value grows over the life of the policy. You can borrow against the cash value while keeping the policy in force. Or you can take out your cash value and cancel the policy. If you no longer need life insurance protection when you reach retirement age, you can use the cash value, if it is of sufficient size, to buy an annuity. The annuity can provide monthly payments for as long as you live. There are several variations of cash value life insurance and annuities.

U. S. Government Bonds. U.S. government Treasury obligations are the safest of all securities. These include EE & HH bonds, Treasury notes, bonds, and bills.

EE Bonds. The federal government sells series EE bonds issued at 50 percent of their face value. When you cash in or redeem the bond, you receive the maturity price. The difference between what you paid for the bond and what you receive is interest. EE bonds sold since November 1, 1982, offer a fluctuating rate of interest. This enables bonds to compete with savings programs offered by financial institutions.

Interest earned on EE bonds is exempt from state and local tax, but they are subject to federal income tax. Federal tax on the yield can be reported as it accrues or it can be deferred. It can be deferred until the bonds are cashed or reach maturity, whichever comes first.

Your employer may permit you to purchase bonds through a payroll deduction plan. This is a convenient way to save small amounts on a regular basis. You may also purchase them from financial institutions qualifying as issuing agents.

HH Bonds. HH bonds are issued in denominations of $500, $1,000, $5,000, and $10,000. They may be acquired only by exchanging EE Bonds. HH bonds pay interest semiannually. That interest is subject to federal income tax in the year received. It is exempt from state and local income tax. If you do make the conversion to HH bonds, you will be able to defer paying taxes on the interest you have already accrued, since you pay taxes on HH bond interest only in the year it is earned.

Thus, you may be able to spread a big one-year tax bite into 10 smaller bites over the life of the HH bond.

Treasury Bills. Treasury bills are sold in minimums of $10,000 (with additional multiples of $5,000) that mature in three months, six months, or one year. Interest rates on three- and six-month bills are established by weekly U.S. Treasury auctions. Rates for twelve-month T-Bills are established by monthly auctions. T-Bills are sold at a discount and can be redeemed for face value (principal and interest) at maturity.

Treasury Notes. Treasury notes are government obligations that mature in 2 to 10 years. Notes are purchased in $1,000 denominations (often a minimum purchase of five is required). Treasury notes are purchased at face value and pay a fixed rate of interest semiannually.

Treasury Bonds. Treasury bonds are notes, except that they mature in more than 10 years. They are purchased at face value and pay a fixed rate of interest semiannually. Treasury bills, notes, and bonds may be purchased from a broker or banker for a fee or from the Federal Reserve or Bureau of Public Debt at no charge.

Corporate Bonds. Many major American companies issue corporate bonds — long-term debts, which may run as long as 30 to 40 years. When a corporate bond is originally issued, it consists of a promise to pay interest at a stated rate (called the coupon rate) plus a promise to repay the full amount of principal on a set date. Interest is generally paid twice a year.

Corporate bonds are usually issued in denominations of $1,000. This is the face (par) value of the bond. Par value is the amount the company agrees to repay to the bondholder when the bond matures. Bonds may, however, trade at a discount (amount less than their face value) or at a premium (amount greater than their face value) depending upon current market conditions, the movement of interest rates generally, and other factors.

While the interest on a bond is fixed, its market value is not. When interest rates rise, bonds lose some of their market value. The loss will not affect you if you hold your bonds until they mature. You may lose some of your investment if you sell early. When interest rates fall, the market value of bonds increases.

Actively traded corporate bonds are listed in the *Wall Street Journal*. They are rated by several private rating agencies. These agencies use a combination of letters A through D to estimate the risk for prospective investors. For example, AAA (or Aaa) is the highest quality bond, while CC or D rated bonds are in default of payment. The ratings are not meant to be a measure of attractiveness of the bond as an investment, but rather how "safe" it is if held to maturity.

Short-term corporate debt is known as commercial paper and is issued most commonly by companies involved in financing matters (banks and other lenders and granters of credit). Commercial paper investments vary, and maturity is generally 90 days. Yield on commercial paper tends to be somewhat higher than on U.S. Treasury issues, with higher-rated issues paying less than those rated lower.

Corporate bonds and commercial paper are available through stockbrokers, mutual funds, and in some cases through investment departments of large banks. Interest earned on corporate debt is subject to both federal and state income taxes.

Municipal Bonds. When cities, states, and other local government units borrow money, their promises to repay are called municipal

bonds or occasionally municipal notes or tax anticipation notes for short-term debt. Minimum denominations vary but are generally much higher than those of corporate bonds.

Interest earned on municipal bonds is exempt from federal income taxes. Further, if the issuing unit is located in your state of residency, interest income will usually be exempt from your state income taxes. Because of this tax advantage, the interest rate paid on municipal bonds is generally lower than that paid on corporate bonds.

As with corporate bonds, municipal bonds are rated as to quality, and their value tends to fluctuate over the years. Municipal bonds are not traded as actively as corporate bonds, and their prices usually are not listed in the daily newspapers.

The higher the rating of municipal bonds, the lower the yield, but the safer the investment. Municipal bonds issued by larger communities are traded on a fairly active basis. But many bonds from smaller communities may not have active buyers and sellers. Consequently, you might have to accept a lower price if you need to sell in a hurry.

While municipal bonds can be of considerable benefit to high-tax-bracket investors, they may offer little or no benefit to lower-tax-bracket investors. If you are in a low enough tax bracket, the tax you would have to pay on normally taxable investments may be so small that your yield on a taxable investment, even after paying taxes, might be better than you would realize in a tax-exempt investment. Unfortunately many people nearing retirement invest heavily in tax-exempt securities. They do so without realizing that once they have retired, they are likely to be in a much lower tax bracket. But once they have made the investment, it may be costly to get out.

Zero Coupon Bonds. A zero coupon bond is sold at an extremely deep discount. It does not pay interest semiannually like an ordinary bond. You receive the face amount when it matures. The difference between purchase price and par value is your interest. You earn interest, but it is not paid until you redeem the bond at maturity. For example, if you pay $377 for a $1,000 bond with annual interest yield of 10 percent that matures in 10 years, you will earn $623. That $623 represents the interest you earn on the $377, plus interest on the interest.

Because the Internal Revenue Service (IRS) expects you to declare average annual gain as taxable income, zero coupon bonds are best used in tax-deferred savings plans like IRAs or retirement plans. This way you do not pay tax until you withdraw the money.

You can buy zero coupon bonds backed by Treasury securities, government agencies, corporations, and municipal governments.

Annuities. Annuities are a combination of investment and insurance. They are products of insurance companies, although some types may be available through stockbrokers. Under an annuity contract, you invest a sum of money with the insurance company, either in one lump sum or in periodic payments. Your earnings accumulate on a tax-deferred basis. At some agreed-upon future date, such as when you reach 65, the insurance company pays you the cash value in a lump sum or begins making monthly payments, which may continue for the rest of your life. With some annuities, the payments continue to your spouse after your death. There are many pay-out combinations from which to choose. The specific terms of annuity contracts differ from company to company, and from plan to plan.

Congress has been observing the tax advantages of single-premium annuities and has taken steps to lessen those advantages in recent years. Annuities are not for everyone, but it is worth your time to investigate their importance in your financial planning.

Mortgage Pools. You may want to pool your money with that of other investors in an assortment of numerous residential mortgages. The most popular program for this type of investing is offered through the Government National Mortgage Association (GNMA, or "Ginnie Mae"), an agency of the U.S. government. Ginnie Mae buys mortgages from lenders such as banks, packages a few dozen into a pool, and then offers certificates to investors that represent a share of ownership in a specific pool of mortgages.

Ginnie Maes are guaranteed by the U.S. government, but this does not mean that their values do not fluctuate. They are complicated investments. For example, if many of the mortgages in a particular Ginnie Mae pool are paid off early, these prepayments can have an adverse effect on the value of your GNMA investment. Therefore, if you decide to own GNMA securities, it is better to own several of them in order to diversify the amount of risk. Unfortunately, the cost of one GNMA certificate is $25,000, making the possibility of owning several of them remote for most people.

To make Ginnie Maes available to more people, mutual fund companies offer GNMA funds, which invest the majority of the portfolio in GNMA securities. Shares in these funds can be obtained for as little as $250.

Other government-related programs offer similar forms of mortgage pool investing. The Federal Home Loan Mortgage Corporation ("Freddie Mac") offers participation certificates and collateralized mortgage obligations. The Federal National Mortgage Association ("Fannie Mae") also offers mortgage-backed securities, but the prices of these individual securities are also high. Few, if any, mutual fund companies offer mutual funds that focus primarily on these securities.

Buying in the Equity Market

As people approach retirement, they usually do not have the time and psychological resilience necessary to recover from financial mistakes or misfortunes. Consequently, before buying, they should determine how much money they can risk losing. If they cannot afford the losses, they should not speculate.

Stocks. Stock is an equity security. When you buy stock, you become an owner of some share of a company's assets. Your shares prosper or decline along with the company. If a company is successful, the price the investors are willing to pay for its stock will often go up. Shareholders who bought stock at a lower price stand to make a profit. On the other hand, if a company does not do well, its stock will probably decrease in value and shareholders can lose money.

Many profitable companies distribute part of their earnings to their shareholders as dividends. Dividends are usually paid on a quarterly basis. As owners, shareholders may have the right to vote on the selection of individuals to serve on the board of directors and other matters of significance to the company.

There are several major categories of stock — blue chip, cyclical, growth, and income. Blue chip stock is stock of a company that has a long history of earnings growth and dividend payments. Cyclical stock closely follows the general level of business activity in the economy. Growth stock is the stock of a company whose earnings are increasing at a faster rate than the increase in the general level of business activity. Income stock is the stock of a well-established company that is relatively mature. The company pays out a substantial part of its earnings as dividends, rather than reinvesting them. Thus, income stocks grow more slowly than growth stocks.

Investors interested in current income will want to pursue income stocks. Investors more interested in capital appreciation and less interested in income will want to pursue growth stocks. Some investors may want to seek a balance of growth and dividend payments.

Preferred versus Common Stock. There are two principal classes of stocks — common and preferred. Common stock dividends are issued at the discretion of the company's management. Preferred stock pays a fixed dividend.

Common stocks can produce income through dividends and capital gains. Capital gains are gains from the sale of a capital asset at a higher price than its original cost. Capital gains are income only when the stock is sold. Many people buy stock expecting the price to increase, thereby allowing them to sell at a profit.

Preferred stock represents a special type of ownership in a company. Purchasers may expect to receive a stated dividend periodically. The amount of this dividend is declared when the stock is first issued. The board of directors of the issuing corporation can elect not to pay this dividend in any period.

Most preferred stock is cumulative. Cumulative means that all dividends not paid in a period accumulate and must be paid prior to giving common stockholders any dividends. Preferred stockholders also have preference over common stockholders if the corporation is liquidated. Because preferred stockholders have these privileges, they normally do not receive any voting rights. Preferred stock is traded in the marketplace, but most people buy it for the dividend return rather than for any anticipated market price appreciation.

Do your homework. All the studying in the world will not guarantee a winner in the stock market. By not studying, however, you may increase your chances of buying losers. The more you study, the more likely it is that you might find situations best suited to your own financial needs. Before you play the stock market with real money, play it on paper for 6 to 12 months. Pick an imaginary portfolio and track your choices. Notice the forces that make prices go up and down.

While you are playing the market on paper, read books, magazines, brokerage house brochures, and newspapers. Interview brokers to find one whose insights, experience, and personality seem right for you. Then, before taking a real plunge into the market, determine and stick to prices at which you will buy and sell.

Mutual Funds. A mutual fund is money pooled by many people for the purpose of investing toward a common goal. Mutual funds combine the dollars of many shareholders to invest in a diversified list of securities. Each share represents a proportionate interest in many individual companies. Mutual funds are popular among shareholders who do not have the background, time, or inclination to select securities personally and chart their investment regularly. Each shareholder gets the benefit that could otherwise be available to only wealthier and more sophisticated investors who have the resources to spread their investments among many business and industries.

Different kinds of mutual funds have different investment objectives:

Balanced funds — Objective is a balanced portfolio that invests in bonds and preferred and common stock.

Income funds — Objective is current income rather than growth of capital. Usually invests in both stocks and bonds that normally pay higher dividends and interest.

Growth funds — Objective is long-term growth of capital. Invests principally in common stocks with growth potential.

Growth and income — Objective is a balance between both income and long-term growth.

Aggressive growth — Objective is the highest possible capital gains.

Special funds — Invest in a narrowly defined sector such as bonds, money market, or gold.

The price of mutual fund shares is called net asset value (NAV). NAV is calculated by dividing the total value of securities that the fund owns by the number of shares that investors have purchased. When securities purchased by the mutual fund increase in price, the net asset value of the fund's shares increases. If the securities held by the fund decrease, your fund's NAV decreases. Your mutual fund performs as the securities it holds performs. The measure of performance is the increase or decrease in the fund's NAV.

Mutual funds can also be classified as load or no-load. No-load funds have no initial sales charge. The mutual fund company sells directly to the public. Load funds charge an initial sales charge ranging from 3 to 8.5 percent. The charge is added to the net asset value per share when determining the offering price. In some cases there may be an annual fee, a fee on reinvested dividends, a charge if you withdraw money from your account or redeem shares. Fee information is included in the fund's prospectus. Load funds are purchased through a broker or other sales agent.

Dollar-Cost Averaging. Dollar-cost averaging is a strategy that can be used to purchase mutual funds or other investments over a long period of time. You invest a fixed amount at regular intervals. After a period of time, you should own more shares than if you had invested the entire amount at the beginning. This happens because you really purchase more shares when the market is low and fewer when it is high. Over the long-run, your average cost per share will be lower than the average price on the dates you made the purchase.

Dollar-cost averaging is most effective in a market that fluctuates over a prolonged period. If the market generally advances, a lump-sum investment made at the beginning of the rise would probably produce larger profits than dollar-cost averaging. On the downside, there is no guarantee that a fund that declines sharply will rise again, so you may have to get out as you would in any other declining investment.

Unit Investment Trust. A unit investment trust is a way you can achieve diversification with a modest investment. An investment company forms a trust composed of a portfolio of professionally selected securities. They typically invest in debt securities. All of the securities are of the same type — all tax-free municipal bonds or all taxable corporate bonds — and have similar maturity dates. Some trusts consist of securities that will mature in six months or one year. Other trusts have an average life of 12, 15, 25, or more years.

Investors buy units of the trust. Each unit costs approximately $1,000. Unit holders receive regular interest or dividend payments. Distributions of interest may be made on a monthly, quarterly, or annual basis.

Real Estate. Investing in real estate (other than residential) is not for the beginner. Knowing how to wisely buy, finance, manage, and sell property takes years of experience. For too long a myth has prevailed that it is easy to make a fortune in real estate. It is far easier to sell books or seminar tickets on the subject than to actually make a fortune. Handled properly, a real estate investment can be fruitful. Handled poorly, it can be a drain not just on your money, but on your time and your psychological well-being.

Careful study is important before you begin. You must determine whether you are best suited to a real estate opportunity that is designed for current income or for possible future appreciation or for tax shelter benefits. The wrong design can be financially detrimental.

If you have the know-how and the energy, you might want to begin a real estate venture on your own. Otherwise, you can choose from package deals offered by brokerage firms, or by local promoters in the form of limited partnerships. Investigate all of these plans very carefully; definite risks are attached to any real estate venture. It is imperative that you know the reputation of any promoters before you deal with them, and it is wise to have your attorney check the limited partnership arrangements before you commit yourself.

Commodities, Metals, Gems, and Collectibles. These items represent pure speculation. In the commodities market, you are placing a bet on the future value of things such as corn, wheat, foreign currencies, interest rates, and an assortment of other items whose price can fluctuate widely. Unless you have a knack for forecasting floods, droughts, wars, and strikes, the commodities market probably has no place in your financial future. For those who have a substantial net worth, a managed commodity account may improve their chances of becoming a successful commodity trader.

Metals (gold, silver, platinum, strategic metals such as molybdenum and titanium) are unpredictable in price and, like other commodities, are subject to all sorts of unusual influences. Gemstones (diamonds, rubies, sapphires) require expert appraisal and keen knowledge of how the marketplace works. Collectibles are more suitable for fun than for profit.

Speculating in these items means that your money is tied up and earning nothing in interest, dividends, or rent. You are gambling totally on price appreciation. Your money is not really working; it is just waiting.

Figuring Certainty Ratings

In evaluating a way of putting your money to work, you must take into account certain criteria with respect to yield, safety of principal, and liquidity. The questions to ask are:

■ How certain am I to receive the expected yield?

■ How certain am I that my principal is safe?

■ How certain am I to be able to liquidate my investment, without delay, getting a full return of my principal?

Rate the following categories of investment on a scale of 1 to 5, with 1 being the lowest and 5 being the highest degree of certainty. Compare your ratings with the suggested ratings listed below.

	Certainty Ratings		
	Yield	Safety	Liquidity
1. Federally insured deposits	_____	_____	_____
2. U.S. government bonds	_____	_____	_____
3. High-rated municipal bonds	_____	_____	_____
4. Medium-rated municipal bonds	_____	_____	_____
5. High-rated corporate bonds	_____	_____	_____
6. Medium-rated corporate bonds	_____	_____	_____
7. Top-quality stocks	_____	_____	_____
8. Medium-quality stocks	_____	_____	_____
9. Low-quality stocks	_____	_____	_____
10. Growth mutual funds	_____	_____	_____
11. Income mutual funds	_____	_____	_____
12. Growth/income mutual funds	_____	_____	_____
13. Good-quality real estate	_____	_____	_____
14. Medium-quality real estate	_____	_____	_____
15. Precious metals	_____	_____	_____
16. Commodities	_____	_____	_____
17. Collectibles	_____	_____	_____

Suggested ratings (Numbers represent in order, yield, safety, and liquidity):

1: 5,5,5	4: 4,3,3	7: 4,3,3	10: 3,2,2	13: 3,3,2	16: 1,1,1
2: 5,4,4	5: 5,4,4	8: 3,2,3	11: 4,4,4	14: 2,2,1	17: 1,2,1
3: 5,4,4	6: 4,3,3	9: 2,1,3	12: 3,3,3	15: 1,1,1	

Choosing a Financial Adviser

When planning where to invest your money, you may wish to seek professional guidance. Financial advisers can give you information to help you choose savings and investments that are right for your lifestyle and family situation. Accountants, bankers, financial planners, insurance agents, and stockbrokers are some of the people who can help you with your savings and investment decisions.

How do you find the right adviser for you? One way is to ask friends or co-workers whose opinion you respect. Ask them to recommend someone knowledgeable in the field of savings and investments.

Before you visit with these experts, gather as much information as you can about savings and investments. Read an introductory book on investments to become familiar with basic terminology and determine your investment objectives. The *Wall Street Journal, Business Week, Kiplinger's Personal Finance, Forbes*, and *Money* are also sources of financial information. After reviewing these resources, you will be more prepared to discuss your savings and investment strategy. Shop around. When choosing a financial adviser, it is a good idea to interview at least three people to be sure you find the right adviser for you. Take the time to meet and talk with the adviser before taking action. The following questions can help you find the right adviser.

- *How many years of professional training have you had?* Look for a degree in accounting, family economics, economics, business administration, or finance. For added assurance, choose someone with a professional designation. A professional designation means that the person has met certain educational and expertise requirements, passed a series of exams, agreed to adhere to a code of ethics, and made a commitment to on-going professional development. Some designations are:
  CFA — Chartered Financial Analyst
  ChFC — Chartered Financial Consultant
  CFP — Certified Financial Planner
  CPA — Certified Public Accountant
  CLU — Chartered Life Underwriter

- *How do you keep up with current trends in your field?*

- *What type of clients do you usually advise, and what income bracket are they in?* Many advisers specialize in a certain area. Learn what area the adviser specializes in and whether he or she specializes in a particular type of client.

- *How long have you (and your company) been in business?* Has the adviser entered the financial services industry only recently? If so, look for related skills acquired from another professional area that add to the planner's credibility and overall abilities.

- *Are you registered or licensed?* For example, financial planners who deal in securities or receive compensation for investment advice should display a license or registration from the Securities and Exchange Commission (SEC) or the National Association of Securities Dealers (NASD). Those who handle insurance should be licensed by the State Insurance Commissioner's Office.

- *How are you compensated? Do you provide a full disclosure of fees and commissions?* Some financial experts, such as insurance agents and stockbrokers, do not charge a consultation fee. They make money from commissions on the products you purchase. Others will charge you an hourly fee for their time. Some will agree to a free visit the first time to determine what your needs are and to see how they can help you.

■ *Have your recommendations outperformed the market in recent years?*

An *accountant* can help you develop your financial plan and goals. An accountant can provide advice on tax planning, investment planning and performance, and financing education as well as retirement and estate planning. Accountants may vary as to how they charge. They may charge a fee, a commission, or a combination of the two. If accountants do not sell products, they can put you in touch with a stockbroker, insurance agent, or whoever else you need to put your financial plan into action.

Your *banker* can provide advice on savings accounts, interest-bearing checking accounts, savings bonds, certificates of deposit, individual retirement accounts, and bonds. Some banks also offer investment services. Bankers are usually paid a salary rather than a commission.

A *financial planner* can analyze your financial situation and recommend savings or investment alternatives that can help you meet your financial objectives. A financial planner can help you with more than choosing savings and investments. The planner can assist you in the following ways:

■ Assess your current financial situation by analyzing your tax returns, investments, retirement plan, estate plan, and insurance policies.

■ Identify financial areas where you may need help, such as building up retirement income or improving your investment returns.

■ Help you develop a financial plan, based on your personal and financial goals, history, and preference.

■ Help you implement your financial plan, including referring you to specialists, such as accountants or lawyers, if necessary.

■ Review your situation and financial plan periodically and suggest changes in your plan when needed.

Financial planners vary as to how they are compensated. Fee-only planners charge a flat fee or an hourly fee for their time. Payment is required whether or not you choose to implement the suggested plan. The planner bases the charge on gathering your financial data, analyzing it, and recommending a plan of action.

Commission-only planners charge no fee for service. They make money through commissions paid by the companies of the investment and insurance products they sell. For example, if the planner sells you a universal life insurance policy, the planner will receive a commission from the insurance company. A planner who relies on commissions might direct you toward the purchase of products that give the highest commission. So be careful when following the advice of a planner who works on commission until you develop a trusting relationship.

A fee-and-commission planner receives payment from both a sales commission and a fee. For example, if the planner receives a commission from the company that sells the product you purchase, the fee you are charged may be less.

Make sure you get a written estimate of the services you can expect and compare the estimate with others. Then choose the package of services that best meets your needs.

Insurance representatives sell products such as whole life, universal, and variable life insurance policies to provide insurance protection while you build up a cash value. A tax-deferred annuity is another investment alternative offered by insurance companies. Insurance representatives work on commission and should be licensed with the state.

Stockbrokers are affiliated with a brokerage firm. Registered representative is the official name for brokers licensed to buy and sell stocks, bonds, government securities, and other investments. Brokerage firms often use other titles such as financial consultants, account executives, or investment executives. In some cases, the brokerage firm will be a full-service organization. In other cases, the broker will be affiliated with a discount service.

Brokers working with a full-service brokerage firm offer numerous investment services. They can analyze your investment needs, goals, and your current assets and develop an appropriate investment plan based on what you consider to be a desirable or acceptable rate of return. Brokers provide research reports on specific securities, and they furnish reference libraries and safekeeping services for your securities. They buy and sell securities for a commission.

Discount brokers only buy and sell securities. So their commissions are lower than those of full-service brokers.

Financial experts give you financial information, but you will have to decide which investment is best for your lifestyle and family situation. Weigh their suggestions carefully before making any financial decisions.

After reviewing the investments options that are available to you in planning for your financial future, you can now relate them to your own personal profile. Some choices will be inappropriate or impossible, but certain ideas for conserving your financial resources will appear tailor-made for you and your family. Only you and your spouse or partner or other family members can decide which investments suit your situation.

You can now proceed to making those important decisions by completing the Action Step that follows. The sample Action Step on the next page is filled in to guide you in your own deliberations.

Investment Planning

Action Step

Example

On the Action Step, list the investment decisions you have made and plan to act on. Remember that these choices have the capacity for ensuring your future financial security or endangering your fiscal well-being. The investments you make now have long-term implications, but remember also that they should be reviewed regularly over the years ahead and amended as your needs and preferences dictate. Use verbs — action words — to describe what you plan to do about your investments.

When you believe your list is complete for the time being, rank your decisions in the right-hand column according to their importance to you, with number 1 being the most important. Use a second sheet of paper to continue your list if needed.

Investment Actions	Rank by Importance
Get coin collection appraised, checking especially steel pennies from World War II	4
Compare CD rates of interest, withdrawal penalties, at area banks	5
Discuss converting life insurance policies to annuities with insurance agent	6
Find kind of U.S. government securities that best fit my own situation	1
Talk with my stockbroker son-in-law about finally investing in the market	7
Start investing in a Keogh plan	2
Find a financial adviser to help with the fine points of savings and investments	3

Action Step

On the Action Step, list the investment decisions you have made and plan to act on. Remember that these choices have the capacity for ensuring your future financial security or endangering your fiscal well-being. The investments you make now have long-term implications, but remember also that they should be reviewed regularly over the years ahead and amended as your needs and preferences dictate. Use verbs — action words — to describe what you plan to do about your investments.

When you believe your list is complete for the time being, rank your decisions in the right-hand column according to their importance to you, with number 1 being the most important. Use a second sheet of paper to continue your list if needed.

Investment Actions	Rank by Importance

THE AARP APPROACH
PLANNING

Plotting out the actions you will take to implement the decisions you have made on your Action Step is the culminating phase of dealing with your investment strategies for the years ahead. Your Master Action Plan, which serves as a "to do" list for making your decisions come to life, is the end product of this unit.

You should list each of your Investment Actions from your Action Step as a Goal Statement on your MAP. Then decide on the sequence of actions that will take you to your desired goal result. The sample Master Action Plan is presented to help you get your own thoughts together on the subject of investments.

Master Action Plan

Goal Statement: *Find best government securities for portfolio*

Actions	Resources	Time Frame	By Whom?
1. Read up on general topic	Library, newsstand, bookstore (Wall Street Journal, Forbes, books)	1 month	Self and spouse
2. Find and attend public lecture on government securities	Newspapers, flyers, posters, other individuals	1 month	Self and spouse
3. Talk to bank officer about such securities	Local bank branch	1 month	Self and spouse
4. See if U.S. savings bonds I currently hold should be cashed in and applied to new security choices	Bank officer, own research	1 month	Self and spouse
5. Decide how much money I can invest in government securities	Own deliberations, research	6 months' research	Self and spouse
6. Make careful purchase of appropriate U.S. government instruments	Money set aside for investment	6 months	Self and spouse

Goal Statement: *Start investing in Keogh Plan*

Actions	Resources	Time Frame	By Whom?
1. Read up on topic	Library, bookstore, IRS, other	1 month	Self and spouse
2. Talk to others	Self-employed individuals with Keogh plans	3 months	Self and spouse
3. Talk to bank officer	Local bank branch	1 month	Self and spouse
4. Talk to stockbroker about firm's offerings	Brokerage firm	1 month	Self and spouse
5. Decide how much income we can put away without access for several years	Own deliberations, research	3 months	Self and spouse
6. Open a Keogh plan	Bank, brokerage firm, other agent	1 month	Self and spouse

Personal Financial Planning

Personal Financial Planning

I t would be unrealistic to view retirement as a single act in time: one day you are working, the next day you are not, and with luck everything will work out all right. Yet many people view retirement this way. It is much wiser, both financially and psychologically, to start planning for your retirement many years in advance. Such long-range planning is the best way to guarantee the lifestyle and financial security you want in the years ahead.

As your actual retirement date draws near, it comes time to review and refine your long-term planning. One effective way to do this is through some short-term planning that focuses on priorities and on current and projected expenses.

Setting priorities is not simply a wishing exercise. Write down every goal, put a price tag on it, and indicate where the money will come from to achieve it. For example, say that two years after your retirement date you want to take a vacation in Hawaii. Start studying the travel brochures now. Talk to a travel agent to discover the price of the trip. Survey your income sources now to determine where the discretionary money will come from to pay for the trip.

The same exercise should be done with all other priorities. These should be separate and distinct from your ongoing daily expenses of housing, food, transportation, and medical expenses. As you progress, you will be able to determine which of your desired goals can be met, which have to be trimmed, which have to be eliminated, and which can be replaced. This Think of Your Future unit channels you into analyzing expenditures, a possibly uncomfortable but nevertheless necessary reality check in planning for the future.

Unit Objectives

- **Assessment:** To assess your current and anticipated expenses as they relate to your plans for the future

- **Alternatives:** To consider alternatives and modifications to your expense patterns that are likely to improve or stabilize your future financial status

- **Responsibility:** To make decisions about your spending and expense patterns that will enable you to pursue your goals

- **Planning:** To make specific plans to follow through on your decisions regarding expenses, remembering to remain flexible and to consult those who share your personal financial life

What Do You Think?

The questions that follow will guide you toward important issues concerning how you spend the income you now have and how you expect to spend the income you anticipate having in the future. You are encouraged to discuss these topics with your spouse or partner, other family members and friends, or anyone else in your support system that you would like to include. When the questions are used as discussion topics in a group setting, you should not feel compelled to reveal private or confidential information.

1. What family members or friends depend on you for partial or full financial support? Do you expect these situations to change (e.g., children will become self-supporting, elderly parents will require additional assistance, friends will find new means of financial support)?

2. Do you know how much money you spend each month? Do you know how much you need to pay your basic bills, without any extras?

3. If your household lost its primary source of income, could you carry on financially with the help of savings, investments, or other assets?

4. Do you regularly use credit cards? Do you need them to get through the month, or do you use them as a convenience? Do you carry large balances, or do you pay each bill in full as it arrives?

For Your Information

Inflation represents one of the great dilemmas of our modern age. It cannot be overlooked, nor can it be predicted. During the late 1970s, the Consumer Price Index (which is the accepted measure of inflation) was in double digits year after year. It has now fallen to well below 5 percent for several years, however. When the inflation rate is high, people are troubled, psychologically as well as financially. When the inflation rate is low, people tend to be too complacent and may fail to take defensive measures against the next round of serious price increases.

A sharp eye must be kept on the trends that signal an increase in the inflation rate. One important indicator is the prime rate — the interest rate major banks charge major borrowers. If the prime rate moves upward two or more times in a six-to-twelve month period, this is a clear warning of price increases across the board. In response, you might wisely begin a modest program of storing nonperishable goods — canned items, paper products — as a way of protecting yourself against price increases. But do so with prudence. Do not tie up too much of your money in inflation-beating hoarding. You might need that money for other purposes.

Retirement Expenses

Consider each category of retirement expenses carefully. Determine how much you are now spending in each category, how much you anticipate spending in future years, how much will be spent if one spouse or partner dies, and how much flexibility you have within the range of your income to adjust these expenditures. Decide also how you can cut on each expense, and how you can substitute if need be. Do not tie yourself down to an arbitrary budget such as national averages. Your expense budget must be created to suit your own individual needs and desires.

Housing. Let's look at the financial angles to some of the issues we discussed in the Housing Planning unit. Retirement, coupled with the empty nest syndrome that occurs when the children move away, motivates some people to think about moving into smaller quarters. This decision is, of course, a personal matter. But the financial aspects cannot be overlooked.

If you have been living for the past years with a low-interest-rate and low-balance mortgage, today's higher home costs may come as a rude shock, particularly if you have to finance any portion of a new dwelling. And you may have to finance more than you anticipate, particularly if you have to take back a buyer's IOU instead of receiving the full value in cash when you sell your house. Also, evaluate the costs of relocating. This includes the need for new furniture, carpets, draperies, moving expenses, and the cost associated with selling your old house and buying your new house (points, appraisal fees, real estate commissions).

If you do decide to sell your current home, determine whether you are better off renting or buying. Consider these pros and cons:

- If you rent, you do not have to tie up any of your capital for a down payment. That capital can be earning money for you.

- Retirement generally means lower income tax brackets. The interest you pay on your home loan is tax deductible to you, but that deduction might not be worth as much. So the advantage of owning versus renting may be much less important to you in retirement. Ask your accountant for an analysis.

- Home ownership gives you the security of knowing you will never be evicted. It does not necessarily protect you from rising home ownership costs such as taxes and insurance. A tenant might always be subject to eviction or rent increases, but local rent control ordinances give the tenant some protection. A long lease with the option to renew also gives renters some protection.

In certain cases, refinancing your existing home loan can cut down your monthly expenses. Each case must be examined on its own merits. Be particularly cautious about assuming an adjustable-rate mortgage loan. A person whose income can be expected to grow is better able to cope with later increases in interest rates than is the retiree, whose income is relatively fixed.

What about making improvements to your existing home? This is often a good way to compromise between staying put and moving. If zoning laws permit, part of your home might be converted into an income-producing apartment. This arrangement can also provide some nearby companionship, which may be desirable in certain circumstances. What used to be the children's bedrooms can be converted into a hobby room or an office.

Retirement affords the leisure time to do many of these renovations yourself. If you are not handy at such matters, it will be necessary to hire outside contractors. Beware of home improvement swindlers, however. Retirees are the most common victims of this multi-billion-dollar-a-year consumer abuse. Be certain you are dealing with reputable people; obtain plans and specifications that detail all the work to be done and materials to be used; get estimates in writing; supervise the work thoroughly. Leave nothing to chance.

You may want to consider moving into a retirement community. Many such communities offer a short-term rental trial period. Take advantage of this offer. Otherwise, if you do not like living in the community, it could be costly to obtain release from a signed contract.

Many retirement communities offer a wide range of leisure activities at a modest cost over and above your basic home loan payments. If you plan to take advantage of these opportunities, the savings can be considerable compared with the cost of these activities in a conventional community. If you are not going to take advantage of those activities, however, you might be spending money needlessly. Analyze your individual situation carefully before you make any decisions on a retirement community.

Decide how you will meet housing costs in the event of a serious illness or the death of your spouse. Will you remain in your own private dwelling? Would it be appropriate to move in with your children or other family members? These are difficult concepts to deal with now, but they will be even more difficult to deal with later if you have not anticipated the possibility of such events. Investigate the costs and facilities at retirement homes or local nursing homes now. You may never have need for these alternatives, but if you do, you will have at least laid the groundwork for a wise decision.

Medical Expenses. Medicare is the health insurance program for persons 65 and older. It is sponsored by the federal government and available through the Social Security Administration. You should apply for Medicare benefits at least three months before your 65th birthday. The government will not automatically enroll you.

Medicare will cover about 40 percent of your health care costs. Consequently, you should explore supplemental health insurance. For most people, this is a medigap policy from a private insurance company. (Some employers' group health insurance programs will continue to provide you with Medicare supplemental insurance in retirement. Check with your personnel office to determine if this applies to you.)

All medigap policies must conform to standardized benefit plans, which enables you to compare policies from different companies. You should understand what Medicare covers and its gaps to determine which medigap policy will be right for you.

For six months after you enroll in Medicare you have the right to buy a medigap policy, regardless of your health. Preexisting conditions cannot be excluded for more than six months on new medigap policies and must be covered from the first day by replacement policies.

If there is a health maintenance organization (HMO) in your area, explore its pricing and service structure. To enroll, you pay a membership fee, which Medicare helps pay, and the HMO pays for all your Medicare-covered health care expenses. In turn, you must go to the HMO for all Medicare-covered health care needs, except in an emergency. Before enrolling in an HMO, you should consider carefully whether you would be satisfied with the choice of doctors offered by the HMO and whether the company is financially stable. If you are not satisfied with an HMO membership, you can disenroll at any time.

In shopping for supplemental health insurance, be certain that you are obtaining the comprehensive protection you need. Many hospital indemnity policies will protect you only in the event of hospitalization and then only for a limited number of dollars per day.

It is also important to consider what arrangements you may need to sustain an independent lifestyle should you become disabled or chronically ill. Long-term care insurance is emerging as one way to help

cover the potentially devastating cost of extended care. Nursing home expenses run higher than $50,000 per year in many locations. This type of insurance usually pays a fixed amount per day for nursing home stays or home health care visits. The amount and duration of the benefits provided vary from policy to policy. This type of insurance is often expensive and can have coverage limitations.

Insurance (Other than Medical). There are several kinds of life insurance from which to choose. Because the terms associated with each kind of policy vary by insurance carrier, discuss these policies in full with a financial planner or insurance representative before selecting one appropriate for you.

Term insurance charges a set premium over a number of years. The benefits are paid to your beneficiaries upon your death. Term insurance has no cash value, so it cannot be borrowed against. The amount of the premium depends on your age at the time you first purchase the policy. The younger you are, the lower your premium will be (because you will be making more payments over your lifetime). Term life insurance must be renewed periodically, usually annually. Your coverage continues as long as you renew the policy. Most term policies will stop covering you once you are 75 or 85.

Whole life insurance has a cash value and can be borrowed against, sometimes at a lower interest rate than would be available at banks. Once a policyholder has reached a specified age, he can receive a lump sum payment from such plans. Some people use whole life insurance as a retirement plan because the premiums paid for such a policy are not taxed until the policy is cashed in. No income taxes are owed, however, if the policy is cashed because of the policy-holder's death.

For someone with a large amount to invest, *single premium whole life insurance* offers one opportunity. Single premium whole life requires that you pay the entire premium in an initial lump-sum payment. It pays you a dividend on the cash value. Before choosing this as an investment, however, discuss the move with an accountant or financial planner.

Universal life insurance is similar to single premium whole life, except that the initial deposit may be paid over a predetermined, but generally short, amount of time such as one year. In addition, dividends may be calculated differently. Both single premium whole life and universal life policies have income tax advantages similar to those of whole life insurance.

During your working years, you may have paid regularly for a whole life insurance program to protect your survivors in the event of your death. For retirees, often much of the need for that protection is over. The children are grown and on their own, and you may have other assets that can protect your survivors in the event of your death. This is the time to consider reducing your life insurance.

You may have built up a substantial cash value in the whole life policies. Review your policies and consider your options.

1. Drop the policy and take the cash. The cash value built up in your policy is yours for the asking. You can take the money and spend it or invest it. You could purchase a deferred annuity. If the cash value exceeds what you have paid into the policy, you may have a taxable gain.

2. Get a paid-up policy. Stop paying premiums and convert the policy to paid-up life insurance. You have the option of a paid-up cash value policy or extended term insurance. Your insurance company can calculate the necessary reduction in face value.

3. Reduce your coverage. If you still need some insurance, but not as much, you can decrease your coverage, and take a proportionate amount of the cash value.

4. Take out a loan. You can borrow your cash value and continue to pay premiums on the policy. You do not have to repay the loan but you do have to pay interest on the loan. The interest is not tax deductible. The loan value will be subtracted from the face value upon your death. Check with your insurance company to determine if this is the right option for you.

Your need for automobile, homeowner's, and umbrella liability insurance will continue in retirement. It is possible, however, to save money on these policies by raising the deductibles. The deductible is the amount you pay before the insurance company pays. In addition, insurance companies offer a number of policy discounts. Discuss the opportunities to save premium dollars with your insurance agent.

Be certain to maintain adequate coverage on your homeowner's (or tenant's) policies. If you have not updated the policy in recent years and do not have an automatic inflation clause, chances are the replacement value of your home may exceed your coverage. In the event of extensive damage, you would suffer a financial loss. Consider purchasing replacement cost coverage on your home and personal property.

Being retired does not mean that you can reduce your liability insurance. With your restricted ability to earn, an adverse decision in a liability case could cut seriously into your personal wealth. It is essential to retain an adequate level of liability insurance.

Transportation. If you were a two-car family before retirement, you can realize considerable savings by becoming a one-car family once the need to drive to work is eliminated. The savings involve far more than just gasoline; you save on insurance, registration costs, maintenance, and repairs. And think of the breather your budget will get if you are able to eliminate a car payment.

The prospect of giving up one car brings an instant negative reaction from most people, because they do not want to give up the freedom that the second car allows. Before you reject this idea, research how much it would cost you to get around via taxis, buses, and ride-sharing. If you are changing your residence, evaluate the transportation costs that you would incur at your new dwelling. If it is easily accessible to shopping and recreation, you might be able to cut your transportation costs.

Annual Expenditures

Head of Household Age 65 and Older

	Percent
Food	17.9
Housing (incl. furnishings, maintenance, utilities, and taxes)	31.8
Clothing and personal care	4.7
Transportation	15.8
Medical care (incl. health insurance)	11.7
Entertainment, reading, education	4.7
Contributions	5.7
Other expenses	7.7

Source: Monthly Labor Review, *May 1993*

Spending Habits Will Change. Almost inevitably, many of your spending habits will change as the retirement routine becomes more familiar. You may find yourself spending more on travel and leisure activities. Your work-related expenses such as restaurant lunches, clothing, and transportation end. Retirees also spend less on insurance and stop contributing to Social Security.

Everyone's situation is different. The amount you spend in retirement depends a great deal on your health and lifestyle. The chart on this page shows how the average over-65 household allocates its money.

The realities of living on a relatively fixed income will provide strong motivation to follow every cost-cutting maneuver available.

Travel, Entertainment, Hobbies. Upon retirement, leisure pursuits can be planned at more convenient times and at lower prices. Attend matinees for movies and shows instead of evening performances. Play golf on weekdays instead of weekends. Travel during the off seasons, when prices are considerably lower. Dine early to take advantage of early-bird or pre-theater specials. It is best to anticipate these changes in your spending habits and incorporate them into your financial plan now.

Since travel is a major pursuit of many retirees, getting the best travel bargains for your money requires homework and a good travel agent. Scrutinize travel advertising carefully. Many deluxe tours offer little more than the stripped down variety at a much higher price. Air fares differ widely from the conventional coach price to the discount price. Since you have more leisure time available, you should take advantage of the discount requirements that will offer you the lowest possible fare. If you are inclined to book a cruise or a package deal at a resort, do so at the earliest possible time. The choicest rooms at the best possible prices sell out quickly.

"Twofers," which are two tickets for the price of one, and senior citizen discount plans are available for many forms of entertainment, including movies, sporting events, amusement parks, hotels, and even some restaurants. Take advantage of them.

Hobby expenses often increase after retirement when you have more time to enjoy them. That enjoyment is one of the benefits of retirement.

Gifts and Contributions. During your working years, you may have been a staunch supporter of local religious organizations, civic groups, clubs, and charities. There is no need to stop now, but you might consider substituting your time and personal services for monetary gifts. In many respects, your time can be worth more to these organizations than your dollars. Giving your time can also allow you to remain active and involved with people you care about.

A Stake for Yourself or Your Children. Have you planned to set aside some of your income, or some of your principal, to start a new business or to help your children get over their hurdles in life? If any of your available dollars will be going into either of these areas, you must carefully evaluate the risks and priorities of doing so. Going into business on your own can entail considerable risk. Giving money to your children is not a matter of risk, but the question arises of how much to give them and when. Might it be better to co-sign a loan for them if they need money, rather than dip into your own capital? Set firm guidelines, but be prepared to change your plans when the need arises.

Dependent Care Expenses. It may become necessary for you to pay some of the expenses needed to care for another person, whether it is a spouse, a parent, a child, or a close friend. This situation can be a heavy drain on your financial and psychological resources. Now is the time to anticipate and plan for these possibilities. Determine if all the parties involved are adequately insured. Decide whether the burden can be shared. Discuss the potential costs with doctors, nursing home administrators, and insurance agents. If the financial needs can be taken care of through insurance or other available assets, you may find the psychological burdens easier to bear.

Debt Repayment. For many families, the biggest item in their budget is debt repayment. This includes car payments, personal loan payments, and credit card debt. It is wise to start a debt elimination program as far in advance of your retirement as possible. This can be done by reducing other expenses and using the extra income to pay bills. In some instances it might be wise to get a home equity loan to pay off all your consumer debts. The interest rate is generally lower, and, if your total home equity is less than $100,000, it is tax-deductible. If this is your choice, be sure to pay it off fast and resist new debt. Do not jeopardize your home!

Tools to Help You Manage Your Expenses

Any of the following devices can be useful when managing your financial affairs.

The Dollar Diet. One of the most common financial dilemmas is finding that there is too much month left at the end of the money. This is largely a budgeting problem that can be remedied if you are willing to discipline yourself. Most people, when called upon to project their current budget, have no difficulty in estimating the major recurring expenses such as house or car payment. But as a rule, most of their other expenses fall into the category known as miscellaneous. This undefined category usually causes quite a problem in the budget. If you could reduce the miscellaneous expenses, you would be on much sounder footing financially. Do it by starting the Dollar Diet. Carry a pencil and notebook with you for two or three months, and every time you spend money, for whatever purpose, record the expenditure in the notebook.

At the end of that period, you will reap these benefits:

1. You will have a clear picture of where money went.

2. You will decide that many expenses just are not necessary.

The Dollar Diet is a self-correcting mechanism for the wayward budget; it costs nothing to try it, and results are guaranteed. Do not wait until retirement to begin.

Trusts. In general terms, a trust is an arrangement in which you turn over your money or property or both to another person who will manage it for you and distribute it according to your instructions. This is frequently done in estate planning. The trustee is generally a bank, often in combination with a lawyer or another person that you have chosen. Trusts can also be used to manage your current finances, though the cost might not be justified unless you have large sums of money to be managed. If your professional advisers feel it wise to create a trust, the trust can be structured to handle your investments and disburse your expenses on a regular basis. This frees you of the worry and time involved in doing these things yourself.

Mutual Fund Withdrawal Plans. If you have money invested in mutual funds, you can arrange to receive a regular monthly check to help you meet your expenses. Be sure that the monthly check does not exceed the actual monthly income that the fund is generating, or you will be dipping into your principal. The more you dip into your principal, the less is left to earn money for you. Before you know it, you could deplete your investment to a dangerously low level.

Financial Advisers. The financial planning industry is relatively new and unregulated. Financial advisers are discussed in detail in the chapter on Investment Planning.

Talking to Others. Discuss your financial status with your spouse, children, siblings, and trusted friends and advisers. Do not let pride or old habits get in the way of acquiring all the information you need. The best investment you can make, at any age, is in knowledge. Seek it, and use it.

ASSESSMENT

Meet Eleanor and Bob Walker

In this Assessment section, we examine the lives of Eleanor and Bob Walker as they approach retirement. After reviewing the description, visualize the Walkers' planning opportunities and challenges. Study the Walkers' financial situation to try to think of some ways the Walkers might have done a better job of preparing for their future. What strategies should they implement now? How can the Walkers decrease their expenses and increase their income?

As you review the Walkers' situation, you may find options that apply to your own financial planning. Take note of those options so you can apply them to your own budget for the future and your Net Worth Statement.

Case Description

Eleanor and Bob Walker are experiencing a very different kind of life from that which their parents knew. The complexity of their lives is unlike anything their families experienced.

Bob Walker, age 60, is a mid-level manager for a manufacturing firm and now earning $36,000 a year. He plans to take his pension at age 65 and move on to a second career as owner and manager of a house painting company. Bob has always enjoyed working on his home and would like to expand to working on other people's homes.

Eleanor Walker, age 55, has taught fourth grade at the local public school for 15 years. She earns $26,000 a year. Eleanor thoroughly enjoys her position and has no plans to retire.

Bob and Eleanor have three children and two grandchildren. Anne, age 30, is their older daughter and has two children. She was recently divorced and is staying with her parents until she can get her life together. She is finishing her training as a physical therapist. John, age 27, received a bachelor's degree in accounting and works for a management consulting firm. He has an apartment in a nearby city. Abby, age 17, is a high school senior who plans to study psychology in college. She does very well in school and hopes to qualify for a scholarship.

Bob's mother, Naomi, has a one-room apartment in an assisted living facility near the Walkers' home. Bob and his brother arranged for the sale of Mrs. Walker's home several months ago, and the proceeds are being used to pay for her care. She is 88 years old and in good health.

Eleanor's mother, Barbara Jackson, is 80 years old and lives by herself in the townhouse that she and her late husband purchased when they moved to be close to Eleanor and her family several years ago. Mrs. Jackson is recuperating from recent bypass surgery after a heart attack and is rather frail.

Bob Walker figures he is eligible for a lump-sum distribution of approximately $150,000 when he leaves his company at age 65. The present value of the pension fund is $108,500. He and Eleanor are not yet sure how to handle this retirement fund, but both of them realize the importance it will play in a comfortable retirement.

Eleanor is enrolled in the state retirement system. She is taking advantage of the state's deferred compensation program and has been saving $100 per month for the past 15 years. It is invested in an income/growth fund worth $32,500. Eleanor projects this tax-deferred fund will grow to $85,000 by the time she reaches age 65.

Bob has a $50,000 face value whole life insurance policy listing him as the owner. He has a $36,000 group term policy provided by his employer. Eleanor is sole beneficiary of both policies. Eleanor has a $10,000 term policy listing Bob as beneficiary.

They have $3,491 in a local credit union. There is $10,000 in Series EE Savings Bonds for Abby's college education, a gift from Eleanor's parents.

The Walkers live in a four-bedroom colonial house located in an attractive part of town. Their house has increased in value to its current estimated value of $156,000. The Walkers purchased the house for $38,000 twenty-two years ago. Their mortgage balance is $15,386, and the monthly payments of $470 include principal, interest, taxes, and insurance.

The Walkers have three cars: a one-year-old economy car, a six-year-old gas guzzler, and a four-year-old import that gets excellent mileage. All are in good working condition. Bob and Eleanor took out a three-year loan for the economy car and still owe $6,006, making monthly payments of $286. They owe $3,638 in credit card debt.

Given what you know about them, what suggestions can you make to help the Walkers enhance their income and reduce their expenses now and after retirement?

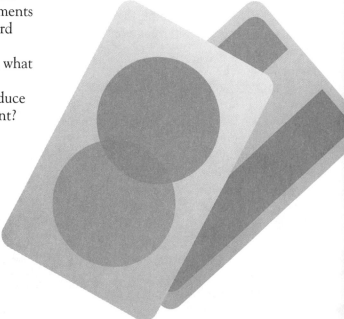

The Walkers' Net Worth Statement

The Walkers' net worth is what they own minus what they owe. Their net worth statement provides a good overview of the Walker family's financial situation.

Walker Assets (what they own)

Cash on hand	$	138
Bank accounts (checking)		1,421
Credit union account		3,491
Savings and loan accounts		
Other savings		
House, market value		156,000
Other real estate, value		
Household furnishings, value		35,000
Automobile(s), blue book value		16,250
Life insurance, cash value		25,000
Stocks and bonds, market value		
IRA plans		32,500
U.S. Savings Bonds		10,000
Money owed the Walkers		
Other assets		108,500
Personal property		4,250
Total assets	$	392,550

Walker Liabilities (what they owe)

Mortgages, balance due	$	15,386
Other loans (bank, credit union)		
Installment debts, balance due		6,006
Credit cards, balance due		3,638
Charge accounts, owed		
Other debts, total owed		
Insurance premium due		
Taxes owed		
Other current bills		
Total liabilities	$	25,030
NET WORTH (assets minus liabilities)	$	367,520

The Walkers' Income and Expense Statement

The Walkers' income and expense statement shows their income and expenses on an annual basis.

Income

Salary/wages	$	62,000
Interest — Credit union account		90
Dividends		0
Total income	$	62,090

Expenses

Deferred compensation program	$	1,200
Mortgage		5,640
Food		7,450
Clothing		3,250
Medical		1,900
Transportation		2,250
Utilities		2,400
Home maintenance		2,350
Appliances, furniture		2,100
Work-related expenses		1,000
Personal items		1,850
Insurance		
Life		500
Health		2,400
Home		0
Auto		950
Education		1,250
Taxes		
Income		13,500
Social Security		3,800
Property		2,800
Sales		1,350
Gifts, donations		1,750
Amusement		2,400
Total expenses	$	62,090

Can We Help the Walkers?

I. Retirement Income Sources

Bob and Eleanor need to get a better picture of their retirement income. They also need to be thinking of their tax options. Some of the questions the Walkers should be asking are:

1. What will be the sources of their retirement income?

   _____

   _____

   _____

   _____

2. How much income will the Walkers receive from each source? How can they find out? What questions do they need to ask?

   _____

3. If Bob decides not to take a company annuity and takes the $150,000 lump-sum distribution, what are his tax options?

   _____

4. What recommendations would you make regarding the Walkers' saving and investment strategies?

   _____

5. Are the Walkers eligible for any tax-deferred retirement accounts? Why? Why not?

   _____

II. The Painting Business

Bob Walker is thinking about using part of his $150,000 lump-sum distribution as start-up funding for his house painting business. He figures that $50,000 would cover the purchase of trucks and equipment, licenses and insurance, salary, and operating expenses until the business is making a profit.

1. What would be the financial implications of this decision? How will it affect their taxes?

   _____

2. Could Bob get a line of credit from his bank to start his business? What are the advantages of starting the company before he leaves his job?

   _____

3. How can Bob and Eleanor maximize their investment return on the remaining $100,000 of Bob's lump-sum distribution?

   _____

4. What additional information do they need to gather to be able to make a decision about the painting company? How might they be able to change or revise their decisions at a later date?

   _____

5. Would Bob be eligible for a Keogh? If so, how much should he invest?

   _____

6. Do they have other options? What would you advise them to do?

   _____

III. Loan for Anne

The Walkers' daughter Anne and her two children, ages 3 and 7, have been staying with Eleanor and Bob for the past four months. They are eager to help Anne at this difficult time in her life, and they are thrilled to have their grandchildren with them. Anne has another year to complete on her degree in physical therapy, and she has been taking summer classes while Eleanor and Abby are available to help with child care. Now Anne wants to move into her own apartment before school begins in the fall and has asked her parents for a $5,000 loan to help her get settled.

1. What additional information do the Walkers need before they can make a decision about this loan?

2. What options does Anne have other than asking her parents for this money?

3. What are the repayment options available for Anne?

4. If parents are able financially to help their adult children, when is it wise to withhold help? Is this one of those situations?

5. What would you advise the Walkers to do? What would you tell Anne?

IV. College for Abby

Abby Walker will be starting college next year. She has not visited any campuses yet but hopes to go away to school. She has $10,000 in savings bonds, but otherwise no large sum of money is reserved for her education. Additional funds will clearly be needed.

1. What additional information do the Walkers need to have before they can decide how to finance Abby's education?

2. What can Abby do to help in this effort?

3. What other resources, including family members, can be called upon for help?

4. How could the services of a professional advisor help? What type of advisor might be best?

5. What would you advise the Walkers to do to prepare for this expense in their financial future?

V. Care for Mothers

Eleanor is very concerned about the health of her mother, Barbara. She spends numerous hours with her each day helping with the activities of daily living. Although her mother owns her townhouse free and clear, her only source of income is Social Security, plus a small amount of interest from a savings account.

1. How will Eleanor care for her mother when school starts and she has to return to the classroom?

   _____

   _____

   _____

   _____

2. Can Barbara continue to live on her own? What other living arrangements might be possible?

   _____

   _____

3. What if Barbara's health deteriorates and she has go to a nursing home for care? Who will pay the costs?

   _____

   _____

4. How will the Walkers manage if Naomi, Bob's mother, becomes ill too?

   _____

   _____

VI. Credit Card Debt

The Walkers have always used credit cards to manage monthly expenses. Since Anne returned home and Barbara had surgery, it seems they are having a difficult time paying these bills. Though they pay the minimum amount due, they can no longer pay the balance in full. Recently, Bob and Eleanor decided to review their credit card debt and they were astounded to find they owed $3,638 to seven different credit card companies. The Walkers' budget is very tight.

Analyze the following options for paying the credit card debt:

1. Contact the Consumer Credit Counseling Service. What can they do for the Walkers?

   _____

   _____

   _____

2. Use the emergency fund savings to pay off the credit cards.

   _____

   _____

3. Take out a home equity loan to consolidate all debt and pay for Abby's college education.

   _____

   _____

4. Bob could earn extra income by painting houses on the weekend.

   _____

   _____

5. What other options do they have? What recommendations would you make?

   _____

   _____

Your Net Worth Statement

Complete your own net worth statement to help in preparation of your Action Step.

Your Assets (what you own)

Cash on hand .... $ _____

Bank accounts (checking) .... _____

Credit union account... _____

Savings and loan accounts .... _____

Other savings .... _____

House, market value .... _____

Other real estate, value .... _____

Household furnishings, value .... _____

Automobile(s), blue book value... _____

Life insurance, cash value.. _____

Stocks and bonds, market value .... _____

IRA plans... _____

U.S. Savings Bonds... _____

Money owed you.. _____

Other assets .... _____

Personal property .... _____

    Total assets .... $ _____

Your Liabilities (what you owe)

Mortgages, balance due .... $ _____

Other loans (bank, credit union) .... _____

Installment debts, balance due... _____

Credit cards, balance due .... _____

Charge accounts, owed .... _____

Other debts, total owed... _____

Insurance premium due .... _____

Taxes owed .... _____

Other current bills .... _____

    Total liabilities.. $ _____

NET WORTH (assets minus liabilities) .... $ _____

Your Income and Expense Statement

Complete your own income and expense statement to help in preparation of your Action Step

Income

Salary/wages .... $ _____

Interest — Credit union account .... _____

Dividends .... _____

    Total income .... $ _____

Expenses

Deferred compensation program .... $ _____

Mortgage .... _____

Food .... _____

Clothing .... _____

Medical .... _____

Transportation .... _____

Utilities .... _____

Home maintenance .... _____

Appliances, furniture .... _____

Work-related expenses .... _____

Personal items .... _____

Insurance

    Life .... _____

    Health .... _____

    Home .... _____

    Auto .... _____

Education .... _____

Taxes

    Income .... _____

    Social Security .... _____

    Property .... _____

    Sales .... _____

Gifts, donations .... _____

Amusement .... _____

    Total expenses .... $ _____

ALTERNATIVES

Cutting Costs

Here are some suggestions for reducing expenses. Check the items that seem to apply to you now or in retirement. Consider other options, too. Then put your plans into action.

Can You Reduce Your Taxes?

Effective tax planning takes advantage of the many ways you can legally reduce your tax bill. This planning could save you thousands of dollars. Listed here are some tax-saving ideas.

- *Individual Retirement Account (IRA)*. You can invest up to $2,000 per year in your own IRA with a bank, mutual fund, or other qualified trustee. The amount you invest may be tax-deductible, and income taxes on earnings are deferred until funds are withdrawn.

- *Spousal IRA*. If your spouse is not employed, you may contribute up to $2,250 per year, split between two accounts.

- *Keogh Plan*. A Keogh plan is for the self-employed and similar to an IRA. The maximum investment each year is 20 percent of your self-employment income or $30,000, whichever is less.

- *401(k) Plans*. Employer-sponsored 401(k) plans allow employees to have a certain portion of their salaries put into an investment program administered by their company. The salary amount invested in the plan is not taxed, nor are earnings on the investment, until funds are eventually withdrawn.

- *Single-Premium Deferred Annuity*. Insurance companies offer these annuities, often through banks and stockbrokers. They allow your investment to build on a tax-deferred basis and may offer other tax benefits. Cashing in the plans early can lead to stiff penalties. Careful shopping and analysis are advised.

- *Income Splitting*. Transferring some income-producing assets to a family member in a lower tax bracket may enable you to shift the tax burden from the higher bracket to a lower one. Get professional advice before taking any action.

- *Profit-Sharing Plans*. Your employer puts a share of company profits into an investment plan on your behalf. The annual investment, and the earnings, are not taxed until the funds are withdrawn.

- *Shift of Year-End Income*. Shifting payment for fees and services or bonuses into the new year makes sense if your income and taxes are expected to be lower in the coming year. You save because you will be taxed at a lower rate next year.

- *Deductions*. Tax deductions for charitable contributions, local property taxes, state income taxes, and other items should be taken in a higher tax year to maximize your savings.

- *Limited Partnerships*. The value of any limited partnership depends on the integrity of the general partners (the promoters), on the quality of the investment being made, and on the specifics of the contract the limited partners (the investors) are required to sign. Before you sign any contract of this type, be sure to get professional advice.

Personal Financial Planning

Cutting Costs

Managing Money

- [ ] Keep track of expenditures to determine how money is being spent.
- [ ] Use credit cards only if paid in full each month.
- [ ] Pay bills early when creditors give a discount for early payment.
- [ ] Comparison shop for insurance premiums.
- [ ] Convert life insurance to a paid-up policy with lower face value when appropriate.
- [ ] Drop life insurance coverage when no longer needed.
- [ ] Pay insurance premiums annually to avoid finance charges.
- [ ] Cover liability risk; buy adequate insurance.
- [ ] Use discount stockbroker.
- [ ] Invest in no-load mutual funds.
- [ ] Contribute clothing to a charitable organization and take tax deduction.
- [ ] Have a yard sale to raise money and get rid of unwanted items.

Food

- [ ] Plan meals for the week, using menus and grocery store ads to make a shopping list.
- [ ] Cut your food shopping trips to one a week — saving gas, time, and money.
- [ ] Use fewer convenience foods.
- [ ] Buy lower-cost generic or store brands of same quality as name brands.
- [ ] Use cents-off coupons.
- [ ] When shopping, compare price unit per pound, ounce, dozen, or package.
- [ ] Buy produce in season.
- [ ] Stop buying "junk" foods.
- [ ] Substitute low-cost protein (beans, peanut butter) for high-cost protein (meats).
- [ ] Stretch hamburger with bread crumbs, oatmeal, or tomato sauce.
- [ ] Prepare your own convenience foods, master mixes, and desserts.
- [ ] Mix instant milk with regular milk, or buy skim milk.
- [ ] Buy items you use often in bulk.
- [ ] Plan oven use by cooking main dish, dessert, vegetable, and bread at same time.
- [ ] Wrap and store foods carefully.
- [ ] Plan use of leftovers.
- [ ] Grow your own fruits and vegetables. Can, freeze, or dry for future use.
- [ ] Cut down on meals away from home.
- [ ] Take advantage of senior citizen discounts and reduced prices when dining out.
- [ ] Join a food co-op.

Housing

- [ ] Relocate to less expensive housing or area.
- [ ] Consider remodeling, rather then moving or building another home.
- [ ] Consider refinancing your home mortgage when interest rates drop.
- [ ] Review your property tax bill carefully and question any discrepancies.
- [ ] Increase your deductible on homeowner's insurance.
- [ ] Plant low-maintenance shrubs and grass.
- [ ] Plant trees, shrubs to cool and protect home.
- [ ] Rent out a room or garden space.
- [ ] Exchange room rent for household help.
- [ ] Turn off air conditioning and open windows in temperate weather.

continues

- [ ] Place plastic over windows in cold weather.
- [ ] Weatherize with caulking, weatherstripping, and insulation.
- [ ] Install electrical load controller to conserve energy to appliances and air conditioner.
- [ ] Install water-saving devices in toilets and showers.
- [ ] Close and turn off heat to rooms not in use.
- [ ] Install window, attic, or roof fan.
- [ ] Adjust thermostat and wear appropriate clothing.
- [ ] Make minor repairs before they become major ones.
- [ ] Buy furniture on sale, at a discount store, auction, garage sale, or secondhand shop.
- [ ] Purchase low-maintenance appliances on sale or at a discount store.
- [ ] Choose appliances with a high energy efficiency ratio (EER).
- [ ] Rent or share household equipment used infrequently.
- [ ] Buy all-purpose cleaning products.
- [ ] Use floor wax sparingly to eliminate need to remove wax buildup.
- [ ] Wash walls instead of painting.
- [ ] Clean, repair, and restore household items yourself.
- [ ] Make draperies, curtains, spreads, slipcovers, and table covers.
- [ ] Make dry flower arrangements from garden flowers, wildflowers, or decorative weeds.

Clothing

- [ ] Determine wardrobe needs and create a clothing budget.
- [ ] Buy clothing on sale or at discount or factory outlet stores.
- [ ] Avoid impulsive clothing purchases.
- [ ] Buy casual, less expensive clothes for leisure activities.
- [ ] Buy color-coordinated clothing that can be mixed and matched.
- [ ] Buy styles, fabrics, and colors that will remain fashionable.
- [ ] Look for quality fabric and good construction in clothing.
- [ ] Check fabric care labels to buy washable, easy-care clothes.
- [ ] Spot-clean clothes promptly and save on cleaning by careful wear.
- [ ] Keep clothes in good repair, remembering a "stitch in time saves nine."
- [ ] Learn to sew.
- [ ] Dress up or modify an outfit you already own.
- [ ] Store clothes properly to protect from sun, moths, mildew, and stretching.
- [ ] Protect shoes and leather items from water and salt stains.
- [ ] Wear old clothes for messy, dirty jobs.

Transportation

- [ ] Repair your old car rather than buy a new one.
- [ ] Time your car purchase, shopping when prices are lower.
- [ ] Buy low-maintenance cars.
- [ ] Keep your car in good running condition for safety and economy.
- [ ] Follow instructions in your car owner's manual.
- [ ] Maintain car by changing oil, air filters, and oil filters yourself.
- [ ] Protect against salt and rust by keeping your car clean and having it undercoated.

Cutting Costs continued

- ☐ Wash and wax your own car.
- ☐ Take advantage of auto repair classes held in your community.
- ☐ Practice good driving habits to save on fuel.
- ☐ Use self-service gasoline pumps.
- ☐ Periodically check oil and water levels.
- ☐ Form a car pool to go to meetings and make shopping trips.
- ☐ Walk more — drive less to save money and improve your health.
- ☐ Plan your trips by making lists of "things to do" and "things to buy."
- ☐ Use less costly public transportation rather than drive.
- ☐ Take a bus instead of a plane.
- ☐ Shop for low-cost air fares.
- ☐ Increase deductibles on auto insurance.
- ☐ Discontinue collision and comprehensive insurance when car value has dropped sufficiently.

Medical Care

- ☐ Maintain good health by eating nutritious food and exercising.
- ☐ Watch weight, because it is costly to put pounds on and costly to take them off.
- ☐ Limit alcohol consumption.
- ☐ Do not use tobacco.
- ☐ Have medical screenings regularly to detect potential problems early.
- ☐ Get second opinions.
- ☐ Question unnecessary tests and X-rays.
- ☐ Buy generic drugs at drug discounters.
- ☐ Review every hospital bill carefully and challenge any discrepancies.
- ☐ Keep good medical records.

- ☐ Own and read a medical guide.
- ☐ Prepare advance directives for your medical care with a living will and durable power of attorney.

Recreation and Entertainment and More

- ☐ Entertain with "potlucks" or inexpensive buffets.
- ☐ Use picnic facilities at parks.
- ☐ Cut recreation costs with activities and games at home.
- ☐ Take advantage of community services such as concerts, fairs, and public tennis courts.
- ☐ Take up less expensive sports and hobbies.
- ☐ Spend vacation camping, renting equipment and a tent or boat.
- ☐ Take advantage of low weekend rates at many city hotels and off-season rates at resorts.
- ☐ Read magazines and books from the library.
- ☐ Cancel book club memberships and magazine subscriptions.
- ☐ Take advantage of low-cost or free community educational opportunities.
- ☐ Maintain an easy-care hairstyle.
- ☐ Barter with skills such as word processing, child care, or yard work.
- ☐ Make gifts or give a gift of your own personal services.
- ☐ Buy gifts and holiday decorations for the next season on sale.
- ☐ Make fewer long distance calls and write more letters.
- ☐ Discontinue unnecessary phone services.

RESPONSIBILITY

In the Assessment and Alternatives sections of this unit, you have learned about the Walkers' expenses and the family's prospects for the challenging years ahead. You have completed your own net worth statement and income and expense statement to provide an overview of your own financial situation.

You should be able to make some definitive choices about your typical expenses and how you will manage them in the future. The Action Step is a handy tool to get these decisions underway, and the completed Action Step on the next page can serve as your model.

Personal Financial Planning

Action Step

On the Action Step, list expenditure-related decisions you want to attend to in the future. Remember that only you can get and keep a handle on how you allot and spend the money you have coming in. The actions you take now to manage your finances will have long-term repercussions for your fiscal future and that of your entire family. Remember also that the decisions made here can and should be reviewed and possibly revised in the years ahead. Use verbs — action words — to describe what you plan to do regarding your expenses.

When you believe your list is complete for the time being, rank your decisions in the right-hand column according to their importance to you, with number 1 being the most important. Use a second sheet of paper to continue your list if needed.

Expense Actions	Rank by Importance
Comparison-shop for groceries between neighborhood market and highway warehouse food store	1
Determine savings if I subscribed to newspapers/magazines instead of getting at newsstand	7
Figure out last year's costs of eating out in restaurants	2
Investigate refinancing home mortgage to lower monthly payments	4
Assess benefits of paying off car loan and credit card debt with home equity loan	5
Prepare household budget for first time ever	3
Make list of last year's "impulse" buys as example for future restraint	6

Personal Financial Planning

Action Step

On the Action Step, list expenditure-related decisions you want to attend to in the future. Remember that only you can get and keep a handle on how you allot and spend the money you have coming in. The actions you take now to manage your finances will have long-term repercussions for your fiscal future and that of your entire family. Remember also that the decisions made here can and should be reviewed and possibly revised in the years ahead. Use verbs — action words — to describe what you plan to do regarding your expenses.

When you believe your list is complete for the time being, rank your decisions in the right-hand column according to their importance to you, with number 1 being the most important. Use a second sheet of paper to continue your list if needed.

Expense Actions	Rank by Importance

PLANNING

The final step in taking control of your expenditures involves setting out step-by-step actions you will take to reach the goals you have listed on your Action Step. Your Master Action Plan is the end product of this unit on analyzing expenditures. It functions as your "to do" list for addressing your decisions on expenses.

You should list each of your Expense Actions from your Action Step as a Goal Statement on your MAP. Then decide on the logical sequence of actions that will take you to your desired goal result. You can use the sample Master Action Plan as a guide in completing your own MAP.

Master Action Plan

Goal Statement: *Comparison-shop for groceries*

Actions	Resources	Time Frame	By Whom?
1. Prepare shopping lists for week's groceries	Own and family input; pantry/refrigerator inventory	6 months	Self
2. Read newspaper grocery ads to make preliminary comparisons	Newspaper	6 months	Self
3. Shop for items at neighborhood market; jot down prices	Shopping list, checkbook	6 months	Self
4. Shop for items at warehouse store; jot down prices	Shopping list, checkbook	6 months	Self
5. Compare price lists from both/all sources	Price lists	6 months	Self
6. Weigh issues of convenience, time, price, atmosphere among sources	Price lists, shopping experience	6 months	Self
7. Decide which items to get at discount on a regular basis	Shopping experience, preferences	6 months	Self

Goal Statement: *Figure out last year's costs of eating out*

Actions	Resources	Time Frame	By Whom?
1. Review last year's charge receipts, credit card bills for restaurant tabs	Personal files	1 month	Self
2. Review last year's calendar/datebook for meals eaten out	Personal files	1 month	Self
3. Make list of dates/costs of meals in restaurants	Personal files	1 month	Self
4. Add up cost of meals; average by month over year	List, calculator	1 month	Self
5. Calculate frequency of meals out	List	1 month	Self
6. Weigh convenience, enjoyment, ambiance against price in deciding if I need to decrease meals out	Dining experiences; preferences	1 month	Self

Legal and Estate Planning

Legal and Estate Planning

At this time in your life, you may be looking at yourself, your lifestyle, and your environment. You are perhaps deciding on what you really want out of life. Uncovering the "real you" can be a great advantage to you as you tackle the difficult decisions that come with sorting out your legal affairs and planning your estate.

Your hard work and unique interests have allowed you to accumulate a lifetime of assets and possessions. Whether they are modest or extensive, you will want your home, your insurance, pension benefits, any savings, stocks, bonds, or other financial holdings, and your personal belongings to be distributed according to your wishes. Only you can make these wishes known, and the most secure and essential way of doing so is in writing. Although no one enjoys thinking about and planning for the distant future, no matter what your age you will experience a sense of relief once you have done so.

Your estate plan will reflect the particular details of your net worth, close relationships, and special causes. No one set of estate-planning tools applies to everyone. Professional guidance can help you choose from the many approaches that are available. Nor is estate planning a once-in-a-lifetime activity. You will want to review your plan regularly to make sure it still meets your needs and wishes.

You may have learned by this point in your life that you are your own best advocate, whether in daily life, medical matters, or legal affairs. Taking a proactive route to efficient and economical estate planning can protect your own interests and those of your loved ones. Keep yourself informed about current laws and various options for structuring your estate. Challenge your financial adviser or estate planner about any suggestions that make you uncomfortable or doubtful.

The future is still in your hands. It will rest easily there if you take carefully considered action on how your legacy will pass to your heirs and cherished associates.

Unit Objectives

- **Assessment:** To assess the dimensions of your total estate; collect the paperwork that verifies your personal, financial, and legal status; and identify the concerns you want to address in planning your estate

- **Alternatives:** To consider means of structuring your estate to best meet your needs and objectives in planning for the future

- **Responsibility:** To make decisions about your estate that will provide for your own future as well as that of your loved ones, remembering to seek professional advice and guidance in doing so

- **Planning:** To make specific plans to carry out your estate decisions, retaining the option to change such decisions as future events or situations warrant

What Do You Think?

The questions that follow will lead you into the many issues you may confront in planning your estate. The questions are individual in nature and more appropriate for personal consideration or discussion with family, friends, or other members of your support system.

1. Have you decided who will receive your property and when? Do you want to give money/property away during your lifetime or have it distributed after your death? Do you have an up-to-date will? What do you consider the best method of property distribution — will, trusts, payable-on-death accounts, something else?

2. Would you be able to maintain your current lifestyle without the income from a full-time job? Would your family be able to maintain this lifestyle if you were no longer on the scene? How can you improve future prospects in this regard?

3. Do you understand what the process of probate involves? Do you wish to help your heirs avoid probate in the event of your disability or death? Do you know how to arrange your legal and financial affairs to accomplish your objectives? Have you done so?

4. Do you know if your estate will be subject to federal estate taxes or to state inheritance or estate taxes? Do you know how to eliminate or minimize these and other levies on your estate? Have you taken the necessary steps to do so?

5. Are you familiar with the various ways in which title to property can be held? Do you know how you hold title to any property you own? Are you aware that the way in which you hold title can affect

your tax liability, eventual distribution of your property, and capital gains payments by your heirs and beneficiaries?

6. Have you made legal, medical, and financial arrangements in the event you become incapacitated? Have you considered how to prepare yourself and your loved ones for such a situation?

7. If you were to become disabled or die, could your spouse, partner, children, or other loved ones successfully manage your financial affairs or the assets you left them? Depending on your level of confidence in their abilities, how could you arrange for proper management of these funds?

For Your Information

Legal and estate planning for the future touches almost every aspect of your life. You will be assigning most of your roles as owner, caretaker, and manager to other parties and will be improving or ensuring their future financial security as a result. At the same time, you want to preserve your own rights to and benefits from your property and investments as long as you wish to retain them. You will need to study carefully, think long and hard, and consult with professional advisers who understand your proposed plans in this area. The subjects discussed here represent the kinds of concerns typically addressed in estate planning.

Family Considerations

You have already covered future sources of income, personal financial management, and investment strategies in the preceding units dealing with your financial affairs. Now you need to carry this knowledge and planning approach a few steps ahead into estate-planning activities. You have estimated your net worth, predictable income, and conceivable expenses. How do you use this information to develop an estate plan?

Your first concern will be for the immediate welfare of your family and other loved ones if something should happen to you. Pension and insurance benefits become payable upon your death to your assigned beneficiaries. Cash bank accounts that your spouse, partner, or other agent can access if you are incapacitated will ensure that mortgage, loan, and other payments are made as required. Contingency plans that can be put into effect if your income-producing ability is lost over an extended period should be part of every estate plan.

Keeping part of your assets liquid and easily accessible — that is, not tied up in property or other investments — is always a good idea. Your family and other loved ones could suffer sudden financial hardship along with grief if most of your estate were to pass to them only through your will. The probate court, which must be approached with an attorney, generally releases only a limited amount of funding for bare necessities in such situations.

Estate planning involves taking a realistic look at the money management capabilities of your spouse or partner, your children, or any other individuals to whom you plan to entrust the proceeds of your life's work. If you have a spouse or partner, *that person should be planning your estate with you* and you should discuss frankly any reservations either of you has about the other's aptitude for sound financial management.

The shape of your estate plan can help shape your children's lives and their subsequent estate plans as well. How much do you want to provide for them, now or in the future? How much can you afford to provide without cutting into your own comforts and security? You should answer these questions in your own mind, and then communicate your thinking to your children. Children who anticipate an inheritance that never materializes, or who did not expect one that does materialize, might shape their lives differently if they knew what to expect.

Why You Need to Plan

If you fail to make a will or specify by other means how you want your property to be distributed, state laws of intestate succession will govern its distribution. Laws vary from state to state. The following example shows how three jurisdictions may distribute property differently in the same factual situation. Here, a man has died without a will, leaving his elderly mother, his wife, and two children:

- In Washington, D.C., the spouse would receive one-third of her husband's estate, while the two children would share equally in the remaining two-thirds. The deceased's mother would receive nothing.

- In Maryland, if the children are adults, the spouse would receive one-half of the estate plus $15,000, while the two children would share equally in the remainder. If, however, one or both of the children are minors, the spouse would receive one-half of the estate and the children would receive the other half. In both situations the deceased's mother would receive nothing.

- In Virginia, the spouse would receive the entire estate as long as there are no children from a previous marriage. The deceased's mother would receive nothing.

Your state might have yet another way of distributing wealth.

Careful estate planning can ensure that your property and assets will be distributed as you wish them to be and with the least cost and aggravation to your heirs.

How Estate Taxes Work

Although most federal estate taxes have been phased out, the following tax liabilities are possible:

- The federal government levies a unified estate and gift tax on certain transfers of wealth between persons other than spouses.

- Some states levy an estate tax.

- Some states levy an inheritance tax, payable by the recipient.

- Although a cash inheritance is not subject to federal income taxes, income generated from investing the inheritance or profits generated from selling it for an amount greater than the value when it was inherited is taxable.

- Profits from the sale of inherited property or earnings generated from inherited property may be taxable as income.

The federal unified estate and gift tax is levied on "taxable transfers": money, real or personal property that a person has passed along either in the form of trusts and gifts while alive or through estate distribution after death. At the time of death, all assets of the deceased are valued at their present value for the purpose of determining tax liability.

You can make gifts of up to $10,000 per person per year to as many persons or organizations as you wish without having to pay federal gift taxes. If both spouses agree in writing to the gift, the annual tax-exempt limit per recipient is increased to $20,000.

Gifts of any amount between spouses are not taxable as long as the spouse receiving the gift is a U.S. citizen. A limited tax-free exclusion of $100,000 pertains to gifts to a spouse who is not a citizen of the United States. If you make gifts in excess of the tax-exempt allowances, the excess will be considered a taxable transfer and may be subject to tax.

The gross estate generally consists of all that the individual owned, plus all that was owed to him or her. From the gross estate are subtracted the debts of the deceased and expenses such as funeral and burial costs, charitable bequests, and the costs of administering the estate. The remainder is the taxable estate.

The amount of the taxable estate can be reduced by the marital deduction, which is that portion of the estate that is left, legally, to the surviving spouse. The marital deduction for bequests to a non-U.S. citizen spouse is limited to $100,000.

After the marital deduction, up to $600,000 of the remaining taxable estate will be offset by the estate tax credit. However, for estates in excess of $600,000 the estate tax is calculated on the value of the entire estate. A credit of $192,800 (the equivalent of the estate tax on $600,000 of assets) will be applied to reduce the tax.

Important: Tax laws are under constant review. Always get the latest information from a tax attorney or tax accountant.

THE AARP APPROACH
ASSESSMENT

What Would You Do?

The case studies that follow describe legal and estate-planning dilemmas that persons might face as they try to plan for the future. These individuals are trying to make decisions that will affect their futures and those of their loved ones.

None of the cases may reflect your life situation, but brainstorming options and solutions to the challenges that face other persons can bring unexpected clarity to your own plans for the years ahead. What would you do if you were in their positions? If you are reviewing Think of Your Future on your own, you may want to discuss these cases with close friends or family members. Group settings for future planning will use the studies for workshop sessions.

Joe Roberts and Ted Martinsen

Joe and Ted have been friends for many years and are now considering buying a house together. They have found an affordable property that is large enough to allow each of them his privacy. The old colonial they have selected will also be able to accommodate Ted's many brothers and sisters and Joe's two children when they come to visit.

The prospective owners will share equally in their down payment, monthly mortgage obligations, and maintenance and upkeep costs of the home. They must now decide how to take title to the house. Neither would want the other removed from the house at his death, but each has close family members who would be likely heirs.

What are Joe and Ted's options?

_____

_____

_____

_____

What are the advantages of each option?

_____

_____

What are the disadvantages of each option?

_____

_____

What do you think they should do? Why?

_____

_____

Agnes Whelan

Agnes has had a successful career as a real estate broker and property manager. She never married and has no children. Her only relatives are a brother and sister-in-law and their three children, who live in a distant state. Agnes has several close friends who have been her "family" over the years. She spends a good bit of her free time with programs that teach adults to read and in working with young people in Junior Achievement projects.

In thinking about her future, Agnes knows she should prepare a will. Her usual business efficiency seems to fail her in this area, however, and she is having trouble accepting that she will never be a wife and mother, that her professional satisfaction will one day come to an end, and that life does not go on forever. Agnes takes some consolation from the knowledge that her brother and his family would inherit her estate if she fails to act, but they would probably not be her choice for sole heirs.

What options are available to Agnes?

_____

_____

_____

_____

What are the advantages of each option?

_____

_____

What are the disadvantages of each option?

_____

_____

What do you think Agnes should do? Why?

_____

_____

Legal and Estate Planning

Diana and Paul Bender

The Benders, married for more than 30 years, have four children and live in a comfortable suburb of a large city. Paul Bender is the long-time manager of a retail chain store in the community. Diana has recently joined the advertising sales staff of the local newspaper. This job allows her the flexibility she needs to supervise the care of the Benders' disabled teenaged son, Rob, the sole survivor of a serious automobile accident.

Diana and Paul have always paid careful attention to their financial security and plans for the future. Their wills, made when all their children were minors, have guardianship provisions and funding to support them. Paul's employer offers a substantial pension plan, and the Benders have saved regularly. Rob's accident and the knowledge that he will need long-term care have now thrown the Benders into a quandary. How can they provide for him, yet be fair to their own futures and those of their three older, now-independent children?

What are the Benders' options?

What are the advantages of each option?

What are the disadvantages of each option?

What would be your recommendation to the Benders? Why?

Sally and Caleb Cyrus

Sally and Caleb Cyrus have assumed informal responsibility for the care of Caleb's elderly mother. At 85, Mrs. Cyrus is relatively healthy, but she lives alone, does not drive anymore, and is often forgetful. Caleb and Sally check in on her daily, do her weekly shopping, take her to doctor's appointments, and in general watch out for her welfare.

Caleb's brother Sam has recently separated from his wife and has gradually moved in with his mother. Sam is going through a difficult time and is not participating in his mother's care. Sally and Caleb have also become aware that Sam has borrowed money from his mother, who is not wealthy by any description and sometimes gets confused.

Sally and Caleb appreciate Sam's problems, but they also fear that Mrs. Cyrus may exhaust her savings in trying to help him. She may need custodial care herself in the future, and her only asset may be her home.

What are the Cyrus family's options?

What are the advantages of each option?

What are the disadvantages of each option?

What would be your recommendation to the family? Why?

The Assessment step in Legal and Estate Planning focuses on information gathering, assembling the necessary personal, financial, and legal paperwork that tells the story of your life. The Inventory of Important Papers that follows will help you accumulate these miscellaneous documents.

Your Legal Check-Up is an exercise that points out common situations and transactions in which you may need legal advice or assistance. Do You Need a Will? presents issues of concern that can be addressed by making out a will.

The last assessment tool, Your Legal Checkup, will help you to review contractual and other legal obligations that you already have and determine how they may affect your plans for the future.

Inventory of Important Papers

Depending on your personal situation, you may have some or all of the documents listed below and perhaps others. When you discuss your situation with your lawyer and/or other estate planning professionals, you may need to bring some of the following. Check the items that pertain to you and then list the location of each item.

Applies to You	Type of Important Paper/Document	Location
☐	Certified birth certificates for immediate family	_____
☐	Adoption papers	_____
☐	Marriage licenses	_____
☐	Social Security cards	_____
☐	Life Insurance policies	_____
☐	Prenuptial agreements	_____
☐	Postnuptial agreements	_____
☐	Divorce decrees	_____
☐	Current family budget	_____
☐	Net worth statement	_____
☐	Your (and your spouse or partner's) will	_____
☐	Your (and your spouse or partner's) living will or health care power of attorney	_____
☐	Disability income insurance policy	_____
☐	Personal property and casualty insurance policy	_____
☐	Deeds to property	_____
☐	Leases to property	_____
☐	Federal income tax returns (past three years)	_____
☐	State/local income tax returns	_____
☐	Itemized list of investments	_____
☐	Gift tax returns	_____
☐	Trust instruments	_____
☐	Employment contracts	_____
☐	Pension benefits statements	_____
☐	Stock certificates	_____
☐	Closed corporation charters, bylaws, minutes	_____
☐	Partnership agreements	_____
☐	Business buy-sell agreements	_____
☐	Business balance sheets	_____
☐	Business income tax returns	_____
☐	Business life insurance policy	_____
☐	Instructions for disposal of personal belongings at death	_____
☐	Business property and casualty insurance, auto insurance policies	_____
☐	Social Security earnings record	_____

If you choose to retire or otherwise change your lifestyle dramatically at some point in the future, your legal rights and obligations can become substantially more involved than they are now. Your margin for error in legal matters can also become narrower. Whatever you do, wherever you go, don't act or sign anything until you *stop*, *look*, *listen*, and *understand*.

In the legal inventory presented here, answer "yes" or "no" to the questions listed. Your answers will help guide you in the plans you are making now, as well as during the years ahead when you periodically review and revise your plans.

Legal Questions	*Yes*	*No*
1. Have you completed your will?	____	____
2. If you are married, has your spouse completed a will?	____	____
3. Have you (and your spouse) reviewed or revised your will(s) in the past five years?	____	____
4. Have you moved to another state since making your will?	____	____
5. Have you prepared last instructions for when you die?	____	____
6. Have you considered assigning health care power of attorney or making a living will?	____	____
7. Do you expect to sell your house?	____	____
8. Do you plan to buy another house or property?	____	____
9. Do you plan to lease or rent a house or an apartment?	____	____
10. Do you hold property in joint ownership?	____	____
11. Do you plan to establish a new business or partnership?	____	____
12. Do you plan to make any major purchases?	____	____
13. Do you plan a late or second marriage?	____	____
14. Do you plan to establish a trust fund?	____	____
15. Will you have power of attorney or be an executor for someone else?	____	____

Do You Need a Will?

Answer these questions by circling either "yes" or "no."

1. Do you want to distribute your property according to your personal wishes rather than according to state law?	Yes	No
2. Do you want to save money by reducing the cost of administration and estate taxes?	Yes	No
3. Do you want an executor who can serve without bond, thereby saving probate costs?	Yes	No
4. Do you want to make a special bequest — to a school, church, fraternal lodge, charity, or some particular person?	Yes	No
5. Do you want to make certain that your heirs can carry on your business without it being tied up in probate proceedings?	Yes	No
6. Do you want to provide for special distribution of your estate if you and your major heir die simultaneously in an accident?	Yes	No
7. Do you want to help ensure that the assets you leave behind will be properly managed and not wasted due to the heirs' grief, gullibility, excessive spending, or lack of financial expertise?	Yes	No
8. Do you want to make sure that your prized possessions (collectibles, jewelry, heirlooms, etc.) will go to persons who will appreciate them?	Yes	No

Note: If you answered "yes" to any of these questions, you should make a will. Your wishes will not be carried out unless you do. If you already have a will, is it up to date, reflecting your present situation? Does your spouse have a will?

Very likely, many of your legal concerns involve contracts that you have already signed. You should keep informed of your rights and obligations, since your future welfare can be affected by such knowledge or lack of it. Here are a number of common contractual and legal matters. Check the documents involved to determine exactly what your current status is. Guessing can prove costly.

1. **Mortgages** (on home or other property)

Does the lender have the right to increase your interest rate?	Yes	No
If you wish to pay off all or part of your mortgage early, do you know what, if any, prepayment penalty you will suffer?	Yes	No

2. **Lease** (on apartment or other property)

Do you have the right to renew when the present lease expires?	Yes	No
Is the length of the renewal lease established in your current lease?	Yes	No
Will the lease renew automatically unless you notify your landlord to the contrary?	Yes	No
Must you give the landlord notice of your intention to renew?	Yes	No
If so, do you know how far in advance of expiration of your lease?	Yes	No

3. **Condominiums**

Can your monthly maintenance fees be increased?	Yes	No
If so, do you know when and by how much?	Yes	No

4. **Safe deposit box**

Does your spouse, relative, or a trusted friend have access to your box should you become unable to act due to illness, incompetence, or distance from home?	Yes	No
Do you know if your state seals safe deposit boxes upon the death of one of the owners?	Yes	No

5. **Savings certificates** (certificates of deposit)

Do you have a record of their dates of maturity?	Yes	No
Will they automatically be renewed unless you give notice to the contrary?	Yes	No
If they are automatically renewed and you want your money before the new certificate has matured, do you know what penalty you will suffer?	Yes	No

continues

6. **Pension, profit-sharing, and Social Security benefits**

   Do you know what your legal rights are to claim benefits under any of these programs:

Pension?	Yes	No
Profit-sharing?	Yes	No
Social Security?	Yes	No

   Do you know how much you can expect to receive from each of these sources when you retire?

Pension	$_____	/month
Profit-sharing	$_____	/month
Social Security	$_____	/month

7. **Life insurance policies**

   Do you know your rights as described in the policies?

a. Can you cash in the policies?	Yes	No
b. Can you borrow against the policies?	Yes	No
c. Can you convert the policies to paid-up insurance?	Yes	No
d. Can you convert the policies to extended-term insurance?	Yes	No
e. If your policy is with your employer, can you continue the insurance when you are no longer employed with your employer?	Yes	No
f. If you can continue your insurance policy, do you remain a part of your former employer's group or are you considered an individual and thus may pay higher premiums?	Yes	No

8. **Health and accident insurance**

Will your group policies terminate when you retire?	Yes	No
Can you continue them by paying the premiums yourself?	Yes	No
Regarding your private policies, do you know until what age and to what extent you are covered?	Yes	No
If you are married, is your spouse covered?	Yes	No
Are your dependents covered?	Yes	No
Do your current policies offer any Medicare supplement provisions?	Yes	No

After completing your legal checkup, go back over the list to determine what subjects you need to investigate and do something about. Your legal well-being is up to you. It is better to try to avoid problems now, rather than have to retain an attorney later.

ALTERNATIVES

After you have determined where you are and what you want to accomplish, you can begin to evaluate your alternatives. No single approach is best for every situation. You will probably find that a combination of estate-planning devices is needed to achieve your desired results. As with all aspects of planning for the future, you should seek out additional information and take an active stance in shaping the years ahead. The Think of Your Future appendix includes publications, organizations, and other resources that may help you pursue certain topics in greater detail than this unit contains.

You should be mindful that federal and state laws are constantly changing and are subject to differing interpretations. Assistance from competent professionals is essential for this and many other reasons as you plan your estate. Professional advice will also help you keep your estate plan up to date as your needs and desires conceivably change in the future.

Your Estate Planning Team

Estate planning is a complex subject, and you should enlist experienced professional advisers to help you make sure that your needs and desires are met in the plan you develop. You will want to consider the services of an estate-planning attorney, a CPA/tax accountant, a financial planner, a life insurance agent knowledgeable in estate-planning concepts, or some combination of these specialists.

Estate-Planning Attorney. An attorney is the only person licensed to write legal documents. If your primary estate-planning concerns focus on drafting a will, creating a trust, using a trust to save on federal estate taxes, or drafting powers of attorney, you will have most need of an attorney. No one attorney is an authority in every aspect of the law, so you will want to find one whose practice specializes in estate planning.

Finding the right lawyer for you is an important exercise. The following suggestions may help in your search:

- Ask satisfied friends about their experiences with specific estate-planning attorneys.

- Ask business associates and other professional advisers like your accountant or financial planner for their recommendations.

- Contact your local bar association or other professional legal organization for a list of attorneys who practice in the area of estate planning.

- As a last resort, check the yellow pages of your telephone directory for a list of lawyers by area of specialization.

- Interview one or more attorneys to be sure you feel comfortable with and are confident in the person you select. Most attorneys offer a free initial consultation, but you will want to determine this beforehand. You will also want to find out the lawyer's fee schedule, payment expectations, and other aspects of the arrangement. You should discuss your preliminary goals and objectives at this first meeting to determine whether the lawyer being interviewed is compatible with your needs.

CPA/Tax Accountant. A tax expert may be the primary professional adviser you need if your main concern is with taxes. This subject would include determining income taxes, figuring estate or state death tax liability, exploring the advantages of tax-deferred investments, and calculating your tax basis on the sale of appreciated assets.

Financial Planner. A financial planner may be able to help you investigate pension and other financial issues, suitable types of investments for your situation, expected pension income/survivorship features, and other matters.

While some financial planners charge a set fee for their services, others earn their living from commissions on the sale of stocks, bonds, mutual funds, insurance, and other financial products. Set fees may range from $500 to more than $5,000 for a master financial plan. Some financial planners will give advice on specific financial concerns, charging hourly fees from $50 to $150 or more.

You need to exercise great care in selecting a financial planner. As a professional field, financial planning is virtually unregulated. Anyone can be called a financial planner regardless of qualifications. You can be in serious trouble if you allow an unscrupulous financial planner to make financial decisions for you.

Although working with a person who has credentials does not guarantee your satisfaction, such information can help you select a financial planner. The following organizations can tell you about the credentials of any financial planner you are considering:

■ American Association of Financial
   Professionals
   P.O. Box 1928
   Cocoa, FL 32923
   305-632-8654

■ Institute of Certified Financial Planners
   Two Denver Highland
   10065 East Harvard Avenue
   Suite 320
   Denver, CO 80231
   303-751-7600

■ International Board of Standards
   and Practices for Certified Financial
   Planners, Inc.
   1660 Lincoln Street
   Suite 3050
   Denver, CO 80264
   303-830-7543

■ International Association for
   Financial Planning
   Two Concourse Parkway
   Suite 800
   Atlanta, GA 30328
   404-395-1605

■ American Society of CLU & ChFC
   270 South Bryn Mawr Avenue
   Bryn Mawr, PA 19010-2195
   215-526-2500

Insurance Agent. A qualified insurance agent who is familiar with estate-planning concepts can help you in matters involving life insurance, disability coverage, and other concerns.

In working with your professional advisers, you will want to remind yourself that the estate plan you are developing is your responsibility and that your and your family's futures are at stake. Regardless of how competent, convincing, and thorough your experts may be, you need to make the decisions on which they operate.

A Will Shows the Way

Your will is the keystone of your estate plan. This legal document, when properly prepared, witnessed, and signed, makes sure that the courts will respect your wishes. A will directs how you want to distribute your assets. If you die without a will (intestate), the state in which you had your principal residence at the time of your death will determine how your assets will be distributed — perhaps against your wishes.

A will also can:

- Name guardians for your minor children.

- Designate a personal representative and alternates to manage and settle your estate according to the instructions you set out in your will. (This personal representative may be a bank or trust company as well as a person.)

- Allow you to choose who inherits or does not inherit your estate. It should be recognized that a surviving spouse has a legal interest to a portion of the deceased spouse's property. This right normally cannot be defeated by a will.

- Distribute your property under probate court supervision.

- Establish a testamentary trust.

When a person dies intestate, the court appoints an administrator to oversee and manage the affairs of the estate. The administrator's duties can include distribution of assets and naming of guardians for children or the elderly. The administrator is someone of the court's choosing, not yours. The court may require the administrator to be bonded to ensure proper performance of the duties. The price of the bond, plus the administrator's fees and other legal fees, can cost your estate dearly — as much as 5–10 percent of your probated assets.

On the other hand, when a person draws up a will, he or she names an executor (in some states, called a "personal representative") to carry out the responsibilities of estate settlement. The executor and guardian is someone you choose, and you may elect to have him or her serve without bond. Powers granted to the executor (such as the right to sell property) can ease the processing of estate matters and minimize court appearances and costs.

The duties of an executor can be extensive, especially if the estate is complex. Choose an executor with care, making certain the person you choose is both willing and able to serve. It is sometimes wise to designate co-executors: an individual or individuals in whom you have personal trust and a bank or an attorney with the needed legal and financial expertise.

To be valid, a will must comply strictly with every requirement of the law of your state. This includes the language, the way it is signed, and the number of witnesses (two in some states, three in others).

A Will for Each Spouse

If you are married, both you and your spouse need to draw up valid wills, because both of you own property: your home, cars, personal goods. Even if one of you has a will, this will not eliminate potential problems. For example, a husband and wife are in a car accident. The husband dies instantly, leaving everything to his wife. She dies several days later without a will. Her estate will be distributed according to state intestacy law. If the couple has no children, the estate will probably go to the wife's relatives.

Hazards of Do-It-Yourself Wills

Don't attempt a do-it-yourself will, either one you write yourself (holographic) or a printed form. Only about half the states recognize "homemade" wills, and many such wills contain imprecise language that breeds misunderstanding. A close family member who has been disinherited may be able to successfully attack a homemade will in court and have the entire document declared invalid. The estate might thus end up being distributed according to the laws of intestacy, with the heirs the deceased intended receiving little or no portion of the estate.

The cost of having a lawyer prepare a simple will need not be high. In terms of peace of mind alone, it may be well worth the investment.

The "Proving" of a Will

Except for jointly owned property passing to the survivor, life insurance proceeds payable to named beneficiaries, qualified plans like IRAs and pension plans with named beneficiaries, U.S. Savings Bonds with designated beneficiaries, and certain trusts, all the belongings of the deceased are subject to a process known as probate. Probate means to "prove" the will — to prove that the document bearing your signature is a genuine statement of how you wish your estate distributed.

In the probate process, the survivors may have to go to probate court (also called "orphans" or "surrogate" court) to present the will. Witnesses may be called in to testify to the will's execution, and the executor must satisfy the court that all bills have been paid, that state and federal death taxes (if any) have been paid, and that creditors of the estate have been notified and given an opportunity to present their claims.

Once the probate procedure has begun, the court may grant the survivors an allowance drawn from the assets of the estate. Beyond that, assets, including savings accounts and safe deposit boxes, may be frozen until the probate process is completed; this could take a year or more. Only after all outstanding bills are paid and the executor has satisfied the court that all other costs and taxes have been settled can final distribution of the estate be made to the heirs.

You can't "beat" probate unless you don't leave an estate or unless you have distributed your assets while alive through a trust set up in conjunction with your spouse. Even joint ownership does not always exclude assets from probate. Probate costs money for attorney's fees, appraiser's fees, court costs for filing papers, and bonding fees (unless the executor is authorized to serve without bond). Added to these expenses are any federal and state estate taxes that are not an actual part of probate costs.

Many states levy estate taxes, which are paid from the proceeds of the assets of the deceased. Some states levy inheritance taxes, which are paid by the recipient of the inheritance.

Estate Planning Checkups

Once you have made a will, don't put it away and forget about it. Review it from time to time to make sure that a revision of tax laws or a change in your status or the status of your assets or heirs will not affect the terms of your will. For instance, you may need to modify your will if you can answer "yes" to any of these questions.

- Have you been married, divorced, separated, or remarried? Has your spouse died?
- Have any of the beneficiaries died?
- Are there any new additions to your family or the families of your heirs?
- Has your executor died or moved away?
- Have you changed residency? (Your will should conform to the laws of the state in which you hold legal residency.)
- Have there been any changes in federal or state laws that might affect your will?
- Have your assets increased or diminished? If you have specified a certain sum to a beneficiary, will there be enough money to cover the bequest?

(You may want to make any bequests as percentages of the total.)

■ Have you changed your mind about any of the beneficiaries? (In some states, if you fail to mention an heir, that heir may still be entitled to a share.)

Where Should You Keep Your Will?

People have stored wills behind paintings and under rugs. Unfortunately, if the originally executed document can't be found, the court may decide that you destroyed it, intending to revoke it. You may want to have your lawyer keep the original, although you do not *have* to give him the original will or even a copy. Keep a copy in your safe deposit box, or leave a copy with a relative. *Do not put the original in a safe deposit box.* Some states require that a safe deposit box be sealed at the renter's death.

Property Ownership

The manner in which you hold title to real estate, bank accounts, stocks and bonds, life insurance policies, pension plans, and other property plays a critical part in your overall estate plan. The kind of title you hold to property can have a dramatic impact on your entire estate planning process. Failing to understand this is one of the most common and most serious obstacles to successful planning for the future.

Five ways of holding title to assets are available: fee simple, joint tenancy with rights of survivorship, tenancy by the entirety, tenancy in common, and community property. Each method is appropriate to certain situations and protects your interests in those situations.

Fee Simple. Fee simple means you own the asset by yourself. You can sell the property or give it away without anyone else's consent. You can distribute the

property after your death to your beneficiaries in a will, provided you recognize a spouse's marital interest; otherwise, the spouse may have a portion of the will set aside. If you do not have a will, the property will go to your heirs-at-law as specified by state law.

Joint Tenancy with Rights of Survivorship (JTWROS). Joint tenancy with rights of survivorship means you own an equal share of the property with one or more other persons. At your death, your ownership share in the property will automatically pass to the other surviving owner or owners of the property, *even if you have specified otherwise in a will or living trust.*

Tenancy by the Entirety. This form of joint ownership is limited to husbands and wives and is sometimes further restricted to real estate. Neither spouse can act alone in disposing of the property.

Tenancy in Common. Two or more persons own shares in the property. When one dies, that share passes directly to his or her heirs, not to the other tenant. You can sell or give away your share independently of the other owners. At your death, your share of the property is disposed of according to the terms of your will. *If a married couple hold property as tenants in common, the surviving spouse does not automatically receive the other spouse's share at death.* The deceased person's percentage must go through probate, even if it is willed to the surviving spouse. Persons with children from previous marriages often use this form of title to ensure that property passes as they intended.

Community Property. The nine community property states — Arizona, California, Idaho, Louisiana, Nevada, New Mexico, Texas, Washington, and Wisconsin — treat the property of married couples differently from the other 41 states. Property accumulated during a marriage is considered community property, with each spouse owning an equal, one-half interest. In these states, property held before marriage and gifts or inheritances received individually after marriage are regarded as separately owned property.

Trusts

A trust provides you with an opportunity to dispose of or manage assets, including property. Basically a trust offers a plan by which a trustee (often a bank) holds your assets for your own benefit or that of your beneficiaries, paying the money at the time and in the manner you specify in written instructions.

For example, you may want to transfer $30,000 to one of your children, but you are concerned that the child might not handle the money prudently. If you want to pass that money along now, not later, you can do so with a trust. You might instruct the trustee to pay income from the fund to your child annually or in a lump sum at a stated time (such as when the child reaches a certain age or upon your death). The trustee receives a fee, and you receive the satisfaction of knowing that the matter will be handled properly.

Trusts can be living or testamentary, revocable or irrevocable. A *living trust* is set up and takes effect while the parties are still alive. A *testamentary trust* is created by will and goes into effect upon your death. For example, your life insurance proceeds could flow into a trust fund upon your death and subsequently be managed by a trustee. A *revocable trust* can be canceled by the person who established it, while an *irrevocable trust* cannot be canceled.

Trusts are not for everyone. Your estate should be large enough to justify the payment of trust management fees.

Furthermore, the initial costs of establishing certain kinds of trusts can be substantial. The offsetting benefits should be discussed in detail with your attorney and the trust officer of your bank or your financial adviser before you take action.

Planning for Incapacity

Your legal and estate-planning activities should also focus on the uncomfortable topic of your own possible future incapacity. Medical and technological advances have led to increased life expectancies and to corresponding increases in the possibility of being alive but incapacitated. While you are fully functioning is the time to make the decisions that will guide you and your loved ones through a period of your incapacity in the future.

Powers of Attorney

A power of attorney is a legal document in which you, the principal, give another person, your agent or attorney-in-fact, legal authority to act for you in matters as simple as writing or endorsing checks or as complex as selling real estate. It can be an especially valuable tool for single persons in the event of extended disability. A power of attorney can be given to anyone you choose, not just to a lawyer, but a lawyer should definitely draw up the documents.

Limited power of attorney allows you to authorize another to act in your stead for a limited period of time or in certain capacities. A *general* power of attorney, which gives the designated person authority to do whatever you can do, should be considered extremely carefully and used only sparingly. Both general and limited powers of attorney terminate upon your incapacity or death.

Creating a *durable* power of attorney enables you to authorize your named agent to continue to act for you in the event of your incapacity. The durable power of attorney, which terminates at your death, can take effect immediately upon signing or can be designed to go into effect upon your incapacity.

Durable powers of attorney generally cover two important areas — finances and health care. A financial durable power of attorney allows your agent to receive your income, pay your bills, manage your property, and handle other financial affairs when you are unable to do so. A health care or medical durable power of attorney, which ideally should be a separate document, charges your agent with making medical decisions for you when you cannot do so yourself. You specify the terms under which both kinds of power would be implemented by your chosen agents.

Advantages of durable powers of attorney include the following:

■ They protect you if you are incapacitated.

■ They are relatively inexpensive and easy to understand.

■ They avoid the necessity of your loved ones' having to petition the probate court to appoint a guardian/conservator to handle your affairs if you are incapacitated.

■ They do not require you to transfer title of your assets.

■ They may be revoked by you in writing unless you are incapacitated.

■ They normally do not have to be filed with any court or government agency.

A Living Will

With the growth of medical technology, a document known as a "living will" is growing in popularity. A living will is a written statement of your wishes regarding the use of any medical treatments you specify. The statement is to be followed if you are unable to provide instructions at the time medical decisions need to be made. This type of will must be signed and dated before two witnesses to ensure that it was signed of the individual's free will, not under pressure. The living will is a document separate from your regular will; it does not involve disposition of your property.

Living wills have been recognized by law in most states, but they are commonly limited to decisions about "life-sustaining procedures" in the event of terminal illness. A durable health care power of attorney is different from and more flexible than a living will in three important ways:

1. A health care power of attorney *establishes a person to act as your agent* if you cannot act, but a living will does not. The advantage of appointing an agent is that, at the time a decision needs to be made, your agent can participate in discussions and weigh the pros and cons of treatment decisions in accordance with your wishes.

2. The health care power of attorney *applies to all medical decisions*, unless you decide to include limitations. The living will normally applies only to particular decisions near the end of your life.

3. The health care power of attorney *can include specific instructions* to your agent about any treatment you want done or want to avoid or about whatever issues you care about most.

In theory, it makes sense to combine the living will and health care power of attorney in one document. However, you will need to be sure that state laws regarding the contents or formalities for signing the two documents are compatible.

Special Considerations in Estate Planning

Guardians for Your Children. If you have minor children or disabled offspring who will be unable to care for themselves in adulthood, you will need to make appointing a guardian for them an important part of your planning. Selecting someone who would pass on your moral, spiritual, educational, and financial values and ethics to your children in your absence will be critical.

The person or persons you are considering for guardianship must be willing to accept this responsibility and must understand what you expect of them if such a situation comes to pass. Your children's future and your peace of mind can depend on a wise choice in this matter. Because a guardian would raise your children until they reach the age of majority, you may want to name a succession of guardians — especially if your children are young — in the event of the death or disability of a designated guardian.

Many parents like to name a couple as co-guardians. As a practical matter, this could create an awkward situation if the couple divorced or circumstances changed in some other way. Assigning custody of your children to one or the other co-guardian could place both them and the co-guardians you selected in a difficult situation. A similar crisis could occur if one of the co-guardians died. You will want to consider your alternatives carefully before you make this decision.

Entering a Second Marriage. If you marry late in life or for a second time, your present heirs and your new spouse might be concerned as to how the marriage will affect their inheritance. One way of settling such

matters may be to draw up a prenuptial agreement. A prenuptial agreement is a written contract entered into by prospective spouses before their marriage that spells out how assets are to be dealt with during and after the marriage. Such an agreement can spell out precisely who owns what and can also allay the concerns of children of previous marriages. It prevents a spouse from successfully challenging your will or any existing trusts and protects the inheritance of your children from a previous marriage. Prenuptial agreements are preferable to contracts made after marriage, which receive varying recognition in different states. Both types of agreement have complicated requirements, and you should seek legal assistance in drawing up whichever type you choose.

For the best protection of all concerned, both parties to a prenuptial agreement should be represented by separate legal counsel, and a full disclosure of each party's financial status should be made to the other party. Lacking these precautions, a disgruntled party could more easily challenge and upset a prenuptial agreement at a later date.

Other Legal Considerations

While most of this section has been concerned with estate planning, there are many other activities and situations that require some understanding of the law. Even if you think you know the specific laws that apply to your situation, you might wish to ask a lawyer's help in interpreting and applying the law properly. Following are some common and not-so-common situations that have legal ramifications.

Making a Contract. The most common legal involvement for most people concerns contracts. A contract is made when (1) someone makes an offer and (2) someone else accepts. For a contract to be enforceable, the participants must agree to exchange something of value — money for services, for example. The details of that agreement are usually spelled out in a written, typed, or printed document.

When you sign a contract, your legal rights and obligations become firmly established. Contracts can include insurance policies (life, health, annuity, property, auto); banking arrangements (savings and checking accounts, safe deposit boxes, loans, savings certificates); charge accounts and credit cards; and agreements to buy, sell, or lease property.

Under the laws of most states, the following types of contracts must be in writing to be fully and legally binding on both parties:

■ A contract extending for more than one year (such as dance lessons for 15 months) or one that is lifelong (such as lifetime support for someone).

■ An agreement made in preparation for marriage (a prenuptial agreement).

■ A loan contract with a bank or finance company.

■ An agreement to establish a trust or an agreement conveying or assigning a trust in personal property.

■ An agreement to employ the services of a real estate agent.

■ Any contract for the assignment of a life, health, or accident policy or a promise to name someone beneficiary of such.

■ A contract to sell any interest in real property or to lease it for more than a year.

Never sign a contract without filling in or crossing out the blanks. (In some states an installment contract with blank spaces is illegal.) A form can be changed after it has been filled out, provided that both parties agree to such a change. If a contract is altered, both parties should initial the changes made on the form.

Caring for an Ill or Incompetent Person. If you have a relative or friend who is unable to handle personal affairs because of illness, injury, mental weakness, intemperance, or drug addiction, you may petition the court to appoint you as a "guardian" or "conservator." Different state laws set forth specific rights and duties and define how one might qualify for either a guardianship (for a child) or a conservatorship (for an adult).

Depending on the circumstances, your duties and obligations may include handling the financial affairs as well as the personal needs of the individual. Considerable responsibility may be involved. Your decision to care legally for another should not be made until all legal and personal ramifications are totally understood. Conservatorship and guardianship end when the ward regains the ability to handle his or her personal affairs or dies.

Another way to help relatives or friends is to have them sign legal documents (drafted by a lawyer) that allow you to act as an agent in certain matters. A special power of attorney limits you to one specific purpose; a general power of attorney authorizes you to transact business in general for the person.

Setting Up a Business. If you establish a small or at-home business, you might be affected by several local laws — zoning restrictions, licensing fees, labeling and food laws — as well as federal laws, particularly federal tax laws. Your lawyer can help you interpret these laws and explain how they apply to you.

Disposing of Business Interests. If you own interest in a business, planning for the management and disposition of your share of that business is a vital part of your legal and estate planning. You will need to resolve several issues, whether you are a sole proprietor, a partner in a partnership, or a shareholder in a corporation.

A *buy-sell agreement* can provide for a smooth transfer of a business owned by more than one individual when an owner leaves the company, becomes disabled, or dies. You can enter into such an agreement with a co-owner or partner in your business to buy your share if you are no longer involved for any of the reasons given. You may make the agreement reciprocal, with your taking on the co-owner or partner's share for similar reasons. Life insurance or other liquid assets should be available to fund the agreement.

Obtaining Consumer Credit. Learn what your rights are when you finance the purchase of expensive items such as cars, major appliances, or furniture. Usually, the seller will retain a security interest in that property if the buyer defaults in payment. In other words, the seller may be able to take back the goods if you don't meet your payment obligations.

Most states have adopted, with some variations, the Uniform Commercial Code. This code sets forth the rights of both seller and buyer by which the seller retains a security interest in property purchased on time. In most cases the lender, banker, or merchant should be able to give you an adequate explanation of your obligations and rights. If you have any unanswered questions, however, you will want to consult an attorney.

The U.S. Congress has passed a number of laws designed to protect consumers, some of them designed especially to protect women. The *Equal Credit Opportunities Act* (ECOA) requires that a woman be given equal footing with a man (income and credit history being equal) when she is considered for creditworthiness. The law also prohibits an individual's being denied credit because of race, religion, or national origin.

In addition to several provisions enabling married women to establish credit histories in their own names, the law contains two other important provisions. First, your creditors cannot terminate your credit automatically should you become divorced, separated, or widowed. (They can, however, ask you to reapply for credit.) Second, if you are nearing retirement, the law says creditors cannot take away your credit cards when you turn 62, as some credit card companies have done in the past.

If for any reason you are denied credit and feel you are being discriminated against when you apply for a mortgage or car loan or want to purchase a major appliance, here are some steps you can take.

The *Truth in Lending Law* requires lenders and others who extend credit to quote all financing costs in terms of annual percentage rate (APR). This is true for almost all common financing transactions. Prior to enactment of this law, interest costs were quoted in a variety of ways, so that it was difficult to compare them. When you shop for a loan, be sure rates are being quoted in terms of APR if you want to keep borrowing costs as low as possible.

The Truth in Lending Law also offers protection to parties signing loan papers. In some cases borrowers now have the right to cancel a contract. In other words, if you sign the papers and then want to back out, you can do so if you take appropriate action within three days.

The *Fair Credit Reporting Act* gives you the right to examine your credit history. If you find that erroneous or misleading information appears in your file, the law sets forth the steps you can take to correct these mistakes. A glance at your credit file every two or three years is wise. Errors may sneak in, and a credit file with "bad marks" on it can weaken your credit record. The Think of Your Future appendix can assist you in contacting a credit bureau.

The *Fair Credit Billing Law* allows you to stop a creditor's demands for payment if you have a valid objection to your bill. Certain steps for accomplishing this are prescribed by law. Firms that bill you for credit accounts (credit card companies, department stores, etc.) are required to provide you with copies of the law from time to time.

Remember, your rights are set forth in these laws, but it's up to you to pursue them. Also keep in mind that asserting your rights successfully often hinges on acting promptly.

Establishing a Credit History. Establishing credit is not difficult for most people with a record of steady employment and prompt payment of debts. But what about the single individual — a widowed or divorced person who has to start from scratch to establish a credit rating? Here are some suggestions.

If you have a steady job, ask your employer to put in a good word for you with the creditor. (The Equal Credit Opportunity Act eliminates the need for anyone to co-sign your transaction.) Another alternative is to open several charge accounts with local department stores and pay your bills on time. The best method for establishing credit reliability, however, is to borrow $500 or so from a bank or finance company and pay it back on time. Put your borrowed money in a savings account. This method will cost you a modest sum in interest payments, but it will provide you with a solid recommendation for future borrowing.

RESPONSIBILITY

Confronting the many choices and challenges that appear when you open the subject of legal and estate planning should illustrate that you are responsible for the consequences of the decisions you make or do not make. You may have realized this fact at other times in your life, but when your own future welfare and the financial and emotional legacy of your loved ones are at stake, responsibility takes on new significance. At this point in your planning for the future, you cannot escape the effects of your own actions or inactions on yourself and your family or other cherished individuals. Even the decision to seek help in attaining your legal and estate-planning objectives resides with you.

You should now be ready to proceed to the Action Step to make some personal decisions about your legal affairs and your estate plan. You may want to use the completed Action Step on the next page as a model to help in your deliberations. Then proceed to complete your own Action Step.

Action Step

Example

On the Action Step, list any and all legal matters or estate-planning decisions you want to attend to in the future. Remember that these activities have significant importance to your own personal welfare and peace of mind, as well as to the future well-being of your loved ones. Also remember that the decisions involved can and should be reviewed and revised if necessary over the years ahead. Use verbs — action words — to describe what you plan to do regarding legal and estate-planning matters.

When you believe your list is complete for the time being, rank your decisions in the right-hand column according to their importance to you, with number 1 being the most important. Use a second sheet of paper to continue your list if needed.

Legal/Estate Actions	Rank by Importance
Make a new will	4
Decide on guardian for minor children	1
Review insurance coverage and beneficiaries to be sure that they are adequate and appropriate	5
Review property titles held or shared. Do they suit our estate plans?	6
Investigate making a living will; if decide to do so, draw one up and sign it	2
Designate specific possessions to go to specific heirs and add to my will	7
Decide on best persons to serve as executor of my will and to receive durable power of attorney in case I am disabled or incapacitated	3

Action Step

On the Action Step, list any and all legal matters or estate-planning decisions you want to attend to in the future. Remember that these activities have significant importance to your own personal welfare and peace of mind, as well as to the future well-being of your loved ones. Also remember that the decisions involved can and should be reviewed and revised if necessary over the years ahead. Use verbs — action words — to describe what you plan to do regarding legal and estate-planning matters.

When you believe your list is complete for the time being, rank your decisions in the right-hand column according to their importance to you, with number 1 being the most important. Use a second sheet of paper to continue your list if needed.

Legal/Estate Actions	Rank by Importance

Confronting your mortality head-on is the essence of legal and estate planning activities. This unit is, for this reason, perhaps the most difficult to complete in the Think of Your Future program. Having completed it, however, you will be free of the nagging need to get your affairs in order. Your affairs will be in order, and you will have a baseline plan to come back to and adjust in the future if you so desire.

The final step in this process involves determining step-by-step actions you will take to fulfill the goals you have listed on your Action Step. Your Master Action Plan is the end product of this unit. It functions as your "to do" list for addressing your legal and estate planning decisions.

You should list each of your Legal/Estate Actions from your Action Step as a Goal Statement on your MAP. Then follow through with the appropriate sequence of steps that will bring you to your desired goal result. You can review the sample Master Action Plan to help you complete your own MAP.

Master Action Plan

Example

Goal Statement: *Decide on guardian for minor children*

Actions	Resources	Time Frame	By Whom?
1. Read up on guardianship, minor children's needs	Library, bookstores, attorney's/advisor's recommendations	1 month	Self and spouse
2. Review own children's needs	Observation of and interaction with own family, environment, lifestyle	6 months	Self and spouse
3. Review possible candidates for guardian	Family members, close friends	6 months	Self and spouse
4. Approach person(s) selected for their approval, input	Family members, close friends	6 months	Self and spouse
5. Decide on willing/ suitable person(s)	Family members, close friends	6 months	Self and spouse

Goal Statement: *Consider living will; prepare it*

Actions	Resources	Time Frame	By Whom?
1. Read up on living wills; get sample	Library, bookstores, family doctor	6 months	Self
2. Discuss with doctor	Doctor, materials read on subject	6 months	Self
3. Discuss with family, close friends	Spouse, children, friends, reference materials read	6 months	Self
4. List pros/cons of living will vs. health care power of attorney	Doctor, lawyer, input from family/friends	1 week	Self
5. Draft the document	Lawyer, materials read	1 week	Self
6. Decide about finalizing and signing document	Lawyer, materials read	1 week	Self
7. Give copies of completed document to doctor, spouse, close friend		1 day	Self

Appendix

Appendix

General Resources

Books

Complete Retirement Workshop. Bureau of Business Practice Editorial Staff. Englewood Cliffs: Prentice Hall, 1993. Comprehensive planning guide that includes financial matters, housing, health, second career, and family matters.

How to Plan for a Secure Retirement. Barry Dickman, Trudy Liberman, and Consumer Reports Books. Yonkers: Consumer Reports Books, 1992. Provides an easy-to-understand reference to retirement planning, focusing on four major areas: income, health care, housing, and estate planning.

Prime Time: How to Enjoy the Best Years of Your Life. Loren Dunton. Hawthorne: Career Press, 1992. Presents a guide to enjoying the "prime time" of life — the years following age 50.

It's Your Future: Midlife and Preretirement Planning. Mary Jo Brzezinski and R. N. Garnitz. Brookfield: International Foundation of Employee Benefit Plans, 1992. Presents an illustrated guide to midlife and preretirement planning.

From Work to Retirement. Marion E. Haynes. Los Altos: Crisp Publications, 1993. A guide to making the transition from work to retirement, including the use of time in retirement, health concerns, and emotional well being.

Retiring on Your Own Terms. James W. Ellison, Doris Reardon, Michael L. Freedman, Herbert Mayo, and Robert F. Palmerton. New York: Crown Publishers, Inc., 1989. A handbook for maintaining financial independence, personal well-being, and health during retirement. Contains numerous retirement planning worksheets.

Pamphlets

A single copy of the following AARP publications is available free. Write to AARP Fulfillment, 601 E Street, N.W., Washington, DC 20049. Specify title and stock number.

Planning Your Retirement (D12322). Provides suggestions on role adjustments, lifestyles, fitness, use of time, working options, housing, financial security, legal affairs, and estate planning.

Focus Your Future: A Woman's Guide to Retirement Planning (D14559). Emphasizes issues of importance to women such as caregiving, in addition to health, financial, legal, and housing options.

A Single Person's Guide to Retirement Planning (D14185). Topics for persons who are widowed, divorced, or who have always been single include establishing a personal support network, planning for extra time in retirement, health, housing, finances, and legal planning.

Organizations

American Association of Retired Persons. 601 E Street, N.W., Washington, DC 20049. A nonprofit membership organization that helps preretired and retired persons age 50 and older make their future years rewarding. It serves their interests through legislative advocacy, research, informative programs, and community services.

Local councils on aging. Many communities have local councils or offices on aging that list local services. Check your telephone directory or call the operator for information and referral service.

State Agencies on Aging, located in state capitals, dispense information about retiring in a specific state. Check your telephone directory.

National Council on the Aging. 600 Maryland Avenue, S.W., West Wing 100, Washington, DC 20024, (202) 479-1200. Conducts and sponsors research and publishes reports on all aspects of aging. Ask for publications list.

National Council of Senior Citizens. 925 15th Street, N.W., Washington, DC 20005, (202) 347-8800. Legislative advocacy organization, with autonomous affiliated clubs throughout the United States. Monthly newspaper reports on activities.

Gray Panthers. National Office, 311 South Juniper Street, Philadelphia, PA 19107, (215) 545-6555. Through 100 local chapters, maintains and inspires pride in being "older." Publishes quarterly newspaper (subscription).

Personal Resources

Books

Beyond Success: How Volunteer Service Can Help You Begin Making a Life Instead of Just Making a Living. John F. and Eleanor Raynolds. New York: Master Media Limited, 1988. A guide to gaining personal satisfaction through volunteer service.

Retirement Careers: Combining the Best of Work and Leisure. Delos L. Marsh. Charlotte, VT: Williamson Publishing Company, 1991. A guide to help the retired person identify, select, and enter a compatible retirement career.

Senior Citizen's Guide to Starting a Part-Time, Home-Based Business. Judy Kerr. Babylon, NY: Pilot Industries, 1992. A guide, in pamphlet form, to starting a part-time, home-based business.

Starting a Mini-Business. Nancy Olsen. Sunnyvale, CA: Bear Flag Books, 1988. Information on how to assess your entrepreneurial qualities, analyze your marketable skills, examine business and economic trends, secure capital, and prepare a business plan.

What Color Is Your Parachute? Richard N. Bolles. Berkeley: Ten Speed Press, 1994. Describes the innovative job search and includes exercises.

Cracking the Over-50 Job Market. Robert J. Connor. New York: Plume, 1992. A job-seeking guide for persons aged 50 and older.

Bed and Breakfast/Country Inns. Old Saybrook, CT: Globe-Pequot Press. (800) 233-6490. Publishes listings of bed and breakfasts and country inns.

Travel Guides by Mobil, Fodor, Frommer, and others are available in bookstores.

Pamphlets

A single copy of the following AARP pamphlets is available free. Write to AARP Fulfillment, 601 E Street, N.W., Washington, DC 20049. Specify title and stock number. Allow four to six weeks for delivery.

To Serve, Not to Be Served (D12028). Tells where to find meaningful volunteer opportunities.

AARP Volunteer Talent Bank Volunteer Brochure (D12329). Computerized volunteer-to-position matching system matches volunteers with AARP programs and those of other select organizations.

A *Winning Resume* (D13961). A summary of general resume skills with special tips for older job seekers.

The First Step (D15084). A booklet for persons who want to start their own business. Outlines major issues to be considered.

Working Options: How to Plan Your Job Search, Your Work Life (D12403). Information on assessing skills, strengthening resumes, interviewing, networking, and setting employment goals.

The following government publications are available through the Consumer Information Center-V, P.O. Box 100, Pueblo, CO 81002:

Starting and Managing a Business from Your Home (146R). $1.75. Gives information about starting a business.

Opportunities in Franchising (173R). $1.00. Helps readers learn about franchise businesses and how to start one.

Your Trip Abroad (#189N). $1.00. Provides tips on international travel, e.g., customs, visas, shots, and insurance.

Organizations

Action. 1100 Vermont Avenue, N.W., Washington, DC 20525. (202) 606-5108. Administers federal volunteer programs, VISTA, RSVP, Foster Grandparents program, and Senior Companion program.

Association of Part-Time Professionals. Flow General Building, 7655 Old Springhouse Road, McLean, VA 22102. A nonprofit membership organization to assist individuals working or planning to work part time.

Elderhostel. 80 Boylston Street, Suite 400, Boston, MA 02116. Will send catalog describing their low-cost, short-term academic programs held in colleges and universities in the United States, Canada, and abroad.

The Great Outdoors. National Park Service, U.S. Department of the Interior, 18th & C Streets, N.W., Washington, DC 20240. Provides information on Golden Age (62+), Golden Eagle, and Golden Access (for permanently disabled) passes as well as other information about national parks.

International Executive Service Corps. P.O. Box 10005, Stamford, CT 06904. Active and retired business executives provide advice on financial management, plant management and production techniques, and marketing.

National University Continuing Education Association. One Dupont Circle, N.W., Suite 420, Washington, DC 20036. Publishes a guide to correspondence schools.

Peace Corps. P-301, Washington, DC 20526. Provides international opportunities for senior volunteers in agriculture, forestry, fish culture, health and nutrition, education, engineering, skilled trades, and business development.

Small Business Administration. 1111 18th Street, N.W., Washington, DC 20417. Supplies information packet on setting up a business. Specify what business interests you. Provides information on SCORE and ACE programs.

SCORE/ACE (Service Corps of Retired Executives/Active Corps of Executives). 409 Third Street, S.W., Suite 5900, Washington, DC 20024. (800) 634-0245. Information on how to use your skills to help new and struggling businesses.

National Park Service. Office of Information. U.S. Department of the Interior, P.O. Box 37127, Washington, DC 20013-7127.

Contact the park you're interested in or write for a brochure on volunteering in national parks.

Volunteer: The National Center. 1111 N. 19th Street, Arlington, VA 22209. A clearinghouse for information on volunteer programs throughout the country.

Health Resources

Books

New Our Bodies, Ourselves: A Book by and for Women. Paula Brown Doress, Norma Meras Swenson, Robin Cohen, Mickey Friedman, Lois Harris, and Kathleen MacPherson. New York: Simon & Schuster, 1992. An updated and expanded edition of a resource guide on women's health issues. Discusses the special concerns of the middle-aged and elderly (aged 40 and older).

Healthy Aging. Robin E. Mockenhaupt and Kathleen Nelson Boyle. Santa Barbara: ABC-CLIO, 1992. Presents a guide to maintaining good health and well-being into the later years.

Who? What? Where? Resources for Women's Health and Aging. National Institute on Aging, Bethesda, MD. NIH Publication # 91-323, 1992. This guide offers an overview of the major health and lifestyle issues affecting women and it helps women identify and locate resources as they plan for and cope with aging.

Forever Fit: A Step-By-Step Guide for Older Adults. Dee Ann Green Birkel and Susan Birkel Frietag. New York: Plenum Press, 1991. Presents a step-by-step physical fitness program for older adults.

50+ Wellness Program. Harris H. McIlwain, Lori F. Steinmeyer, Debra Fulghum Bruce, R.E. Fulghum, and Robert G. Bruce, Jr., New York: John Wiley and Sons, 1990. A complete program for maintaining nutritional, financial and emotional well-being for mature adults.

Is It Hot in Here or Is It Me? Gayle Sand. New York: Harper Collins, 1993. A personal look at the facts, fallacies, and feelings about menopause.

American Heart Association Cookbook. New York: Ballantine Books, 1991. Heart-healthy recipes for lowering cholesterol in adults.

Aquacises. Miriam Study Giles. Lexington: Mills and Sanderson, 1990. A guide to restoring and maintaining mobility through water exercises.

Pamphlets

A single copy of the following AARP pamphlets is available free. Write to AARP Fulfillment, 601 E Street, N.W., Washington, DC 20049. Specify title and stock number. Allow four to six weeks for delivery.

A Handbook About Care in the Home (D955). Describes the range of home health care services and how to assess home care agencies.

Have You Heard? (D12219). How to cope with various hearing impairments.

Healthy Questions (D12094). How to select and talk to doctors, dentists, vision care specialists, and pharmacists.

Pep Up Your Life (D549). An exercise program designed specifically for persons over 50.

Getting the Most from Your Medications (D12083). Provides a pocket-size

personal medication record; includes tips on nonprescription drugs.

Action for a Healthier Life: A Guide for Midlife and Older Women (D13474). Focusing on the areas of prevention, detection, and treatment, this pamphlet includes recommendations for actions that every woman can take to help prevent, detect, and treat disease.

Organizations

Mental Health Association. 1021 Prince Street, Alexandria, VA 22314, (703) 684-7722. A national voluntary citizens organization working to combat mental illness and promote mental health. Publishes numerous books and booklets on all phases of mental health. Ask for publications list. Chapters in local areas.

American Heart Association. National Center, 7320 Greenville Avenue, Dallas, TX 75231. Offers many reports and brochures on all phases of heart disease and positive/preventive care (exercises, diet, and more). Write to request publications in areas of your special interest.

Social Resources

Books

Caregivers' Roller Coaster: A Practical Guide to Caregiving for the Frail Elderly. Billie Jackson. Chicago: Loyola University Press, 1993. A self-help guide for caregivers of frail elderly persons.

Answers: A Divorce/Separation Survival Handbook. Woodbridge, NJ: Divorce Support Services, 1991. How to survive after a divorce or separation.

Being a Widow. Lynn Caine. New York: Arbor House, 1988. Examines the experience of widowhood and provides advice for dealing with the emotional, psychological, social, and practical problems.

When Women Retire: The Problems They Face and How to Solve Them. New York: Crown Publishers, 1992. Offers recommendations on special concerns for women in retirement such as caregiving for children, spouse, or aging parents.

A Book For Couples. Hugh & Gayle Prather. New York: Doubleday, 1989. A guide to marital relationships.

Rights of Passage: How Women Can Find a New Freedom in Their Mid Years. Elinor Leng. Los Angeles: Lowell House, 1991. Topics covered are the challenges of being part of the sandwich generation, the void when children leave home, marriage in transition, and changes in sexuality.

The Grandparent Book. Linda B. White, M.D. San Francisco: Gateway Books, 1990. A sourcebook to bring grandparents up to date on the many changes in birth, child rearing, and family roles that have taken place in the past several decades.

Pamphlets

A single copy of the following AARP pamphlets is available free. Write to AARP Fulfillment, 601 E Street, N.W., Washington, DC 20049. Specify title and stock number. Allow four to six weeks for delivery.

On Being Alone (D150). Offers information for the newly widowed on topics such as emotional response to grief, housing concerns, finances, and adjustment to the loss of a spouse.

A Path for Caregivers (D12957). Helps individuals who provide care for older persons to identify their needs and develop a plan to meet them.

Divorce After 50 — Challenge and Choices (D12909). Helps midlife and older women examine the issues related to divorce.

Tomorrow's Choices (D13479). A guide to help individuals and families plan for important decisions related to aging such as health care, finances, and legal matters.

Miles Away and Still Caring — A Guide For Long-Distance Caregivers (D12748). A guide for persons who care for a loved one from a distance.

Organizations

Women Work! The National Network for Women's Employment. 1625 K Street, N.W., Washington, DC 20006, (202) 467-6346. Serves as national clearinghouse for information of use to displaced homemakers. Refers women to about 600 local programs across the country.

Widowed Persons Service. AARP, 601 E Street, N.W., Washington, DC 20049. An outreach program in which trained widowed volunteers offer support to newly widowed persons in over 230 communities nationwide.

Housing Resources

Books

50 Healthiest Places to Live and Retire in the United States. Norman D. Ford. Bedford, MA: Mills and Sanderson, 1991. Rates and describes the 50 healthiest places to live based on both man-made health factors, such as urban stress and pollution, as well as natural health factors, such as climate, elevation, and natural beauty.

50 Fabulous Places to Retire. Lee and Saralee Rosenberg. Hawthorne: Career Press, 1991. Describes places that meet the following criteria: scenic beauty, good weather, affordable living costs, and quality services.

Long Term Living: How to Live Independently as Long as You Can and Plan for the Time When You Can't. Susan Polniaszek. Reston, VA: Acropolis Books, 1990. Provides a guide for planning for long-term care and housing in retirement.

Should Mom Live with Us? And Is Happiness Possible If She Does? Vivian F. Carlin and Vivian E. Greenberg. New York: Lexington Books, 1992. Provides advice to middle-aged children and their aging parents contemplating living in the child's home.

Sunbelt Retirement: The Complete State-By-State Guide to Retiring in the South and West of the United States. Peter A. Dickinson. Washington, DC: Regnery Gateway, and distributed by National Book Network, Lanham, MD 1992. Provides current and comprehensive information on planning for retirement in the Sunbelt states.

Housing America's Elderly: Many Possibilities, Few Choices. Stephen M. Golant. Newbury Park: Sage Publications, 1992. Examines the housing options available to older people in the United States.

Retirement Income on the House: Cashing in on Your Home with a Reverse Mortgage. Ken Scholen. 1992. Order from the National Center for Home Equity Conversion, Suite 300, 1210 E. College Drive, Marshall, MN 56258. Provides a detailed and comprehensive guide to cashing in on a home with a reverse mortgage for retirement income.

Pamphlets

A single copy of the following AARP pamphlets is available free. Write to AARP Fulfillment, 601 E Street, N.W., Washington, DC 20049. Specify title and stock number. Allow four to six weeks for delivery.

Buying a Home: What Buyers and Sellers Need to Know About Real Estate Agents (D14783). Guide to assist home buyers and sellers in obtaining high-quality services from real estate agents at a lower price.

A Guide to State Energy Assistance Offices (D1024). Lists addresses of state offices for low-income energy assistance, weatherizing assistance, office on aging, state energy office, and state energy conservation program.

Home-Made Money (D12894). Describes how basic types of home equity conversion plans work, gives examples of how they can be used, discusses their advantages, disadvantages, and availability.

The Doable, Renewable Home (D12470). Identifies and explains design concepts, products, and resources that can make an existing home more comfortable for its older occupants with physical limitations.

The following publication is available from the Consumer Information Center-V, P. O. Box 100, Pueblo, CO 81002:

When You Move — Do's and Don'ts (433N)
1974. 6 pp. 50 cents. Presents important considerations when planning for a move whether you hire professionals or do it yourself, and tells how to handle a loss or damage claim.

Organizations

American Association of Homes for the Aging. 1050 17th Street, N.W., Washington, DC 20036. Provides list of nonprofit homes belonging to the organization.

Department of Housing and Urban Development (HUD). Information Center, 451 7th Street, S.W., Washington, DC 20410. Provides pamphlets about the department's programs. Has free brochure on housing for the elderly.

Home Manufacturers Councils of National Association of Home Builders. 1201 15th Street, N.W., Washington, DC 20005. Provides information on planning and building economical retirement housing.

National Climatic Center. Federal Building, Asheville, NC 28801. Supplies data on the climate of any state or city. Fees begin at $4.70 and vary depending on information requested. Write or call (704) 259-0682.

Financial Income Resources

Books

Can You Afford to Retire? Robert J. Doyle, Kenn Tacchino, Ted Kurlowicz, Neal Cutler, and Jeff Schnepper. Chicago: Probus Publishing, 1992. Responds to frequently asked questions about financial planning for retirement.

Planning to Retire in Comfort: How Much to Save, Invest and Tax Strategies: Work Sheets. David L. Gibberman. Chicago: Commerce Clearing House, 1992. Explains how to retire in comfort by saving, investing, and using various tax strategies.

Retiring Right: Planning for Your Successful Retirement. Lawrence J. Kaplan. Garden City Park, NY: Avery Publishing Group, 1990. Presents a complete guide for planning a financially secure and successful retirement.

Your Parents' Financial Security. Barbara Weltman. New York: Wiley, 1992. Presents information and strategies that can be used to plan for the financial security of parents.

What Every Woman Should Know About Her Husband's Money. Shelby White. New York: Turtle Bay Books, 1992. Provides a financial survival guide for married women.

You Can Afford to Retire! The No-Nonsense Guide to Pre-Retirement Financial Planning. William W. Parrott and John L. Parrott. New York: New York Institute of Finance, 1992. A guide to pre-retirement financial planning.

Comfort Zones: A Practical Guide for Retirement Planning. Elwood N. Chapman. Los Altos, CA: Crisp Publications, Inc., 1985. Straightforward advice on essential topics ranging from attitude and use of leisure time to comprehensive financial planning.

Your Retirement Benefits. Peter E. Gaudio and Virginia S. Nicols. New York: Wiley and Sons, 1992. One in a series of personal wealth building guides by the Institute of Certified Financial Planners. Includes pensions and other retirement plans.

Making the Most of Your Money. Jane Bryant Quinn. New York: Simon & Schuster,

1991. Smart and practical ways to create wealth and plan your finances. Specific chapters on investing and retirement planning.

Social Security Manual. William Thomas III, editor. Cincinnati: National Underwriter Company, 1993. Provides accurate and authoritative Social Security information.

Pamphlets

A single copy of the following AARP pamphlets is available free. Write to AARP Fulfillment, 601 E Street, N.W., Washington, DC 20049. Specify title and stock number. Allow four to six weeks for delivery.

Social Security: Crucial Questions & Straight Answers (D13640). Answers commonly asked questions about the Social Security system.

A Woman's Guide to Pension Rights (D12258). Explains basic pension rights and suggests questions to ask.

Look Before You Leap: A Guide to Early Retirement Incentive Programs (D13390). A framework to help study the pros and cons of early retirement packages.

A Primer on Financial Management for Midlife and Older Women (D13183). A primer to help women take control of their lives by taking control of their money.

Government Publications

Your Pension: Things You Should Know About Your Pension Plan. Describes the major provisions of the private pension laws — what they are, how they operate, and the rights and options of pension plan participants and beneficiaries. To request a free copy, write to the Pension Benefit Guaranty Corporation, Coverage & Inquiries Branch, Insurance Operations Department, 2020 K Street, N.W., Washington, DC 20006-1806.

The following publications are available free from the U.S. Department of Labor, Pension and Welfare Benefit Administration (PWBA), Room N-5666, 200 Constitution Avenue, N.W., Washington, DC 20210:

What You Should Know About the Pension Laws. Provides a detailed description of the rights, safeguards, and guarantees of the private pension laws.

Facts about the Joint and Survivor Benefits of the Retirement Equity Act. Emphasizes the special transitional rules of the Retirement Equity Act that enable former employees with vested benefits to provide a preretirement survivor annuity or a joint and survivor annuity for a spouse.

Know Your Pension Plan. Explains various aspects of pension plans and includes checklists for participants to fill in important information about their plans.

Money Management Booklets. Money Management Institute, Household International, 2700 Sanders Road, Prospect Heights, IL 60070. $1.00 each or the 12-booklet set for $8.00. Booklets offer basic information on various consumer subjects, including food, clothing, recreation, housing, credit, and financial planning.

Organizations

Social Security Administration. 64401 Security Boulevard, Baltimore, MD 21235. Contact your local SSA office for booklets on the various Social Security programs.

Pension Rights Center. 918 Sixteenth Street, N.W., Suite 704, Washington, DC 20006. A variety of pension booklets are available at a nominal cost including a series on your pension rights at divorce under the civil service retirement system, the military retirement system, private pensions, and Social Security.

50 Plus. 850 Third Avenue, New York, NY 10022. Offers seven inexpensive retirement planning guides including ones on financial planning and on working in retirement.

Investment Resources

Books

Terry Savage's New Money Strategies For the 90s: Simple Steps to Creating Wealth and Building Financial Security. Terry Savage. New York: Harper Business, 1993. Offers step-by-step strategies for creating wealth and building financial security.

Retire Prosperously. C. Colbourn Hardy for J.K. Lasser Institute. New York: Simon & Schuster, 1989. A guide to all aspects of retirement living with emphasis on building financial security.

The IRA Book: The Complete Guide to IRA's. Robert Krughoff. Washington, DC: Center for the Study of Services, 1984. A guide on how to invest retirement funds, whether to roll pension funds into an individual retirement account, and when to retire.

Where to Put Your Money. Peter Passell. New York: Warner Books, 1984. Presents a variety of investment options for the small investor. Includes investment company addresses and phone numbers.

Everyone's Money Book. Jordan E. Goodman and Sonny Block. Chicago: Dearborn Financial Publishing, Inc., 1993. Money management with chapters on investments including mutual funds and software options.

New Strategies for Mutual Fund Investing. Donald D. Rugg. Homewood: Dow Jones-Irwin. Comprehensive book on investing in mutual funds.

Pamphlets

Before You Say Yes: Fifteen Questions to Ask about Investments. #614N. 1985. 3 pp. Free. Consumer Information Center-V, P. O. Box 100, Pueblo, CO 81002. Outlines guidelines to help you invest wisely, particularly when buying commodities. Also gives information about protection against fraud and swindlers.

Buying Treasury Securities at Federal Reserve Banks. Available from the Federal Reserve Bank of Richmond, Public Services Department, P. O. Box 27622, Richmond, VA 23261. 42 pp. Free.

The following publications are available from the Internal Revenue Service. See your telephone directory for the office in your area or use the toll-free telephone number found in the instructions for preparing Tax Form 1040:

Tax Benefits for Older Americans (D554)

Tax Information on Individual Retirement Accounts (590)

Tax Information on Pension and Annuity Income (575)

Tax Information on Self-Employed Retirement Plans (560)

Organizations

Investment Company Institute. 1600 M Street, N.W., Washington, DC 20036. Provides listings of money market and mutual funds by investment objective, with toll-free telephone numbers. Their catalog describes a wide variety of free materials on investment topics.

Moody's Investors Service. 99 Church Street, New York, NY 10007. Offers financial data and a rating service and publishes standard references on several types of investments.

No-Load Mutual Fund Association. 11 Penn Plaza, Suite 2204, New York, NY 10001. Provides a free list of no-load mutual fund organizations. A free catalog also lists other services.

Standard and Poor's Corporation. 25 Broadway, New York, NY 10004. Offers financial data and a rating service, and publishes standard references on several types of investments.

American Association of Individual Investors. 612 N. Michigan Avenue, Chicago, IL 60611. Provides excellent newsletters and seminars through its local chapters.

The Savings Bond Informer. P.O. Box 9249, Detroit, MI 48209. (800) 927-1901. Provides statements to holders of U.S. Savings Bonds outlining interest rates, values, and timing issues. The fee for a statement is based on the number of bonds included in the statement.

Magazines

Money and *Kiplinger's Personal Finance.* Each of these magazines gives good investment information in layperson's language.

Other magazines presenting useful information concerning business and financial topics include *Barron's, Business Week, Financial World, Forbes, Fortune, Harvard Business Review, Nation's Business,* and the finance/business sections of *Newsweek, Time,* and *U.S. News and World Report.*

Newsletters

The Retirement Letter. Peter A. Dickinson, ed. Phillips Publishing, Inc., 7811 Montrose Road, Potomac, MD 20854. Published monthly.

Over-55 Financial Management Letter. Prentice-Hall, Inc., Englewood Cliffs, NJ 07632. Published biweekly.

Kiplinger's Retirement Report. Kiplinger Washington Editors, Inc., 1729 H St., N.W. Washington, DC 20006-3938. Published monthly.

Financial Planning Resources

Books

Comfort Zones: A Practical Guide for Retirement Planning. Elwood N. Chapman. Los Altos, CA: Crisp Publications, Inc., 1989. Offers straightforward advice on essential topics ranging from use of leisure time to comprehensive financial planning.

On Your Own: A Widow's Passage to Emotional and Financial Well-Being. Alexandra Armstrong and Mary R. Donohue. Chicago: Dearborn Financial Publishing, Inc., 1993. Helps widows to cope with the enormity of their loss as well as deal with their financial affairs.

The Dow Jones–Irwin Guide to Retirement Planning. Homewood: Dow Jones–Irwin, 1989. Explains in detail how to develop savings habits, organize records, do personal financial statements, and invest wisely.

Retirement on a Shoestring. John Howells. San Rafael, CA: Publishers Group West, 1992. Offers strategies for saving money on rent, utilities, and home ownership.

Your Parents' Financial Security. Barbara Weltman. New York: Wiley, 1992. Presents information and strategies to plan for the financial security of parents.

Consumer Reports Buying Guide. Mt. Vernon: Consumers Union. Published annually. Presents facts and unbiased ratings on all types of insurance: homeowners, automobile, and health insurance.

Life Begins at 50: A Handbook for Creative Retirement Planning. Leonard J. Hansen. Hauppage: Barons Educational Series, 1989. Manual offers personal and financial advice for prospective and current retirees, and includes worksheets.

Money-$aving Tip$ for Good Times and Bad. Walter B. Leonard and the Editors of Consumer Reports Books. Yonkers: Consumer Reports Books, 1992. Hundreds of budget-wise strategies that will help stretch your dollars to new lengths.

Pamphlets

A single copy of the following AARP pamphlets is available free. Write to AARP Fulfillment, 601 E Street, N.W., Washington, DC 20049. Specify title and stock number. Allow four to six weeks for delivery.

Medicare: What it Covers, What it Doesn't (D13133). A summary of Medicare benefits, including the appeals process.

The following government publications are available from the Consumer Information Center-V, P.O. Box 100, Pueblo, CO 81002:

Consumer Credit Handbook (591N). 1982. 44 pp. Free. Tells how to apply for credit, what to do if you are denied, and how consumer credit laws can help you.

A Consumer's Guide to Life Insurance (592N). 1983. 21 pp. Free. Presents a comprehensive guide to different types of policies, costs, and coverage. Includes a glossary of commonly used terms.

Fair Credit Billing (491N). 1978. 3 pp. 50 cents. Describes how to resolve a billing dispute on credit card purchases.

Fair Credit Reporting Act (420N). 1980. 3 pp. 50 cents. Explains how to check the data in your credit file and what to do if you are denied credit because of incorrect information.

Fair Debt Collection (421N). 1983. 4 pp. 50 cents. Tells methods of debt collection that are prohibited by law and where to complain.

Organizations

Board of Governors of the Federal Reserve System. Publications Services, Washington, DC 20551. Administers regulations affecting a wide variety of financial activities. Provides booklets about credit rights and other consumer credit information.

American Council of Life Insurance. 1850 K Street, N.W., Washington, DC 20006. Produces a variety of publications available to consumers concerning life insurance, home and health insurance, and money management.

Legal Planning Resources

Books

Financial Choices: Making End-of-Life Decisions. Lee E. Norrgard and Jo DeMars. Santa Barbara: ABC-CLIO, 1992. A guide for terminally ill persons and their families on the issues involved in and the resources available for making end-of-life decisions.

What Every Senior Citizen Ought to Know: Taxes, Benefits, Health Care, Estate Planning Basics. Chicago: Commerce Clearing House, 1992. Provides basic information on wills, trusts, and other estate planning concerns.

To Will? Or to Trust?: That Is the Question. J. David Gratwohl and Mario Risso. San Mateo, CA: Chicken Little Press, 1991. An easy-to-understand, large-print guide to living trusts.

Estate Planning Guide. Martin M. Shenkman. New York: Wiley, 1991. Explains how to provide for your family's future.

Thy Will Be Done: A Guide to Wills, Estates, and Taxation for Older Persons. Eugene J. Daly. Buffalo: Prometheus Books, 1990. A guide containing general information on preparation of a will, estate administration, and estate taxation.

Estate Planning: A Basic Guide. Edward F. Sutkowski and Karl B. Kuppler. Chicago: American Bar Association Section of General Practice, 1990. Discusses preparation of wills, appointing trustees, avoiding probate, and more.

Your Vital Papers Logbook. San Francisco: Harper Collins. This booklet helps to organize personal documents with forms for tax returns, bank statements, property deeds, and much more to help handle personal affairs. This book was developed by AARP to provide an easy-to-understand way of keeping track of important paperwork. It also contains useful information about making a living will, filing claims for Social Security benefits, and a section to chart the family tree.

Plan Your Estate. Denis Clifford. Berkeley: Nolo Press, 1990. Contains sample forms and explains laws of every state except Louisiana.

Medicaid Planning Handbook: A Guide to Protecting Your Family's Assets. Alexander A. Bore, Jr., Boston: Little Brown, 1992. A handbook for Medicaid planning, including asset protection through the use of gifts, trusts, prenuptial agreements, and other tools.

Pamphlets

Legal Counsel for the Elderly, a department of AARP, specializes in the delivery of legal services to older persons. LCE publications are for sale and must be ordered from the following address: Legal Counsel for the Elderly, P.O. Box 96474, Washington, DC 20090-6474. Be sure to include the stock number and a check or money order payable to LCE, Inc. (D.C. residents add 6 percent sales tax).

Organizing Your Future: A Guide to Decision-making in Your Later Years (D13877). $12.95. This 100-page book clearly describes the legal tools available so you can exercise control over major life decisions should you become incapacitated. Topics include joint ownership, powers of attorney, trusts, wills, living wills, elder abuse, representative payees, guardianships, conservatorships, and long-term financing.

Planning for Incapacity: A Self-Help Guide.
$5.00. A useful and complete state-specific guide to medical decision making. The following state editions are currently available: AL, AZ, AK, CA, CT, DC, FL, GA, ID, IL, IN, IA, KY, LA, MD, MA, MI, MO, NV, NY, NC, OH, OK, OR, PA, SC, TN, TX, VA, WA, WI.

Where to Write for Vital Records. Consumer Information Center, Pueblo, CO 81009, 1984. $1.50. A state-by-state directory of vital statistics offices and sources for birth, death, marriage, and divorce certificates.

You and Your Living Will. 1985. Free. Everything you need to know about living wills. Order from: Society for the Right to Die, 250 West 57th Street, New York, NY 10107.

A Consumer's Guide to Probate (D13822). Provides general information on probate common to all states. Order a free copy from AARP Fulfillment, 601 E Street, N.W., Washington, DC 20049. Specify title and stock number. Allow four to six weeks for delivery.

The following pamphlets are available from the Order Fulfillment Department, American Bar Association, 750 North Lake Shore Drive, Chicago, IL 60611. Each costs $2.50 plus $1.00 for handling:

Your Rights Over Age 50

The American Lawyer: How to Choose and Use One

Landlords and Tenants: Your Guide to the Law

Your Guide to Consumer Credit and Bankruptcy

Law and Marriage: Your Legal Guide

The following pamphlets are available free from the Federal Trade Commission, Public Reference, Washington, DC 20580:

Equal Credit Opportunity. Explains the law that provides all consumers an equal chance to receive credit.

Fair Credit Billing. Explains how the Fair Credit Billing Act helps consumers resolve disputes with creditors and ensures fair handling of credit accounts.

Fair Credit Reporting. Describes the provisions of the Fair Credit Reporting Act.

Women and Credit Histories. Explains women's credit rights under the law and how women who have never had credit can start building a good credit record.

Organizations

Legal Counsel for the Elderly. 601 E Street, N.W., Washington, DC 20049. National legal resource center administered by AARP. Specializes in expanding and improving legal services for older persons, providing money management services for the disabled poor, protecting the rights of institutionalized seniors and those subject to guardianship, and securing benefits for low-income elders.

National Legal Aid and Defender Association. 1625 K Street, N.W., Washington, DC 20006. National headquarters of an organization that gives free legal service to poor persons in civil or criminal cases and to state and local units of government.

Commission on Legal Problems of the Elderly. 1800 M Street, N.W., Washington, DC 20036. Provides legal services to the elderly. Offers many free publications.

National Senior Citizen Law Center. 2025 M Street, N.W., Suite 400, Washington, DC 20036. Supports legal services programs on behalf of elderly poor clients. Particularly concerned with Social

Security, pension plans, Medicare, Medicaid, and nursing home rights.

Equal Employment Opportunity Commission. 2401 E Street, N.W., Room 5214, Washington, DC 20506. Call (202) 634-6423. Provides information and assistance regarding your rights under the Age Discrimination in Employment Act (ADEA).

Credit Bureaus

Use these addresses to complain about errors or obtain copies of your credit report. Although each of these credit bureaus charges a fee for a copy of your credit report, any of them will send you one copy free if you have been denied credit.

TRW ($7.50)
TRW Consumer Assistance Center
P.O. Box 749029
Dallas, TX 75374
(800) 392-1122

EQUIFAX (formerly known as CBI) ($8.00)
P.O. Box 740241
Atlanta, GA 30374
(800) 685-1111

Trans Union ($8.00)
25249 Country Club Boulevard
P.O. Box 7000
North Olmsted, OH 44070
(800) 851-2674

Master Action Plans

Master Action Plan

Goal Statement:

Actions	Resources	Time Frame	By Whom?

Goal Statement:

Actions	Resources	Time Frame	By Whom?

Master Action Plan

Goal Statement:

Actions	Resources	Time Frame	By Whom?

Goal Statement:

Actions	Resources	Time Frame	By Whom?

Master Action Plan

Social Planning

Goal Statement:

Actions	Resources	Time Frame	By Whom?

Goal Statement:

Actions	Resources	Time Frame	By Whom?

Master Action Plan

Housing Planning

Goal Statement:

Actions	Resources	Time Frame	By Whom?

Goal Statement:

Actions	Resources	Time Frame	By Whom?

Master Action Plan

Income Planning

Goal Statement:

Actions	Resources	Time Frame	By Whom?

Goal Statement:

Actions	Resources	Time Frame	By Whom?

Master Action Plan

Investment Planning

Goal Statement:

Actions	Resources	Time Frame	By Whom?

Goal Statement:

Actions	Resources	Time Frame	By Whom?

Master Action Plan

Goal Statement:

Actions	Resources	Time Frame	By Whom?

Goal Statement:

Actions	Resources	Time Frame	By Whom?

Master Action Plan

Legal and Estate Planning

Goal Statement:

Actions	Resources	Time Frame	By Whom?

Goal Statement:

Actions	Resources	Time Frame	By Whom?

Master Action Plan

Goal Statement:

Actions	Resources	Time Frame	By Whom?

Goal Statement:

Actions	Resources	Time Frame	By Whom?

Master Action Plan

Goal Statement:

Actions	Resources	Time Frame	By Whom?

Goal Statement:

Actions	Resources	Time Frame	By Whom?

Master Action Plan

Goal Statement:

Actions	Resources	Time Frame	By Whom?

Goal Statement:

Actions	Resources	Time Frame	By Whom?